THE APHASIA THERAPY FILE

The aphasia therapy file

edited by

Sally Byng
City University, London, UK

Kate Swinburn
Roehampton Rehabilitation Unit, London, UK

Carole Pound
City University, London, UK

Psychology Press
a member of the Taylor & Francis group

Psychology Press, Publishers
27 Church Road
Hove
East Sussex, BN3 2FA
UK

1002450895

British Library Cataloguing in Publication Data

A catalogue for this book is available from the British Library

ISBN 0-86377-566-7 hbk

Cover design by Leigh Hurlock

Typeset by Facing Pages, Southwick, West Sussex
Printed and bound in the United Kingdom by Bookcraft Ltd, Midsomer Norton, Somerset

We would like to acknowledge the fundamental contribution made to aphasia therapy in the UK by Eirian Jones, through her inspirational teaching and personal example.
This first edition of the Aphasia Therapy File *is dedicated to her with gratitude.*

Contents

List of contributors   ix

1. **Introduction to the *Aphasia Therapy***
    File   1
    Aims of the *Aphasia Therapy File*   2
    Criteria for submission   2
    About the studies in this volume   3
    Acknowledgements   6
    References   6

PART I: ALTERNATIVE FORMS OF
OUTPUT

2. **Introduction to Part 1: When there's no**
    spoken output   9
    Psycholinguistic profiles   9
    References   11

3. **Needs, function, and measurement:**
    Juggling with multiple language
    impairment   13
    Deborah Harding and Carole Pound
    Introduction   13
    Aims of the current therapy study   14
    Background issues   14
    Assessment   15
    Therapeutic intervention   16
    Outcome: Language and beyond   29
    Social, cultural, and emotional factors in
        psychosocial transition   30
    Acknowledgements   33
    Footnote   33
    References   33
    Appendices   35

4. **Drawing on the semantic system: The use**
    of drawing as a therapy medium   41
    Jon Hunt
    Background   41
    Assessment   42
    Conclusions and implications for therapy   46
    Therapy   46
    Evaluation of therapy and conclusions   56
    Emotional and psychosocial aspects   59
    Acknowledgements   60
    References   60

5. **Increasing effective communication**
    using a total communication approach   61
    Richard Lawson and Maggie Fawcus
    Introduction   61
    Previous speech and language therapy   61
    Social history   63
    Group therapy   63
    Rationale for therapy   64
    Treatment strategies   64
    Outcomes   68
    Acknowledgements   71
    References   71

PART 2: WORD RETRIEVAL THERAPIES

6. **Introduction to Part 2: Therapies for word**
    finding utilising orthographic relay
    strategies   75
    Strengths and strategies   75
    Outcomes/functional change/
        generalisation   76
    Teasing out strands of therapy and change   76

Intensity of therapy 77
References 77

7. **An intensive strategy-based therapy programme for impaired spelling** **79**
Jane Mortley
Background to the single case study of MF 79
Assessment 80
The stages in therapy 81
The therapy outcome 86
The therapy process 86
Discussion 87
Conclusions 91
Acknowledgements 91
References 92
Appendix 92

8. **Naming therapy for an aphasic person with fluent empty speech** **93**
Morwenna White-Thomson
Background 93
Initial observations and assessments 93
Therapy 95
Summary 98
References 98
Appendices 99

9. **A treatment programme for an impairment in reading function words** **101**
Jenny Sheridan
Language investigations 101
Therapy 1 102
Therapy 2 103
Summary 104
References 104

PART 3: "BEYOND THE SINGLE WORD" THERAPIES

10. **Introduction to Part 3: Therapies addressing impairments in processing verbs and sentences** **107**
References 109

11. **Doing something about a verb impairment: Two therapy approaches** **111**
Jane Marshall
Introduction 111
Spontaneous speech analysis 112
Verb and noun production 113
The design of the therapy study 116
The first therapy programme 117
The second therapy programme 123
Emotional aspects 129
Footnote 130
References 130

12. **Early stages in treating a person with non-fluent aphasia** **131**
Alison Greenwood
Introduction 131
Therapy 136
Evaluation of therapy 139
References 141

13. **"Who ends up with the fiver?"—a sentence production therapy** **143**
Jane Marshall
Introduction 143
Assessment 145
Therapy 146
Evaluation 149
References 149

14. **An informal example of a successful therapy for a sentence processing deficit** **151**
Kate Swinburn
Introduction 151
Single-word assessment 152
Sentence-level assessment 152
Therapy 153
References 157
Appendices 158

Author index 161
Subject index 163

List of Contributors

Sally Byng, Department of Language and Communication Science, City University, Northampton Square, London EC1V 0HB.

Maggie Fawcus, 63 Golden Square, Tenterden, Kent TN30 6RN.

Alison Greenwood, Amersham Hospital, South Buckinghamshire HP7 0JD.

Deborah Harding, West Kent Neurorehabilitation Unit, Sevenoaks Hospital, Hospital Road, Sevenoaks, Kent TN13 3PG.

Jon Hunt, Southmead Hospital, North Avon Healthcare Trust, Westbury on Trym, Bristol BS10 5NB.

Richard Lawson, Speech and Language Therapy Department, Royal Leamington Spa Hospital, Heathcot Lane, Heathcot, Warwickshire CV34 6SR.

Jane Marshall, Department of Language and Communication Science, City University, Northampton Square, London EC1V 0HB.

Jane Mortley, Aphasia Computer Team, Speech and Language Therapy Research Unit, Frenchay Hospital, Bristol BS16 1LE.

Carole Pound, Department of Language and Communication Science, City University, Northampton Square, London EC1V 0HB.

Jenny Sheridan, 110 Chatham Road, London SW11 6HG.

Kate Swinburn, Speech and Language Therapy, Community Neurorehabilitation Team, South West Community NHS Trust, Roehampton Rehabilitation Unit, London SW15 5PR.

Morwenna White-Thomson, Southmead Hospital, North Avon Healthcare Trust, Westbury on Trym, Bristol BS10 5NB.

1

Introduction
to the *Aphasia Therapy File*

This edition of the *Aphasia Therapy File* marks the first in what will be a regular publication providing a resource of ideas about therapy for speech and language therapists working with people with aphasia. The purpose of the *File* is to disseminate, encourage, and facilitate writing about therapy interventions for aphasia by the people who implement the therapy.

The idea for this publication emerged some years ago from a question asked by a practising speech and language therapist about where she could send a small case study to be published, which she considered would be of interest to other clinicians. The dilemma was that, if she published the study in a professional magazine it would have meant that it lost its ready accessibility for clinicians to reference and that there would have been constraints on length. However, if she sent it to an academic journal, it had probably to conform to a conventional journal format, having a literature review and considerable theoretical discussion and interpretation. The therapist in question did not have time to do the amount of research necessary to permit this within the constraints of her clinical job and felt that the therapy she had done was not on a large enough scale for such a publication, nor could

she write in as much detail as she wished about the therapy in such a forum.

The literature usually comprises one of a number of types of therapy study. These might be studies of the implementation of a therapy technique with a group of individuals where the therapy and the responses of the aphasic people are only described in outline. Alternatively there are a number of examples of in-depth theoretical studies of aphasic people with specific language impairments for which therapy is provided, which are then followed by detailed discussion of the theoretical implications for understanding of the language impairment. Yet again, the study may be a model experimental study to show the very specific effects of an intervention on a specific problem and to account for those effects.

Although this is something of a caricature of the literature, it serves to demonstrate that there is currently little space for more discursive description of what therapists do and why, and how what they do is shaped by the individual with aphasia. Most therapists find that, however they set out to achieve something, it is changed by the reaction/response of the aphasic person. Thus, the published studies that concentrate either solely on the nature of the language impairment or the implementation of a specific predetermined therapy procedure do not reflect therapy as it happens with most therapists, in the UK at least.

The rationale then for providing these in-depth therapy studies, outside the confines of a traditional academic or professional journal or textbook, is to allow therapists a different medium for discussion of their work, which perhaps fits the implementation of therapy better than conforming to existing styles. The purpose behind these studies is to allow therapists to write about what they actually did when working with a specific client, in ways that conform by and large to their own style.

It seemed also that there was a need for a resource for practising clinicians who wanted ideas about what to do in therapy, backed up by some evidence of the effects of those ideas. This publication therefore represents a half-way house—a permanent reference resource in which therapies which are explicit in their design, rationale, implementation, and measurement of outcome are described, but without the requirement necessarily to reference other literature or draw theoretical as well as clinical conclusions. This not only makes the material more easily accessible to busy clinicians, but also provides a realistic medium for therapists to communicate the outcome of their work.

AIMS OF THE *APHASIA THERAPY FILE*

The *Aphasia Therapy File* was conceived as a resource about implementing therapy, with the following aims:

- to provide working clinicians with a forum for publishing good quality real-life case studies detailing the effects of speech and language therapy
- to provide a forum for publication unconstrained by the usual demands of academic research journals
- to provide an accessible resource of ideas and directions to take in aphasia therapy

- to encourage the publication of evidence about the effectiveness and utility of a wide range of types of therapy, reflecting real-life needs of people with aphasia
- to support the development of forms of writing about therapy that provide clear guidance to other clinicians about how to apply the same approach
- to provide a resource of material about therapy for academic and clinical researchers, which might support parallel research development.

It is intended that there will be an addition to the *File* annually, comprising an additional set of therapy studies. A cumulative index and list of contents will be included, so that therapists can keep extending the resource at a reasonable cost. The editors will encourage submissions from clinicians and also receive speculative submissions, much in the way that academic journals operate. All submissions will be reviewed, using external reviewers where necessary.

The *Aphasia Therapy File* will reflect clinical practice; clinicians have different therapeutic styles, which are demonstrated in the written presentation of those therapies. There is therefore no "house style" nor preferred length or scale of study. Rather we want to stimulate the publication of as wide a variety of studies as possible and avoid constraining the type of material that clinicians submit for publication. A personal style of writing is acceptable, including use of the first person singulars which can seem a more natural medium when writing about therapy.

CRITERIA FOR SUBMISSION

There are some explicit criteria that studies published in the *Aphasia Therapy File* should meet, as follows:

- a clear description of the nature of the communication impairment and/or disability of the aphasic person or group of people who are the focus of the study

- preferably a transcript of spoken language to assist the reader in familiarisation with the aphasic person in question
- an explicit rationale for the type of therapy implemented
- a clear description of the therapy itself: the materials or resources used (if any), the tasks implemented, the type of facilitation techniques or strategies etc. employed
- if possible, a transcript of a sample from a therapy session to exemplify a specific aspect of therapy (as in Hunt, Chapter 4; Mortley, Chapter 7; and Marshall, Chapter 11; in this volume)
- a detailed account of the evaluation of the intervention
- the evaluation should include a description of the impact of the intervention on the everyday life of the aphasic person.

Not all the studies included in this edition meet all these criteria: in this edition the studies included are of varying length, style and scope. We considered that it was important to publish material currently available from clinicians, with the expectation that the publication of an increasing number of case studies will stimulate future submission of studies from therapists. We hope that some of the existing studies will serve as role models and allow clinicians increasingly in the future to refine the presentation of the therapy study, outside the constraints of more traditional forms of publication.

Studies need not document only therapy for the impairments caused by aphasia; therapies for disabling aspects of aphasia could also be included. Our use of the terms "impairment" and "disability" are largely in accordance with the World Health Organisation, 1980, classifications. Within this framework, impairment refers to abnormality of function and disability reflects the consequences of impairment in terms of functional activities. In line with the views of some disabled groups, including some people with aphasia (e.g. Ireland, 1995), we have chosen not to employ the term "handicap", but to include issues of social role and lifestyle within a broadened concept of disability. This will be evident in this volume in particular in the chapter by

Harding and Pound (Chapter 3). Therapy that involves relatives and friends or other health and social care professionals could also be included. Contributions by clinicians who discuss how, in retrospect, they would have made modifications to the therapy, will be welcomed, especially when those modifications are made explicit.

ABOUT THE STUDIES IN THIS VOLUME

The studies are grouped loosely according to the aims of the therapy, although there is of course considerable overlap between studies even in different parts. Each part is introduced briefly by a review of the studies to be included, pulling out the common and interesting themes raised, and referring to other current literature where relevant. This is intended to put the studies into a context for therapists with limited reading time.

This first edition of the *Aphasia Therapy File* is divided into three parts, organised around the basic focus of the therapy, although the parts are not mutually exclusive, and all the studies address some common issues and raise common themes. Most of the studies concern therapies aimed primarily at the language and communication impairment. This does not mean that we believe this to be the sole primary area for intervention in aphasia, but rather it reflects the nature of the studies submitted.

The therapies for the language impairments described in this volume come from what has emerged over the past decade as the predominant theoretical background for work on the language impairment in aphasia therapy in the UK. That is, they are all based on an interpretation of the underlying language impairment within a simple cognitive neuropsychological/psycholinguistic model of language processing. The authors assume a basic working knowledge of this kind of model (typical of therapists in the UK), which they use as a point of reference for the explanation of the language impairment and the formulation of aspects of impairment to be addressed in therapy. The fact that this is a characteristic of these studies does not mean that all future submissions will have to conform to this tradition. It merely represents the current predominance of this approach in the UK. Provided therapy studies meet the criteria listed earlier (i.e. explicitness about the person, impairment, and disability, the rationale for therapy, and the therapy itself) they will be accepted for consideration.

A further assumption clearly evident in these studies is the need in each case to address the language impairment itself, in addition to or in support of work to address the functional, social, and emotional impact of that impairment. Each case highlights primarily the work that was undertaken to ameliorate the language and/or communication impairment, but most of the studies also discuss the relevance of this therapy to functional communication. The authors largely take a position (sometimes unconsciously) that there is a continuum between therapy for the impairment and therapy to assist in communicating more effectively and efficiently in everyday life. Often we find these two concepts polarised in the literature—these studies demonstrate the necessary reliance of functional communication strategies on developing the language and communication skills underlying those strategies.

There is not necessarily anything particularly original or unusual about these studies—the aphasic people, the therapies, and the therapeutic dilemmas presented will be familiar to most speech and language therapists/pathologists. We believe, however, that much of the discussion of these latter two issues has not before reached the literature. Here, each author describes in some detail the therapy that they undertook, providing a reasonably detailed rationale for the activities undertaken. The majority of the studies talk the reader through the thinking that the therapist went through as she/he decided what to do next, often with considerable frankness (e.g. Hunt, Chapter 4) about the lack of certainty about what they should be doing, and also in hindsight with some regrets about what they did not do. We hope that this will be an important feature of the *Aphasia Therapy File*. So often, published therapy studies make it look as though the therapist was quite sure what to do and what the predicted outcomes would be at the outset. *Real* therapy is more like a voyage of discovery—the therapist starts on a course of action, in discussion

with the aphasic person and perhaps those around them, with, often, only a hunch that this will be effective.

These studies also indicate how determining a course of action is not a one-off occurrence. Most of the studies pick up the therapy after other therapies had already been implemented (usually by other people), often to little or no effect. They demonstrate how therapists change course or re-evaluate what they are doing in the light of the aphasic person's response, both in linguistic and emotional terms. We believe that providing a description of the therapists' thought processes in both setting about and re-evaluating therapy will be of interest to experienced therapists and students alike.

Thus, the therapy studies published here do not represent new therapies. Rather we hope that they will help therapists to reflect on their practice, to assist in more detailed analysis of why someone may or may not be able to make use of the therapy provided. They may provide ideas for further developing therapy tasks or reorientating familiar ones to address a difficulty more subtly or more directly. These studies also represent real-life therapies, where the therapists cannot implement or pursue lines of thinking that they think to be of primary importance, because of intervening factors, be they social, psychological, cultural, or logistical (e.g. Harding and Pound, Chapter 3).Changes made under these conditions are even harder to bring about than those achieved under optimal therapy conditions (which are often those described in the literature). All but one of these studies (Marshall, Chapter 11) was carried out during the course, and within the constraints, of "normal" clinical practice in typical UK National Health Service speech and language therapy services.

None of these studies describes complete therapeutic interventions. In almost every case further intervention is indicated, but some of the authors describe the complexity in determining what that further intervention should be. For example in D's case (Harding and Pound, Chapter 3), it is clear that he is going to need further support in both using his developing communication skills and in adapting to his new identity and lifestyle. However, how that intervention can be provided is hard to determine given the social and cultural constraints. Some of the studies (especially those by Harding and Pound, Chapter 3; Hunt, Chapter 4; Lawson and Fawcus, Chapter 5; and Marshall, Chapter 13) bring out the complex relationship between therapy for the language impairment and addressing psychological, emotional, and social issues. Marshall (Chapter 11) and Hunt (Chapter 4) both indicate how the depressed status of the women they worked with seemed to impair their ability to use the often considerable communicative strengths at their disposal.

The importance of providing emotional support to people adapting to life with aphasia from very early on post onset of the aphasia seems critical. What is devastatingly apparent is how intractable and destructive the depression accompanying aphasia is; the distress experienced by so many of the people described here is palpable. No wonder it has been so difficult either to establish that therapy is effective, or to bring about carryover of changes to communication skills outside the clinical environment—anybody grappling day by day with such mind-numbing depression and anxiety would find it hard to take on any new behaviours. Even where therapy has been both effective and appreciated, the depression can seem to block further change or use of new communication skills. The need for more attention to the psychological effects of aphasia has been so regularly reiterated but seems as yet to be so little developed.

However, Lawson and Fawcus (Chapter 5) describe a more positive interaction between enhancing communication skills and psychological state. They cite how TS's wife considered that the establishment of some means of communication for TS had improved the mental health and well-being of them both, in the estimation of his wife keeping them both out of psychiatric care. The role of therapy for communication impairments and disabilities in maintaining and promoting general and mental health has not been well described in the literature, and could represent an important role for therapy in future as health promotion moves high onto the political agenda in health care delivery.

Some interesting general issues about therapy for language impairments emerge across these studies. For example a number of the studies use written language as a route into enhancing other forms of communication—speech, gesture, drawing. It is interesting how many of the aphasic people described here had relatively strong written language in comparison to spoken language, but how few of them were exploiting this strength until the therapists made them aware of it. There seems so often to be a heavy focus on spoken production in therapy—"point to and it's a ...?" therapy as described by Audrey Holland (personal communiction)—which seems to be quite unfounded. The value of strengthening semantic and auditory input skills as a foundation for production comes across strongly. In fact in many of the studies, change in output produced as a result of strengthening input seems to be a feature. The strong relationship between gesture and spoken output also comes across in a number of the studies—an observation that is not new. There is a flavour of Schuell (Schuell, Jenkins, Jiminez-Pabon, 1964) and Wepman (1953) to many of the approaches to therapy described here, even if it is not overtly acknowledged. What is different, however, is the tailoring of the implementation of the therapy to meet specific needs, rather than a blanket "this is how to treat aphasia" type of approach. Here we see how treatment is modified and modulated according to the person's need/response.

A robust similarity between all the studies is the exploitation of observed communication strengths as a foundation for the development of a therapy strategy. In almost every study, the therapist discusses an observation of some skill remaining to the person, however isolated or minimal. The adaptation of this skill into a therapy approach is one of the most elegant, subtle, and under-appreciated aspects of the therapeutic art. What might seem to be an impenetrable maze of communication impairment can provide a clear avenue in to the centre of a strategy for addressing that impairment, in the hands of a skilled therapist.

The studies in this edition also illustrate the complexity of identifying change through use of outcome measures. What may seem small insignificant gains, in terms of quantitative measurement, can, to the person concerned and their family, be of considerable importance, as is so well exemplified by TS and his wife (Chapter 5). Outcome measures must have some means of capturing the qualitative changes and improvements that happen during the course of therapy. Attribution of changes is of course always a difficult issue. The difficulty of placing the cause of changes should not deter us from describing what has happened to people during the course of therapy, even if it is not clear how closely related those changes are to the intervention implemented. Valid and reliable outcomes measurement remains a hugely difficult enterprise for everyone involved in health and social care. Descriptive, qualitative accounts can be an acceptable cogent adjunct to traditional quantitative measures. From these kinds of accounts, related to the perceptions of aphasic people about the nature of important criteria for change, new approaches to measurement may emerge.

Therapists are usually working simultaneously on a variety of levels, juggling at one and the same time attempts to understand and tackle the communication impairment and address the multiple needs of the individual recovering from, and adapting to, life with aphasia (Byng, Pound, & Parr, 1999). We hope that this first volume of case studies illustrates the complexity of the multifaceted nature of therapy for aphasia

ACKNOWLEDGEMENTS

Many of the studies published here have previously been presented at conferences and symposia organised by the British Aphasiology Society (BAS). We would like to pay tribute to the work of BAS in stimulating not only the study of aphasiology in Britain but also maintaining and developing clinical interest and understanding for a population for whom therapy services are constantly under threat. The *Aphasia Therapy File* will maintain a close link with the activities of BAS and will aim to provide the forum for publication of many of the therapy studies presented during the course of its activities.

REFERENCES

Byng, S., Pound C., & Parr, S. (1999, in press). Living with aphasia: A framework for therapy interventions. In I. Papathanasiou (Ed.), *Acquired Neurological Communication Disorders: a Clinical Perspective.* London: Whurr Publishers.

Ireland, C.M. (1995). One hundred years on from Freud's paper on Aphasia. In C. Code & D. Muller (Eds.), *The Treatment of aphasia: From theory to practice.* London: Whurr Publishers.

Schuell, H.M. Jenkins, J.J., & Jiminez-Pabon, E. (1964). *Aphasia in adults: Diagnosis, prognosis and treatment.* New York: Harper & Row.

Wepman, J.M. (1953). A conceptual model for the processes involved in recovery from aphasia. *Journal of Speech and Hearing Disorders, 18,* 4–13.

World Health Organisation (1980). *International classification of impairments, disabilities and handicaps.* Geneva: WHO.

Part I

Alternative forms
of output

2

Introduction to Part 1:
When there's no spoken output

What do we do when we try to work with aphasic people who have no useable spoken output? There is no doubt that aphasic people who have no spoken communication present the clinician with a range of challenges, for example: How will alternative communication strategies be introduced; what non-verbal form of communication is best for that person; how can a clinician facilitate choice for the aphasic person; how can the clinician help ease the aphasic person, their family, and friends through the realisation that speech is no longer a viable option; will the outcome of intervention be satisfactory and/or effective for the aphasic person, their communication partners, and the therapist? The three case studies in this part demonstrate varied responses to these taxing questions and examine how successful intervention is possible in a variety of settings, using different techniques with differing clients.

The three aphasic people discussed were all relatively young (between the ages of 56 and 64). When therapy commenced they were between 7 and 12 months post stroke and all were, not surprisingly, devastatingly disabled by their aphasia in terms of functional communication and emotional consequences of the language loss and its

sequelae. Each person had intensive "outpatient" therapy (twice, three times weekly, or on a twice-daily basis) over an extended length of time ranging from 18 weeks to 8 months, one within a group setting and two on an individual basis.

PSYCHOLINGUISTIC PROFILES

All three people had no useable expressive language; however, their psycholinguistic profiles were by no means identical. Both people described by Lawson and Fawcus (TS; Chapter 5) and Harding and Pound (D; Chapter 3) had significant impairments in auditory comprehension including poor acoustic analysis. Harding and Pound's client had fluent, neologistic speech whereas Lawson and Fawcus's client had a single expletive as his sole output. Hunt's client, Joan (Chapter 4), was severely non-fluent, with an unreliable yes/no response only, but with good functional comprehension. When examining the route of written language, again the profiles of these three people differed. Hunt's client made some functional use of limited orthographic output, whereas the other two aphasic people had no written output at all. All the authors postulate that a deficit in phonological processing contributed substantially to their client's lack of speech. As is often the case with non-speaking clients, an element of articulatory dyspraxia was apparent but none of the authors ascribe their client's lack of verbal expression to this late-stage articulatory sequencing deficit.

Semantic representations and/or access appear to be relatively well preserved in all three dysphasic people discussed. It could be that this preservation of semantic representation is crucial to successful therapy for this group of aphasic people and in each case was incorporated into therapy. This work mainly required output in various modalities from within constrained semantic categories (such as definition or details of an item within a semantic category) or between semantic categories (such as odd man out or charting tasks). Without preserved semantic representations and degrees of access and recall, this level of work may have been ineffective. Semantic activation may not have been sufficient to stimulate phonology (whether intact or partial). However, in each case it was strong enough to allow for activation and selection of an individual target within the semantic system in preference to items related to it in meaning, through some form of icon, be it a gesture, a drawing, or a written symbol.

The focus of therapy input for each client was different, despite them all being non-verbal. Harding and Pound chose to work at the impairment level using a structured psycholinguistic approach concentrating on input phonology and semantic levels of representation. They dovetailed this with functional work using word charts and a book containing word lists used within the rehabilitation unit. Lawson and Fawcus used a number of tasks aimed at practising preselected non-verbal modalities and then moving on to a total com-munication approach where TS chose to combine drawing with some gesture/mime and pointing. Joan worked with Jon Hunt extensively on drawing to express herself. The tasks varied in their focus from drawing picture names within semantic categories through to unconstrained free drawing constantly encouraging ever more sophisticated

written output. Though the input and output focus was different all the authors chose to focus the aphasic person's attention on semantic properties in some form or another.

As discussed previously, although each of the aphasic people did not have a functionally comprehensible means of communication through spoken output, they were not the same in many other ways. The authors all focused on work that played to each person's individual strengths, maximising these to facilitate functional communication however this was achieved for their particular client; for TS this was through total communication relying mainly on pointing, gesture/mime, and drawing. Lawson and Fawcus point out that TS was already beginning to use non-verbal modalities in an attempt to communicate prior to their intervention. They reasoned that he should be encouraged to explore all possible channels of communication and exploit success in communication using a small group setting to facilitate these aims. Communicating through drawing and writing seemed the most appropriate avenue to pursue for Joan who had previously rejected gesture. Hunt hypothesised that Joan had difficulty "assembling semantic representations in conditions of low constraint" and that the most appropriate therapy was one that required her to "access semantics for output whatever the medium". He emphasises that writing and drawing had showed the most potential and were most acceptable to Joan and her husband and so these became the preferred output modality. D, through maximising auditory and written comprehension abilities, was able to use his reading abilities as a route to a written word communication strategy. Harding and Pound demonstrate that all output tasks were demanding and distracting for D. They therefore chose to focus therapy on facilitating access to semantics via reading, in anticipation that the improvements in semantic processing would develop to underpin all routes to output.

All the therapists identified the strengths and limitations of the aphasic people and chose therapies that minimised their difficulties and maximised their strengths. With regard to the chosen mode of communication as Lawson and Fawcus point out "aphasic people, as a general rule, select the alternative mode of communication which is most effective and most comfortable for them", the role of the therapist therefore is to clarify the options and facilitate choice and maximise the necessary underpinning skills. It is significant that in two cases, successful therapy only started after other therapies had finished. How was it that these people were offered further therapy? Is access to therapy something of a lottery?

It is perhaps not surprising that all the clients discussed sustained their strokes at least seven months prior to treatment. Had the type of work described been introduced earlier in the recovery and adaptation process, it is questionable whether it would have been so successful. It may well be that there is a critical period for work that focuses on non-verbal communication, and introduction before this period will meet with resistance or lack of understanding of why alternative therapies are necessary. Sacchett, Byng, Marshall, and Pound (in press) investigated prepositional drawing introduced to significant effect to seven aphasic people. All aphasic people had "little or no spoken or written output" but benefited from com-municative drawing therapy. They were all at least one year post stroke when this therapy began. Certainly there is no significant evidence yet that introducing alternative forms of communication early or late makes a significant difference to the ultimate uptake and use of other modalities, but timing for this type of intervention is an area that might benefit from further research and development.

Degree of acceptance and reliance on a non-verbal means of communication and the impact on the identity of the non-verbally communicating person must vary from person to person and the three people in these case studies demonstrate this varied response. For TS, perhaps the most severely impaired and disabled of the three, "the burden of communication still rested heavily on his partner". However, according to his wife, he was "no longer the passive, negative and depressed man who commenced intensive therapy … his drawings are very good and his actions tell me a lot. He comes

home and is doing splendidly". This quotation highlights the preventative role therapy may have, enhancing the mental health of both TS and his wife. TS's impairment was unchanged but, by focusing on alternative communication strategies, Lawson and Fawcus were able to show how the negative emotional consequences of the aphasia can be significantly reduced and a positive outlook introduced after the year of negativity that had preceded it for TS and his wife. Joan and her partner communicate well "given the circumstances", apparently using pen and paper, though Hunt observed that, in practice, yes/no question and answering was their habitual mode of communication. Hunt feels, however, that Joan "continues to grieve greatly for her loss … it is highly questionable the extent to which Joan … has accepted her new life and identity". Finally, Harding and Pound draw a distinction between the differing gains in impairment, disability, and social role and identity for their client. D "had altered his impairment and disability to a level where communication … was far more successful than on admission. However, we feared that an inability to address D's changed role and interaction of this role with home and work would lead to considerable difficulties".

Despite the changes brought about by all the interventions, the authors agree that for aphasic people relying on alternative means of communi-cation, success is relative. But what is the alternative for these people? What other interventions would be realistic, feasible, and acceptable? What these case studies suggest, however, is that therapy relating to identity and social role is as crucial as communication therapy for this population *and* their families and friends.

REFERENCE

Sacchett, C., Byng, S., Marshall, J., & Pound, C. (in press). Drawing together: Evaluation of a therapy programme for severe aphasia. *International journal of disorders of communication and language.*

3

Needs, function, and measurement: Juggling with multiple language impairment

Deborah Harding and Carole Pound

INTRODUCTION

The case of D, a 56-year-old postmaster with multiple language impairment following a left middle cerebral artery infarct, is discussed. Reputed to have been a great orator in his first language, Punjabi, he is also said to have been a fluent speaker of English. D presents now with severe fluent expressive dysphasia and a similarly severe auditory comprehension impairment. Written material is more readily understood, though unreliable and laboured beyond single words. He is largely dysgraphic demonstrating little success in written output beyond writing his own name. In the initial weeks of the current study, D also demonstrated a certain degree of cognitive inflexibility. In terms of physical disability following the stroke, D had a mild right-sided weakness affecting upper limb function to a greater degree than lower limb. He was also reported to demonstrate some perceptual deficits affecting his ability to manipulate everyday objects, such as cutlery.

D had previously enjoyed playing sport at a competitive level. He had spent much of his young adult life in Kenya where he had worked as a game warden, a part of his social history of which he was especially proud. He lives with his wife and has a married daughter. In his local Sikh community, in which he was actively involved, he was clearly well liked and respected. Indeed, it was not hard to see why! D was cheerful, generous spirited, and highly motivated while he was at the rehabilitation centre, making him a popular character with both staff and fellow patients.

The Speech and Language Therapy intervention described took place 7 months after the onset of D's stroke, during the time that he was a patient at a neurological rehabilitation centre. He had previously received Speech and Language Therapy on the Stroke Unit at the hospital where he was initially admitted and subsequently, once a week, as an outpatient until the time of his admission to the neurological rehabilitation centre.

AIMS OF THE CURRENT THERAPY STUDY

The primary aim of the current therapy study is to outline the Speech and Language Therapy intervention undertaken with D, while he was a patient at the rehabilitation centre. The rationale of the more specific aspects of therapy will be considered with reference to the outcomes of speech and language therapy assessments used to evaluate D's language impairments, and in the context of D's social situation, bilingualism, and the emotional impact of his communication disability. The outcome of therapeutic intervention will be discussed both in terms of post-therapy language assessments, with additional consideration being given to more functional qualitative measures. There will be some discussion of the impact on therapy of aspects of impaired non-language cognition.

The combination of D's various communication and non-language cognitive impairments, coupled with his bilingualism, presents interesting therapeutic challenges. Case descriptions such as his are not, however, unique and therapists are doubtless equally varied in the approaches they adopt with such patients! Our therapeutic intervention with D has had both ups and downs and it is hoped that sharing this with other clinicians may act as a catalyst for fruitful discussion of the therapeutic issues relating to multiple language impairment.

BACKGROUND ISSUES

Family

Clearly an early aim of intervention was to involve D's family as centrally as possible in the therapy process, not least because of the cultural and bilingual issues, which we required assistance with.

D lived with his wife JD, a warm and friendly woman. Seemingly, she had always taken a back-seat role compared to D in the running of their post office, yet since his stroke and despite her own ill health, she had apparently assumed responsibility for the day-to-day management of the business and awaited further recovery in D's language before taking any major decisions as regards its future. Although communication between D and JD was enormously difficult and often unsuccessful, when seen with her husband JD always maintained a tolerant, good-natured attitude towards him, and one imagined that they enjoyed a very solid relationship prior to, and since, the stroke. D maintained a protective, dominant role in his relationship with his wife. This manifested itself both in his obvious concern for her being burdened and over-tired by working in the shop and also by his reluctance to allow us to contact her to arrange meetings or discuss what was happening in therapy. On occasions when we did meet with her, she tended to listen attentively to what was said, though was seldom forthcoming with questions or in providing other than basic details about D's lifestyle at home and in the community. Throughout, her attitude to us was one of deference and gratitude.

A more powerful character in challenging what therapy would achieve and when, was D's elder brother, in Britain on an extended vacation. His anger and distress at seeing D transformed from witty orator and raconteur to, in his opinion, psychologically disturbed and depressed invalid, was very apparent. He had numerous misconceptions about D's condition which he reiterated at subsequent meetings, even after comprehensive explanation and discussion. These included, for example, the fact that surgical interventions might "cure" D's dysphasia and that the recurrent utterance, /duːkaːn/ ("shop" in Punjabi), reflected D's constant concern as regards the business.

The third principal character in D's family circle was his married daughter, RD, an intelligent, confident woman, who, while D was attending his previous hospital therapy, had been the key person for liaison with the family. This may have been due to JD's difficulty in leaving the shop or may have been because RD was the most anglicised member of the family, next to her father. She had married a non-Sikh, which had resulted in a distancing from her parents until the time of D's stroke when the family unit had pulled together once more.

Her input to D's rehabilitation faded at the arrival of D's brother and she had minimal input to the therapy process throughout D's admission. She did, however, take an active role in discharge planning and follow-up.

In summary, there were a number of complex, fluctuating dynamics that appeared to affect the free-flow of information from the core family and home setting to the therapy context. The impact of these aspects and the related cultural and bilingual issues will be discussed later.

ASSESSMENT

As mentioned, D presented with multiple language impairments. His speech was fluent and littered with neologisms and phonological paraphasias (see Appendix 2). The impression gained, from the function words and identifiable paraphasias D used, was that his output had its foundations in English. However, it was not always apparent to what extent the neologistic output resembled his first language, Punjabi. Indeed, one of the more recurrent utterances heard in D's conversation was [du:ka:n] meaning "shop" in Punjabi. D also gave the impression that he had considerable difficulty understanding speech. It looked as though he had to concentrate very hard when listening to a speaker, he was easily distracted, at times found it almost impossible to stop himself speaking, and he frequently got the "wrong end of the stick". It was sometimes possible to clarify aspects of a conversation by writing down relevant key words, again, in English, suggesting that it may be possible to employ therapy tasks using written words as stimuli. D showed almost no ability to write, beyond attempting his own name.

D's bilingualism clearly complicated the task of evaluating his language, however, our impression was that his output, at least, was based on English.

To satisfy ourselves further, we asked D and his family whether they felt it would be appropriate to work in English. Having ascertained that this could be beneficial, we set about more formal assessment. With D's purchasing authority agreeing initially a period of 8 weeks' rehabilitation at the centre, we wanted to assess as thoroughly but as swiftly as possible. The key areas we wanted to clarify as a result of our informal observations were as follows:

1. The extent of D's ability to understand spoken English.
2. The extent to which D's ability to understand written English was superior to his understanding of speech.
3. The extent of D's naming difficulties, again comparing spoken and written.
4. D's auditory perception.

Elements of the PALPA (Kay, Lesser, & Coltheart, 1992), the three-picture version of the Pyramids and Palm Trees Test (Howard & Patterson, 1992), and the TROG (Bishop, 1982), were chosen. The assessments used to evaluate D's language impairments before therapy are summarised in Table 3.1. Our impression that D's ability to understand written words was superior to his understanding of speech was confirmed, although both are impaired. It is similarly clear that D does, indeed, present with multiple language impairment. It is important to note that D was very conscious of being "tested". He tried enormously hard throughout but also became very agitated, frustrated, and distressed if he suspected he was doing badly, or, in the case of the output assessments, when he could see he was not doing well.

Obviously, it is not just the scores that tell us about D's impairments, but exactly how he went about the tasks, and how he arrived at his responses. Considering first the input tasks, with the spoken word-to-picture matching task, on initial assessment, D made errors across the distractor types. Thirteen of the errors were either unrelated or visual distractors, with the remaining 11 errors equally distributed across close and distant semantic distractors. Of the three errors made on the written word-to-picture matching assessment,

TABLE 3.1

Details of Speech and Language Therapy initial assessments

Assessment	Initial Assessment
Minimal Pairs (PALPA)	15/40
Spoken word-to-picture matching (PALPA)	16/40
Test for Reception of Grammar (TROG) (spoken)	17/32
Written word-to-picture matching (PALPA)	37/40
TROG (written)	25/40
Pyramids and Palm Trees (3-picture version)	34/52
Spoken picture naming (PALPA)	2/40
Repetition (PALPA)	2/40
Written naming (PALPA)	0/25

two were in selecting the close semantic distractor and one in the selection of the visually related distractor. The auditory discrimination assessment used required the selection of one from three pictures in response to spoken input. The picture array includes the target, a picture for a minimally different word, and one for a word different by two distinctive features. D's errors consisted of 15 erroneous selections of the minimally different distractor and 10 of the distractor differing by two distinctive features from the target. There was no clear pattern reflected with respect to the position of the phonemic change in the distractor items and similar numbers of errors were made for high and low frequency lexical items. With the TROG assessments, D was very slow and gave the impression that he was selecting his responses by a process of elimination.

D evidently found the output tasks demanding. Examples of his responses in the spoken naming and repetition assessments, and a transcription of his spontaneous spoken output is presented in Appendices 1 and 2. Attempts at oral reading of single words produced similarly neologistic and perseverative responses. D was unable to attempt written naming of pictures and on only 3/20 occasions successfully produced the target word from an anagram of appropriate letter tiles. He was, however, able to identify the first letter from a selection of three on 17/20 occasions.

In summary, the assessments administered confirmed our working hypothesis of (1) severely impaired auditory input, with impairments at or around the acoustic analysis stage and subsequently in accessing the semantic system, (2) relatively preserved access to single word semantics via the written channel, and (3) impaired output affecting spoken and written naming. Although his spoken word output difficulties may have been partly the result of reduced semantic specification, poor reading aloud and repetition suggested difficulties in lexical access/retrieval and later stage phonological assembly also.

THERAPEUTIC INTERVENTION

In order to outline the various aspects of therapy undertaken with D it has been necessary to describe the rationale and therapy tasks in a very formal and modular way. In reality, the therapeutic intervention was much more integrated in nature. It was often impossible to follow rigid hierarchies, and in some cases a single task was considered to address a number of different aspects of both D's language impairment and his communication disability.[1] Furthermore, specific emotional and social aspects of D's communication disability tended to be addressed throughout the therapy course, and often in response to issues raised in therapy sessions, rather than in isolation. Indeed, the multidimensional and integrated nature of D's speech and language therapy, reflect the clinical picture of interactive, multiple language impairments.

The period of assessment revealed, as anticipated, D's severe and widespread impairments of both language comprehension and expression. Therapy focused on three key areas: semantic knowledge, phonological processing, and functional communication strategies, with many tasks capitalising on D's relatively preserved ability to comprehend single written words. A total of 18 weeks' Speech and Language Therapy was given as part of a general neurological rehabilitation package while D attended the rehabilitation centre.

The "Therapeutic Timescale" (see Fig. 3.1) summarises the communication therapy input across the 18-week period. Speech and Language Therapy was on a twice-daily basis with sessions lasting 40 minutes each. D was typically seen by two different therapists (the authors), assisted by a range of students. For the first 8 weeks, while D was an inpatient, he also received daily occupational therapy and physiotherapy.

Impact of impaired non-language cognition

Before considering in more detail the various aspects of communication therapy undertaken with D, it is necessary to discuss the impact of D's cognitive rigidity and inflexibility on assessment and therapeutic intervention. As can be seen from Fig. 3.1, this rigidity and inflexibility was a specific factor impinging on language assessment and therapy during the first 9 weeks of Speech and Language Therapy. Tasks often required repeated demonstration each session and, indeed within sessions. Performance on tasks was very variable and it is possible to identify a hierarchical pattern of behaviours with respect to this aspect of D's performance:

1. Difficulty with a given task, presented by the same therapist, within the same therapy session.
2. Difficulty with a given task, presented by the same therapist, across different therapy sessions.
3. Difficulty only occurs for given, familiar tasks when presented by unfamiliar therapist, (i.e. a therapist involved with D's rehabilitation, but one who did not generally present that exercise).
4. Able to perform familiar therapy tasks with a range of therapists.

FIGURE 3.1

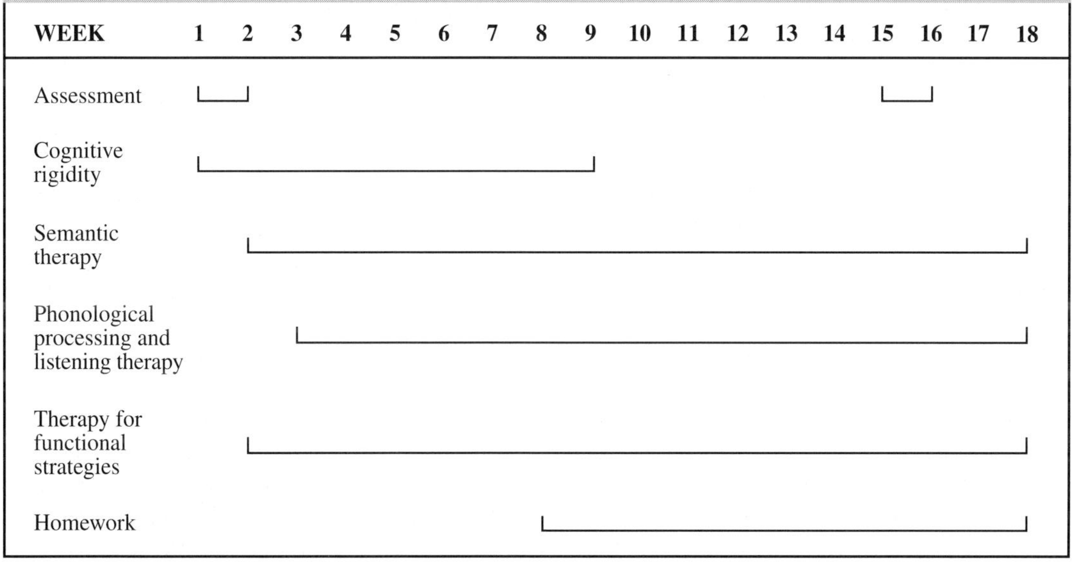

Timescale of therapeutic intervention.

Behaviours 1 and 2 were evident until week 5 of rehabilitation, with behaviour 3 persisting until the end of week 6. Interestingly, in week 6, in spite of this developing flexibility and ability to change set in semantic tasks (see later), D was on one occasion completely unable to perform a written-word semantic task previously performed without error, when the items were presented in a different order. It was not until week 9 that D proved able to perform familiar therapy tasks with a range of therapists.

Semantic therapy

Rationale
Reference to the section on assessment will reveal that D's performance was generally impaired for tasks considered to require access to semantic information. However, it seems that he was more readily able to access such information via some inputs as compared with others. D's performance on the spoken word-to-picture matching task was much poorer than his performance on either the written word-to-picture matching task, or the three picture version of Pyramids and Palm Trees. However, this was, no doubt, largely due to D's additional auditory input difficulties at an earlier acoustic analysis stage (see later). The need to build on D's strengths (i.e. partial ability to draw on semantic knowledge), was agreed and therefore therapy targeting semantic aspects of language processing was commenced in the second week of therapy.

Aims
- To achieve reliable comprehension of single written words with the hope that comprehension of spoken words might also improve.
- To achieve possible extended effects from improved semantic processing ability to enhancing naming and output (see, for example, Scott, 1987).

Predicted outcomes
- Improved performance on Pyramids and Palm Trees test.
- Improved performance on word-to-picture matching tasks for written and potentially spoken stimuli.

Therapy tasks
A range of tasks, predominantly requiring access of semantic information from pictures and/or written words, were used to target semantic aspects of language processing. Different types of task were employed and these will be described in turn later. Each task employed stimuli and a mode of input corresponding to D's own hierarchy of difficulty:

> Pictures only
> Pictures + written words
> Written words only
> Pictures + spoken words
> Written words + spoken words

However, after the first few sessions working on this aspect of language processing, it was not always necessary to work rigidly through the hierarchy. Wherever possible topics of specific interest to D were used, e.g. sport, travel, religion, food, family. Therapy did not focus on a specific set of words, but rather on a specific set of topics.

Categorisation tasks
These tasks made up the main part of the semantic therapy. Examples of actual exercises are shown in Appendix 3. From week 2 to week 6 all tasks involved sorting of either pictures or written words into specified categories. Tasks included:

1. Semantic – co-ordinate based, employing two and later three, related co-ordinates, e.g. Household vs. Garden items, Cities vs. Countries.
2. Attribute based, with stimuli all within word class, e.g. Hot vs. Cold, Light vs. Heavy
3. Concept based (wider semantic fields/across word classes): (a) Unrelated, e.g. Food vs. Hospitals, (b) Related e.g. Christianity vs. Hinduism, Kenya vs. Britain.

Intriguingly and perhaps unusually, the degree of semantic relatedness of stimuli did not appear to be a parameter of difficulty for D, while broader conceptual judgements were apparently more challenging. Hence, the concept-based tasks were considered more taxing for D than the attribute-based tasks, even where the target categories are apparently unrelated. It was felt that this pattern reflected the more convergent, concrete nature of D's language and non-language cognitive processing and the restricted way in which he was able to draw on his semantic knowledge.

By week 6, D was much better able to switch set in sorting tasks and it was possible to use one set of stimuli for two different sorting tasks, e.g. Famous People, (a) Male vs. Female, (b) Sport vs. Politics.

In week 7, D began to be able to perform tasks involving the categorisation of spoken words presented by the therapist and the work targeting semantic processing could begin to be integrated with the listening work developing as part of the therapy addressing phonological processing.

Charting tasks

For these and remaining tasks described in this section on semantic therapy, stimuli were largely written or spoken only. Given D's apparent difficulty organising and relating specific features of semantic knowledge, these tasks were introduced in week 4. In these tasks D is presented with a chart with a number of different properties or qualities, for example:

NEAR	X	FAR
ENGLAND	AFRICA	INDIA
TOWN	COUNTRY	COUNTRY
VISITED	X	NOT VISITED
FLY	WALK	DRIVE

D was then required to indicate for written words presented singly, which of the characteristics on each line best described the named item. For the example chart illustrated, the stimuli words would be place names, e.g. Birmingham; Kenya.

Other semantic tasks

Odd man out. Using pictures or written words, D was required to indicate which item did not belong, for example:

easy: CUP PLATE BATH FORK SAUCER
hard: WEDNESDAY THURSDAY FRIDAY
JUNE SATURDAY

Difficulty was judged according to the semantic relatedness of the distractors.

Sentence-category task. D was required to identify which word in a written sentence belonged to the category indicated at the beginning of the sentence, for example:

FLOWER: *The man gave the rose to his wife.*
FOOD: *The rice was boiling in the big pan.*

Definitions. D was required to select the written word that matched the written definition, for example:

long yellow fruit:	ORANGE BANANA
	APPLE LEMON
place of worship:	GURU GURDWARA
	SIKH GRANTH SAHIB

There was no strict hierarchy for these tasks, for example D's performance was sometimes better with tasks involving the selection of a specified word from a sentence (presumably because of the number of redundant words in this task), whereas on other occasions it seemed that D became so fixed on the sentence that he could not perform the task. It was certainly noticed that when tasks involved words considered to be of functional relevance to D, such as family names, D was often worse than if the same task was presented with more personally irrelevant words. We suggest that this was in part because of the additional emotional overload that accompanied the processing of such words, but also D often appeared confused as to whether the therapist was trying to converse with him or whether she was presenting him with a therapy task.

As D progressed it became possible to give many of these semantic exercises as home assignments, requiring less one-to-one supervision and guidance. Furthermore, in the later weeks, therapy became increasingly integrated. Tasks aimed at developing functional communication strategies often required the use of semantic processing, and later semantic categorisation tasks using spoken input, clearly incorporated the use of listening skills developed as part of the auditory discrimination work.

Outcome of semantic therapy

Quantitative improvements were seen in the following assessments involving semantic processing:

> Written word-to-picture matching
> Spoken word-to-picture matching
> Pyramids and Palm Trees (three-picture version)

The results of these pre- and post-therapy assessments are illustrated in Fig. 3.2 (see also Table 3.2, p. 29).

D's performance on the Pyramids and Palm Trees test did improve as anticipated, as did his ability to comprehend single written words reliably. In addition, D demonstrated a marked improvement in his ability to comprehend single spoken words. The more qualitative aspects of D's enhanced communication skills are discussed in the general summary of outcome at the end of the therapy section.

Therapy for phonological processing

Rationale

Support for the need to target aspects of phonological processing in D's therapy was both qualitative and quantitative. Informal observation provided the qualitative rationale, the "therapeutic intuition"! As mentioned earlier, D's fluent spoken output presented largely as neologistic jargon with some *conduite d'approche* and phonological paraphasias, which he was completely unable to self-monitor. He seldom recognised if, in the course of a string of speech, he produced a correct target word and he was constantly distracted by his own incorrect, perseverative repetitions of both words and neologisms. D demonstrated most frustration about his inability to express himself effectively. His insight into his poor comprehension was less apparent, perhaps highlighted by the fact that D seldom, if ever, requested repetitions.

Consideration of the assessments carried out in the first few weeks of D's stay at the rehabilitation centre provide the quantitative rationale for therapy targeting phonological processing. First, his poorer performance on spoken vs. written word-to-picture matching tasks, in the light of a very poor performance on a task of minimal pair discrimination, suggested that in addition to a semantic element, impaired acoustic analysis also affects his comprehension of speech. Further support for a phonological processing impairment comes from D's near inability to repeat spoken words (although clearly this must be considered in the context of generally impaired output).

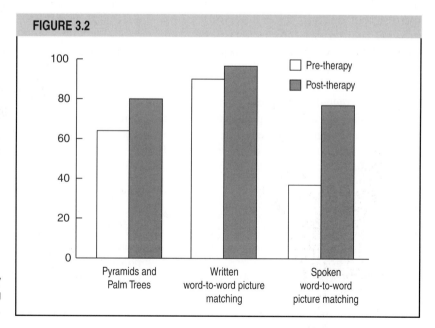

FIGURE 3.2

Pre- and post-therapy assessments requiring semantic processing.

Aims

- Improve listening skills.
- Improve self-monitoring.
- Switch of emphasis from output to input to:
  - (a) improve insight into comprehension difficulties
  - (b) encourage D to reduce meaningless, ineffective verbalisation (jargon)
  - (c) encourage D to request repetitions.

Predicted outcomes

- Improved performance on minimal pair judgements.
- Constraint of verbal output.
- Improved self-monitoring.
- Possible improved comprehension of single spoken words.

Therapy tasks

The hierarchy of difficulty for auditory discrimination-based tasks was, by necessity, led by D's ability to construe and follow task demands at a structural rather than a linguistic level. Early interference, for example of spoken output, which D clearly saw as the end aim of all tasks, or difficulty comprehending same/different concepts, led to a range of presentations and responses on a similar task being explored in the early days of therapy. Frustratingly for both D and the therapist, massive inconsistency across tasks and sessions, resulting from both the interplay of these linguistic and structural elements, and D's emotional response to failure, meant clear hierarchies of difficulty were not easy to develop in the initial phase of phonological therapy (see Jones, 1989 for an alternative, more structured approach to listening/monitoring therapy). Broadly speaking, however, task content and requirements followed the order outlined next.

Word and picture minimal pairs

Task 1. In this task, D was presented with two pictures and the corresponding written words. D was then required to point to the picture corresponding to the spoken word provided by the therapist. On initial trials the distractor was a real word differing by at least two distinctive features from the name of the target item, as shown in Fig. 3.3.

On later trials, the distractor differed from the target by only one distinctive feature, e.g. TIN vs. PIN. A pointing response was required for these tasks. D was not required to make verbal responses and was encouraged to remain silent.

Task 2: In task 2, D was presented with one picture and its corresponding written word only. In these tasks he was required to indicate yes/no (spoken word), in response to the spoken word, which may or may not have been the correct spoken target, provided by the therapist. As D's ability to follow the task with grossly dissimilar CVC words (consonant-vowel-consonant) developed, a more

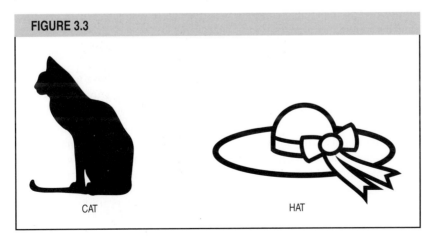

FIGURE 3.3

CAT   HAT

Example of word and picture minimal pair item.

structured hierarchy of difficulty for CVC distractors was adopted as follows:

Non-word, at least two distinctive features different, word initial consonant change

Non-word, one distinctive feature different, word initial consonant change

Real-word, at least two distinctive features different, word initial consonant change

Real word, one distinctive feature different, word initial consonant change

Real word, at least two distinctive features different, word final consonant change

Real word, one distinctive feature different, word final consonant change.

In initial trials, the therapist presented D with the target word spoken in isolation; in later trials the target word was preceded by "Is it a…". In both instances D was required to respond by answering yes/no.

Outcome for word/picture minimal pair task

Tasks 1 and 2 formed the core of the therapy for phonological processing. As mentioned previously, D's difficulty following the structural components of the task, and therefore the lack of consistency and reliability within and across sessions for the same task and stimuli, were confusing and distressing for both D and therapist. For example, he could vary from a success rate of 50–95% accurate within one session for the same task. Interestingly, at the same time D demonstrated a similar level of inconsistency/inability to hold on to concepts. For example, with respect to apparent revelations he expressed about his communication difficulties, he appeared to understand an aspect of his limitations in a morning session, for example, yet was totally bewildered by the same aspect in the afternoon. Not until week 3 was a clearer pattern of phonological processing difficulties emerging and a sufficient degree of consistency to press on with this therapeutic approach in a more linguistically useful way. However, a useful offshoot of the many misunderstandings and communication failures about the hows, whys, and wherefores of the therapy tasks prompted much productive discussion (in written and diagrammatic form), about the

nature of D's language processing impairments, and strengths, and their wider implications.

Written word auditory discrimination tasks

From week 9 onwards, it was possible to introduce a number of auditory discrimination tasks without the need for pictures:

Written word minimal pairs. This task was, essentially, a minimal pair discrimination task. Initially D was presented with two phonologically/visually similar written words. He was requested to point to the word that the therapist said, for example:

written words:	BEER	DEER
spoken word:	DEER	
written words:	BEAR	PEAR
spoken word:	BEAR	

Written word minimal sets. Once D was successful with the written word minimal pairs, the task was extended to give a choice of three written words, for example:

written words:	RAKE	CAKE	LAKE
spoken word:	LAKE		

In the previous tasks each of the targets were carefully modelled allowing D to make the auditory visual association. He was also encouraged at this stage and throughout the task to pay attention to word-initial lip position as a further cue. Informal attention was therefore given to visual as well as phonological aspects of distractors in the set.

Outcome for written word auditory discrimination tasks

Although performance on the above tasks showed confusing variations on a day-to-day basis, D progressed from an average of 60% to 90% accurate on the phonologically similar pairs and subsequently on the triads. He demonstrated an equivalent level of performance with word-initial and word-final changes until increased attention to lip reading cues returned the advantage for word-initial tasks. Over this period D also demonstrated improved ability to (1) ask for repetitions when unsure of the input, and (2) inhibit his own output so that full and undivided attention was focused on the listening aspect of the task.

Miscellaneous tasks for auditory perception

As the date of discharge from the centre approached a wider range of tasks targeting auditory perception were introduced. As far as possible these tasks used words of functional relevance to D, e.g. names of friends and family, places regularly visited by D, etc. The following variables were included in these tasks but were not introduced in any specific hierarchy.

Word length. Initially, in these tasks D was required to point to one or three short lines beneath a mono- or polysyllabic written word, to indicate whether he judged words spoken by the therapist to be long or short. Subsequently, written words only were used. Word length was varied in terms of number of syllables and words were sometimes semantically similar and sometimes not.

1. Phonologically similar, semantically un-related words, e.g. car vs. carton.
2. Phonologically similar, semantically related words, e.g. football vs. footballer.

This task was then extended to include triads of phonologically (+/− semantically) related sets of one, two, or three syllable words or compounds with D required to point to the written version of the spoken word, for example:

"BACK":	BACK BACKWARD
	BACKWARD POINT
"SUNDAY":	SUN SUNDAY
	SUNGLASSES

Phonological similarity, bisyllabic words. In these tasks D was required to point to a written word corresponding to the word spoken by the therapist, given a choice of two written words. The written words could be solely phonologically similar or, in addition, semantically related, for example:

1. Phonologically similar, semantically unrelated – DAUGHTER vs. DOCTOR.

2. Phonologically similar, semantically related—MOTHER vs. BROTHER.

Identifying phonemic variation
Task 1. In these tasks D was required not only to detect the therapist's mispronunciations, but also to correct the written word such that it corresponded with the word spoken. D was presented with a word written with Scrabble tiles, together with a selection of three letters from which to choose in order to correct the word, for example:

Spoken word TIN

Consonant distractors were kept as visually and phonologically dissimilar as possible and location of change was maintained at word-initial consonant position. Ten spoken target presentations per minimal set were given.

Task 2. As D became more proficient in the listening component of the task, and in an attempt to incorporate more explicit work on production and self-monitoring, D was encouraged to produce two of the four alternatives at the end of each set. After listening to therapist models of the target, D was asked to produce the same word, for example.

Target: PIN
Therapist: "pin...pin...pin"
D: —

As D's productions at this stage were closer approximations to the target, they enabled discussion, using the visual prompts of the Scrabble tiles, as to the relative accuracy of D's attempted repetition.

Outcome of miscellaneous tasks for auditory perception and detection of phonemic variation
Both these sets of tasks featured in the later weeks of therapy while D was at the rehabilitation centre. D clearly experienced greater difficulty where tasks

involved both phonological similarity and personal significance, e.g. brother vs. mother, though varying word length also increased the difficulty although he gradually progressed from a 65% to a consistent 95% success rate. He also appeared to perform less well on personally related material despite more distant phonological links, in contrast to more neutral but semantically related stimuli, suggesting that the abstract less emotionally laden content of stimuli may have helped him to maintain full attention on the nature and structure of the task. This is in contrast to studies suggesting that use of personally relevant information enhances auditory comprehension (see, for example, Wallace & Canter, 1985). Incorporation of the production and monitoring aspects of the word monitoring tasks had limited success at a specific, "spot the segment error", level. However, it proved useful, (1) as a concrete demonstration of how all the listening work had, as predicted, resulted in more target-related repetitions, which D was now able to identify as more or less closely related to his intended word, and (2) as a constrained outlet for spoken production, which D had been desperate to work on throughout therapy.

General outcome for therapy for phonological processing

Qualitatively, the following improvements were observed on discharge and evident on informal comparison of admission and discharge videotaped sessions:

- Ability to listen to speaker, highlighted by:
  (a) more accurate responses to requests
  (b) asking for repetitions
  (c) ability to switch between spoken (watching the speaker), and written forms of input.
- Ability to self monitor, highlighted by:
  (a) fewer perseverations and consequently fewer self-distractions
  (b) increased ability to recognise when he has said a correct word.

Quantitative evidence of improved auditory perception comes largely from D's improved performance post therapy on the minimal pairs assessment and spoken word-to-picture matching. The results of these pre- and post-therapy assessments for spoken word input are illustrated in Fig. 3.4 (see also Table 3.2, p. 29).

FIGURE 3.4

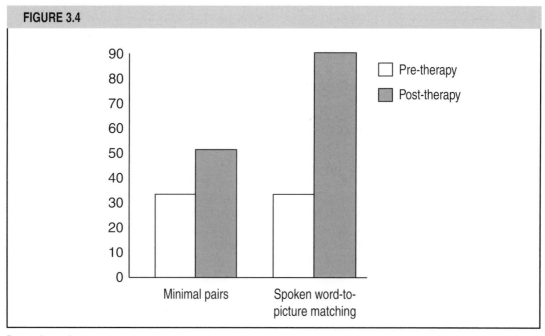

Pre- and post-therapy assessments.

The mismatch between still limited success levels on the minimal pairs test (where D was asked to point to one of three phonologically related pictures), and his superior performance on treatment tasks requiring a similar response to one of three written words, may be due to the distracting influence of pictures, or his lack of familiarity with the type of assessment task at this stage in therapy. As discussed previously the improved performance on the spoken word-to-picture matching assessment can also be attributed to an improved ability to access semantic representations for spoken words, as a result of the therapy for semantic processing. Perhaps the more striking improvement in spoken word comprehension can be explained as a result of a combination of improved acoustic analysis and more effective retrieval of semantics for spoken words.

Therapy for the development of functional communication strategies

Rationale
Prior to his stroke, D had been a skilled communicator in both English and his first language, Punjabi. At the time of his arrival at the rehabilitation centre, 8 months after his stroke, he and his family presented as very distressed and highly frustrated by the level of communication breakdown they were experiencing. It appeared that neither D nor his family had developed a reliable way to communicate, or deal with communication failures. In addition, D's communication difficulties were having an adverse impact on other therapy sessions at the centre (i.e. occupational therapy and physiotherapy). The severity of D's impairments, especially expressively, meant that in less structured settings spoken or written attempts to communicate were likely to be, at best, ambiguous. The early introduction of some communication strategies therefore seemed essential. Furthermore, it was felt that early consideration of alternative methods of communication aside from speech and writing would minimise the sense of "failure" or "last resort" which may be encountered when such measures are introduced later in therapeutic intervention.

Options for alternative communication strategies

Gesture. D was, on rare occasions, able to use gesture to express himself effectively. Early attempts to evaluate the possible usefulness of gesture as a form of expression, quickly demonstrated that, once focused on, D's gesturing became confused, disorganised, and far from functionally useful.

Pointing to written words. D's relatively preserved ability to recognise and understand single written words was being used routinely during therapy sessions, to clarify D's attempts at spoken communication, with some success. This option was pursued most actively during the 18-week therapy period, for the following reasons.

1. This was the method of choice being used to clarify communication in Speech and Language Therapy sessions.
2. It was envisaged that work towards a written word communication chart or book could be linked to the more impairment-led therapy, in particular the work on semantic processing with written words.

Aims
To be able to use communication charts with written words collated in a small file to express needs and to interact with familiar others.

Therapy tasks

Identifying how to introduce the strategy
Mistakenly, it was assumed that D's ability to perform, with relative success, the written word-to-picture matching task in assessment, would mean that he could perform a range of tasks involving written word-to-picture matching. The previously discussed cognitive inflexibility and rigidity again seemed to play a part as D's success varied. For example, he proved quite unable to match single written words to items identified in a composite picture, while readily (except for the occasional semantic error) able to match the same written word to a target picture given a choice of one or two pictures. Once again it was unclear whether it was

the introduction of a novel task utilising familiar stimuli which baffled D, or whether he was unsuccessful for some linguistic reason. Either way, if D was to be able to develop the skills necessary to use a strategy of pointing to written words as a form of communication we anticipated a need for utilising a more flexible approach. Furthermore, he would need to be able to recognise that the same occurrence of a given written word could be used to refer to a number of different occurrences of items or concepts. Mental flexibility and semantics emerged then as central to the development of this strategy. The fact that we might be working on two of D's impairments while also, hopefully, addressing a key aspect of D's communication disability seemed clinically sound. As will be seen, many of the tasks developed to address this aspect of therapy can also be considered as tasks requiring semantic processing and increased cognitive flexibility.

Other aspects of therapy for written word communication strategy

The need to link with D's family and other professionals in the rehabilitation centre was evident. Other disciplines were asked for word sets which we could work on, that would be relevant to their sessions with D. Where possible, joint sessions were arranged with that discipline. At meetings with the family the idea of a written word communication chart or file was discussed, and both D's wife and brother were asked to provide word lists that they considered would be useful to work on.

Hierarchy for therapy and details of the therapy tasks

It was considered that progressing through the following hierarchy of therapy tasks would facilitate the development of the communication strategy:

1. *Written word-to-noun picture matching (and vice versa).* Initially these tasks would be of a "Pyramids and Palm Tree" type format, i.e. D was required to match a written word to one of two distantly semantically related pictures, or a picture to one of two distantly

semantically related words. As D became more able to perform these tasks the semantic distance between target and distractor would be decreased.

2. *Written word-to-action picture, (and vice versa).* These tasks were essentially the same as the tasks for written word-to-noun picture matching except that verbs and action pictures were used. At this stage all the action pictures were of single actions only.

3. *Written word-to-picture arrays (and vice versa).* In these tasks arrays of pictures would be used. In the first couple of trials, D would be required to match a single written word to one of three semantically related pictures. Unlike the first word-to-picture matching tasks described, the distractor pictures could be either distantly or closely semantically related to the target picture. Once successful, arrays of four related pictures would be added. As with the previously described tasks, D would also be required to match a pictured object to an array of written words. Picture or written word arrays could be all object/nouns, all actions/verbs, or a combination of both.

4. *Matching subject-verb-object written word combinations to action pictures.* D would be presented with an action picture under which was written a choice of three alternatives for subject, action, and object. The object of this task was to begin to demonstrate to D that pointing to a written word could be expressive or communicative.

5. *Written word-to-aspects of composite pictures.* Like the previous task, the object of this exercise was to further demonstrate the more creative possibilities of pointing to written words as a communication strategy. In the first instance D would merely be required to identify the part of a composite picture corresponding to a single written word presented.

6. *Word charts with composite pictures.* At a later stage, D would be required to point to words arranged as in task 4 to describe a

specified aspect of a composite picture. An example of this exercise is given in Appendix 4.

Tasks 4-6 could be presented as either a written worksheet, or, as a PACE-type task.

7. *Word charts around unit/outside of unit.* It was envisaged that word charts could be developed for particular activities that D was involved in as part of his therapy and activities/people that he would be involved with at home. D would be encouraged to use the chart in sessions to request things he needed, and to give accounts of activities to those who had not been present at a particular therapy session.

8. *Word book around unit.* Ultimately, communication charts would be collated in a small "Filofax" type file. Clearly, this would involve added cognitive and organisational demands, e.g. the need to recognise which page was relevant in a given situation and locating the appropriate page.

Outcome of therapy for alternative communication strategy

D's progress through the hierarchy of tasks described above was neither as smooth nor as modular as the documentation might suggest. Tasks 4 to 6 were intermingled within therapy sessions, and it was necessary to add further tasks as progression from one task to another, in some cases, proved problematic. Furthermore, the degree to which D's functional ability to communicate was enhanced proved difficult to measure, despite quantitative evidence that D could perform the tasks in the therapy hierarchy. Therapy for the development of the alternative communication strategy began in week 2 of the Speech and Language Therapy intervention at the rehabilitation centre. By week 5 D was sufficiently successful with tasks 1–5 for attempts to be made to use written words to communicate in more functional settings, i.e. tasks 6, 7, and 8 in the proposed hierarchy. In week 5 the first joint sessions with the Occupational Therapist were undertaken with the aim that D might use simple charts with written

words to perform a functional activity in the Occupational Therapy Workshop. In consultation with the Occupational Therapist, D had indicated that he would like to practise preparing simple hot snacks and drinks as part of his upper limb function rehabilitation. It was decided that D could use a communication chart with relevant words to request equipment and ingredients when working with the Occupational Therapist in the kitchen and that, if this proved successful, to describe what he had done later to a person who had not been present. It was quickly apparent that there was a gulf, for D at least, between matching words and pictures to each other in a structured therapeutic task, and using what essentially appeared to be the same set of skills to communicate more creatively. D was completely unable to use words written on a card to ask for anything and in fact became agitated and distressed.

It seemed, once again, that D's cognitive rigidity contributed to his difficulty in applying the same principles to different tasks. Or was it simply that D was puzzled to find the Speech and Language Therapist in the Occupational Therapy Department and the Occupational Therapist presenting communication exercises? For this reason, in weeks 5 and 6 further tasks were developed, introduced, and worked on with D, in conjunction with the Occupational Therapist. The familiar tasks of written word-to-picture matching (nouns and/or verbs) were reintroduced and combined with tasks of written word-to-object and written word-to-person performing an action. It was enormously beneficial to work in conjunction with another therapist at this point as it made it possible to model the exercises for D before he attempted them. His confidence returned, and by week 7 he was able to use charts with a limited selection of written words to request equipment and materials, e.g. saw, screwdriver etc., for a woodwork project, when working in the Occupational Therapy Department and to later "talk" about activities he had been involved in, e.g. tell the Speech and Language Therapist what sport they had played in the recreation group. By week 11 the communication charts were collated in a small file. D demonstrated proficient use of the file to communicate by week 14 and it was possible to confirm this by video-taping D interacting with unfamiliar people.

So far the outcomes might be considered as quantifiable evidence that D had mastered skills necessary to be able to use a written word communication strategy of some kind. However, as previously mentioned, the degree to which D's functional ability to communicate was enhanced is less convincing. D, his wife, and his brother appeared to welcome the idea of the communication book, yet the names of family and friends, where they lived, and places D had travelled to were largely all that were forthcoming when his family were asked for ideas for the book, with all contributions in English. Furthermore, the fact that D's family home was some distance from the rehabilitation centre, coupled with his family's business and other commitments, made it difficult for members of his family to attend therapy sessions to see what was being done so that they might adopt similar strategies at home. Additional evidence that D did not see the written word charts as a method of choice for communicating in novel situations came from a shopping trip organised as part of his therapy. Two sessions had been devoted to preparation for communication in the shop using a chart, but when therapist and D arrived in the shop, D produced a list he had copied, a perfectly acceptable and successful strategy! Whether D would have seen the idea of presenting a written list to the shop assistant as communicative earlier in therapy is hard to say.

Post-therapy assessments

As can be seen from Fig. 3.5 and Table 3.2. D's performance on all input assessments carried out before therapy improved (with the exception of the written TROG, which is unsurprising given that therapy had focused almost exclusively on single word input). On reassessment with the written word-to-picture matching, D performed perfectly. Furthermore, he selected almost twice as many correct target pictures in the spoken word-to-picture matching assessment. On this assessment, one error was the selection of a visually related distractor but all other errors were made with semantic distractors, perhaps suggesting that D could now recognise the spoken word sufficiently to be able to access semantic information more reliably. D's performance on the minimal pairs assessment was

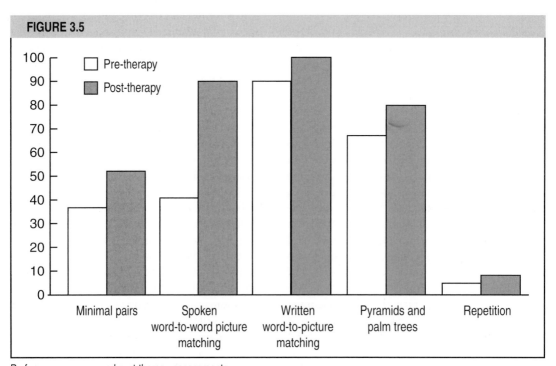

FIGURE 3.5

Performance on pre- and post-therapy assessments.

TABLE 3.2

Pre- and post-therapy assessments

Assessment	Initial Assessment	Re-assessment
Minimal Pairs (PALPA) Chance=13/40	15/40	22/40
Spoken word-to-picture matching (PALPA) Chance=8/40	16/40	36/40
TROG (spoken)	17/32 Chance=8/32	23/40 Chance=10/40
Written word-to-picture matching (PALPA) Chance=8/40	37/40	40/40
TROG (written) Chance=10/40	25/40	20/40
Pyramids and Palm Trees (3-picture version) Chance=26/52	34/52	40/52
Spoken picture naming (PALPA)	2/40	Not formally assessed
Repetition (PALPA)	2/40	3/40
Written naming (PALPA)	10/40	Not formally assessed

not qualitatively different from the pre-therapy assessment, although he managed to select more target items.

D was more successfully able to contribute to spoken conversation post therapy (see Appendix 6). However, with the exception of repetition (see Appendix 5), single word output tasks were not formally reassessed or were abandoned owing to D's distress and difficulty breaking perseverative patterns. D appeared to have increased insight into his difficulties in these tasks and to press on with the entire assessment when little change was evident, seemed like assessment for assessment's sake. Comparing D's single word repetition pre and post therapy reveals subtle qualitative changes (see Appendices 1 and 5). This may reflect a combination of improved acoustic perception and non-specified output processes.

OUTCOME: LANGUAGE AND BEYOND

In order to gauge D and his family's own perspective on therapy-induced change, at a discharge interview, D and his daughter were asked to complete a simple rating scale, marking levels of ability/disability pre- and post-intervention (see Appendix 7). Both pre- and post-therapy scales were completed retrospectively. Reassuringly, each of the areas of change highlighted in the clinical observation and assessment were corroborated by them. Both D and his daughter noted significant changes in spoken word comprehension and oral expression, with minor improvements in reading and no change in writing, which had not been a focus of treatment. Both also reported marked change in D's level of confidence in communicating with friends and family. Across the ratings there was a tendency for D to rate his performance as worse that his daughter's perception, though agreement as to amount of change was largely consistent.

Another form of outcome measure which was completed as part of standard procedure at the rehabilitation centre was the Functional Assessment Measure (FAM; Forer, 1990). This is a multidisciplinary outcome measure which aims to quantify improvement in functional levels of performance across a range of physical, cognitive, linguistic, emotional, and behavioural parameters (see scoresheet in Appendix 8). Within our clinical setting, the therapy team is required to score patients on the 1–7 scale 10 days after admission and again in the week of discharge. Within the communication section of the FAM, scores are allocated to the component processes of comprehension, spoken and/or non-verbal expression, reading, writing, and speech intelligibility. An example of guidelines for scoring spoken expression would be:

1. Able to express basic needs and ideas less than 25% of the time or does not express basic needs appropriately or consistently.
2. Able to express basic needs and ideas about everyday situations 50% to 74% of the time.
3. Able to express complex or abstract ideas without difficulty.

As can be seen from the discharge scores on the communication section, the measure again reflected the clinically observed improvements in those language areas addressed in therapy. The predicted goal scores set shortly after admission highlight both a degree of uncertainty at that time as to the target areas for treatment and also an element of over ambition regarding our ability to dramatically influence aspects of D's communication within the timescale to which we were working.

Post-therapy scores also reflect subtle shifts in problem solving ability, i.e. D's slightly less rigid approach to tasks (though note the over estimation of abilities on this and other sections on admission), and an ability to take a more active though still very limited role in his employment context.

Less clear is the picture that emerges (or not) from the section on the FAM covering psychosocial adjustment. The initial high scores on the sections relating to emotional behaviours (designated as including frustration, depression, anxiety, agitation) and adjustment to limitations reflect, in part, D's outward cheerfulness and reduced awareness of the extent and impact of his communication disability on himself and others. However, they seem, with hindsight, a poor reflection of the well of frustration and distress which, whilst always under fragile control, became increasingly evident as our relationship with D developed. As is the case in the scoring of many other clients with reduced language ability and/or lack of insight, the validity and usefulness of assigning therapists' subjectively determined ratings to a client's internal state should be fundamentally questioned. This is an even greater problem when scores must be assigned

before the therapy team have had an opportunity to develop any real therapeutic relationship with the client.

However, as therapists, we see consistently one of our aims of intervention as supporting a client and their family throughout the difficult transition from non-disabled to disabled identity, from pre-stoke roles and lifestyles to revised family and social structures with all the emotional pulls and upheavals which that may entail. In an attempt to evaluate the impact of our intervention on these less readily quantifiable areas of D's disability and lifestyle, the following section will provide more qualitative, descriptive, and largely subjective detail of other aspects of our involvement with D.

SOCIAL, CULTURAL, AND EMOTIONAL FACTORS IN PSYCHOSOCIAL TRANSITION

What impact had our intervention had on D and his family at a more emotional, socially relevant level? Our initial aims of therapy included providing D and his family with access to information and support regarding the nature and consequences of his condition. Much therapy time was directed at simple, repeated explanation of why D was experiencing this confusing array of receptive and expressive language impairments. This was often in response to D's bewildered questioning of "But why … I want to know" when he compared his erratic, tortured performance on a simple language task to his ability pre-stroke to competently chair or minute meetings at the Temple, deal with complex business transactions, and be the witty life and soul of family gatherings.

Understandably, as insight and self-monitoring increased, D began to express a feeling that his language was getting worse rather than better. A touching example of this was when, shortly prior to discharge, he brought along to a therapy session a copy of the minutes he had written up from the Temple AGM not long before his stroke and brandished them with the words "Look, this was me, this was me!" In spite of the fact that, at discharge, both D and his daughter indicated that they felt they had acquired a sound knowledge base about the nature of his communication disability (see Appendix 7), D's struggle to understand the practical and emotional reality of his disability remained embryonic.

Although D had begun to reintegrate into the life of the Temple at a social level, his inability to take a more leadership role, or even to read and repeat simple prayers was clearly a source of great distress. D was also greatly concerned by the extra burden which his incapacity was putting on his wife in terms of the day-to-day running of the business, not to mention the longer-term financial implications of his absence from work. However, following D and his family's lead, little "therapy" time was spent on these issues. Social work involvement, including a home visit, helped clarify basic benefit issues but support of a more emotional level was not apparently something which the family were seeking from our input. The shop, the Temple, and family life were all clearly central to D's life but there was always a sense that his presence with us was for work on and information about his language. From D and his family there was a strong sense of respect for us as professionals and reluctance to interfere with our business or schedules. Meanwhile D's assertive protection of his wife from any extra commitment which might take her away from the shop or add to her workload led, in turn, to a reluctance on our part to pester the family for a greater amount of attendance at therapy sessions or informal meetings.

Given this polite mutual respect for our own territories, and the additional cultural, linguistic, and therapeutic factors noted next, it is perhaps unsurprising that our role and potential for facilitating real change on a psychosocial level were limited.

Cultural issues

D's Sikh background evidently represented a central focus of his life. Although he at first appeared somewhat bemused by our interest, he undertook with great pride the difficult task of educating us about the life and customs of the Temple, bringing in useful pamphlets and reference materials. As a therapy team we attempted to be sensitive to D's religion and social conventions, though the ease with which D and his family participated in Western conventions, e.g. offering Christmas cards and presents of wine, meant that it was all too easy to overlook and underestimate culturally determined difficulties to balance two-way communication about D and his lifestyle. This quiet acquiescence to Western culture on D's part and subtle reminders of institutionalised racism on ours were perhaps most obvious in joint sessions with Occupational Therapy. On one occasion for example, having chosen to follow a pizza recipe, D happily followed the Occupational Therapist's lead in layering the pizza base with ingredients including ham. Despite suggestions that he may prefer a vegetarian version, D was reluctant to offend anyone by not using the meat. However, on preparing to eat the finished dish, and with the therapist elsewhere occupied, D discreetly removed the offending pieces of ham and concealed them under the uneaten remains of the pizza crust. Similarly, his deference to Western ways so as not to contravene social "norms" was visible in the way he offered no objection to struggling to use cutlery in his dyspraxic right hand despite the fact that at home the family reported that he chose to eat with his hand in the traditional way.

D's approach to therapy and his relationship with therapy staff also reflected a strong sense of prevailing codes and roles. He presented himself each day punctually and eager for the work we would direct. Not afraid to express his displeasure at lateness, cancellations, or interruptions, and by no means a passive participant in therapy, there was nonetheless an implicit assumption that we were fully responsible for orchestrating the "cure" for his dysphasia which would enable him to return to work and "normal" life.

The power of this implicit association between medically based rehabilitation and "cure" was perhaps more noticeable in the attitude of D's wife and brother. D's wife rarely questioned any of our interventions, being receptive in a quiet, grateful way to any of our proposed ideas. Transport difficulties, work commitments, and D's desire not to involve her any more than necessary meant that she did not attend therapy sessions. When asked for information or ideas about relevant situations and vocabulary which might prove useful in therapy she appeared unable to generate material, perhaps finding the gulf between the real-life home or work context to the busy but sterile clinical setting as difficult to bridge as we did. Reassurances from her that we were doing the right thing, our own desire not to pressure her in any way, and D's staunch protection of her from time-consuming involvement with us, meant that we maintained a warm but, on an information basis, rather unproductive relationship with JD.

D's elder brother, although more overtly challenging of our plans for D's therapy and language prognosis, found it equally difficult to cross the boundary between linguistic impairment (and its cure) and the relationship between communication and life. His disappointment at there being no quick medical fix was profound and his ability to appreciate our focus on small, transitory therapy goals or our interest in D's life beyond the centre walls was perhaps a further factor in our dissatisfaction at adequately addressing wider issues of communication and coping strategies for the outside world.

As in many other cases, it seems that our role was defined by our client as language-based only and maintaining a rather narrow focus of therapy seemed neither inappropriate nor inadvisable, given our awareness of cultural and individual no go areas. However, it is interesting to reflect on how cultural factors contributed, in this case, yet another layer to the complex dimensions of power and role as they operate within the therapeutic relationship.

Bilingual issues

Linguistically, similar issues complicated the therapy process. Knowing that D spoke Punjabi in the home and in much of his social world, we were anxious to learn more about his linguistic environment and, where possible, incorporate Punjabi sections into the communication book. Again, however, we were largely unsuccessful in this aim. D and his family insisted, and we had no reason to doubt, that his English had been of a very high standard prior to his stroke. All requests for words in Punjabi met with the response that it was not necessary to concern ourselves with Punjabi as his English was so good and currently was of a similarly impaired level as his first language.

Furthermore, both D and his family emphasised the importance of improving his English as a prerequisite for any return to work. Indeed, D appeared somewhat confused that we might want to incorporate non-English vocabulary into communication activities though he was happy, on occasion, to attempt social conversation in Hindi with an Indian Occupational Therapist at the centre.

There was a strong sense that we were constrained by and operating within well-defined roles and contexts and the language of our context and involvement was very firmly English. Given our non-existent skills in Punjabi and our decision not to involve a link worker (due to issues of timing, access, and D's difficulty in switching between different therapists) this was hard to challenge! However, this situation did little to blur the sharp edges between communication work in the clinic and carry-over at home, and naturally led us to fear for the use of the communication book at home.

In terms of language recovery, when D's daughter was asked to rate improvements in English and Punjabi post-therapy, she reported no perceived differences across the two languages except for an impression that perseveration on the predilection word /du:kan/ remained evident in Punjabi whilst it had virtually been eradicated from English. This parallel pattern of language recovery in bilingual individuals is well documented in the literature (see, for example, Paradis, 1987).

Psychosocial transition and aphasia therapy: Disappointments and challenges

Although 18 weeks of aphasia therapy is an undeniably meagre period of intervention in which to expect major shifts in lifestyle adjustment, particularly with a man of such high standards and pre-morbidly developed communication skills, the intensity and warmth of our therapeutic relationship with D had led us to anticipate, or at least wish, for a more optimistic outcome for D. We felt confident that our input had altered his impairment, as measured by the clinical assessments, and disability (in the WHO, 1980 classification sense), to a level where communication with a range of familiar people, with externally imposed structure and strategies, was far more successful than on admission.

However, we feared that our inability to address D's changed role and interaction of this role with home and work would lead to considerable difficulties on discharge. His assumed identity of the past 18 weeks as a sociable, physically able "worker" and well-liked personality at the centre was coming to an end and one sensed D itching to get back to his business, where he could, at least in part, resume the leadership role of before. Given his wife's quiet deference to his position and judgement, the departure abroad of his elder brother and the impending arrival of his daughter's first child, the earlier constraining influences were no longer in place. An additional concern of ours was his persisting marked decline in language performance when performing activities which had any degree of physical or cognitive demands operative concurrently, or when attempting to participate in communication about emotive, real-life issues. Indeed these anxieties proved well-founded when, at regular periods after discharge, telephone calls from both D's wife and daughter expressed concern and frustration at apparent declines in effective communication as D took on increased workloads in the shop and at home.

On reflection, one might question either the validity of treating an aphasic person in a protected setting such as a rehabilitation centre, which is so removed from reality or, as in D's case, the wisdom of trying to incorporate more "functionally" relevant components of therapy into our treatment programme. Yet, adhering to a more abstract, impairment-based focus for language therapy had clearly paid dividends as, for example, Sacchett and Marshall (1992) have asserted elsewhere in the debate about functional communication. Perhaps more importantly our discussions about D and his therapy remind us of the need to be flexible and reflective of the different tools we bring to therapy, the different timings of their application, and the fluctuating needs and expectations of our client. This may seem self-evident in theory, but the reality of organisational, therapeutic, and self-imposed constraints has an insidious habit of side-tracking the best-laid plans (not to mention the flying by the seat of your pants approach to therapy!). A more realistic appraisal of our own roles and limitations with respect to D and his

social milieu may have alleviated our ultimate unease at discharging him without the communication skills or psychological preparation to cope with a largely unchanged environment, or they with him. Yet, it may be precisely this uncomfortable challenge of questioning, and defining our role as agents of language, communication, and social change, which will best serve the future of aphasia therapy.

ACKNOWLEDGEMENTS

We would like to thank D for his humour, commitment, and constant drive to do and know more which prompted our many puzzled but therapeutically "growing" discussions. We would also like to thank our colleagues at the Wolfson Medical Rehabilitation Centre for helpful comments and discussions, and especially Jenny Sheridan and Nancy Craven for commenting on an earlier draft of this chapter.

FOOTNOTE

1. Throughout this chapter, our differentiation between the notions of impairment and disability is largely in accordance with the World Health Organisation, 1980, classifications, which forms the basis of some approaches to outcome measurement currently being explored by speech and language therapists (e.g. Enderby, 1992). Within this framework, impairment refers to abnormality of function, and disability reflects the consequences of impairment in terms of functional activities. In line with the views of some disabled groups, including some people with dysphasia (e.g. Ireland, 1993), we have chosen not to employ the term "handicap", but to include issues of social role and lifestyle within a broadened concept of disability.

REFERENCES

Bishop, D. (1982). *Test for reception of grammar.* Oxford, UK. Medical Research Council.

Certner Smith, M., & Morganstein, S. (1988) *Thematic picture stimulation – pictures and worksheets for clients with aphasia or head injury.* Tuscon, Arizona. Communication Skill Builders Inc.

Enderby, P. (1992). Outcome measures in speech therapy: Impairment, disability, handicap and distress. *Health Trends, 24,* 61–64.

Forer, S. (1990). *Functional assessment measures— Revised.* Santa Clara, CA: Santa Clara Valley Medical Center.

Howard, D., & Patterson, K. (1992). *Pyramids and palm trees.* Bury St. Edmunds, UK: Thames Valley Test Company.

Ireland, C. (1993). *Disabling barriers, enabling processes:Dysphasia from the inside out.* Paper presented at the British Aphasiology Conference, Warwick, UK.

Jones, E. (1989). A *year in the life of EVJ and PC.* In E. Jones (Ed.), Advances in aphasia therapy in the clinical setting. Proceedings of the Cambridge Symposium on Aphasia Therapy. London: British Aphasiology Society.

Kay, J., Lesser, R., & Coltheart, M. (1992). *Psycholinguistic assessments of language processing in aphasia.* Hove, UK: Lawrence Erlbaum Associates.

Paradis, M. (1987) *The assessment of bilingual aphasia.* Hillsdale, NJ: Lawrence Erlbaum Associates Inc.

Sacchett, C., & Marshall, J. (1992). Functional assessment of communication: Implications for the rehabilitation of aphasic people: Reply to Carol Frattali. *Aphasiology, 6,* 95–100.

Scott, C. (1987) *Cognitive neuropsychological remediation of acquired language disorders.* Unpublished MPhil thesis, City University, London.

Wallace, G., & Canter, G. (1985). Effects of personally relevant language materials on the performance of severely aphasic individuals. *Journal of Speech and Hearing Disorders, 50,* 385-390.

World Health Organisation (1980). *International classification of impairments, disabilities and handicaps (ICDH).* Geneva, Switzerland: Author.

APPENDICES

Spoken naming and repetition of single words (pre-therapy)

Target	Naming	Repetition
comb	most of them…	/wəʊm/
mountain	this one…	/wəʊkʃu/
screw	/dɪklein/…/deik/	/wəʊptju/
glove	/dukan/…that one	/subjə/
belt	/dukan/	/subtə/
cow	/zɔl/	/sau/
fork	we had them here just now…/zeik/	/saebiəʊ/
chair	/siks/	/sɛks/
bread	/sik/…/kliks/	/zɛbz/
shoe	/sɪflas/…this one's down	/zu/
elephant	/həʊkei/	/zaiŋ/
bird	/blu/	+
brush	/dukaen/	/jɔks/
thumb	/dɪkərɛts/	/vʌn/
scissors	/dɪs…/	/saiks/
toaster	this morning…all the time	/zɛgwɔ/
watch	/wɔksəl/	/wɔkjɔ/
dog	+	/zɔtʃ/
foot	first like…	/zɔks/
knife	/druk/	/zaits/

Examples of spontaneous speech (pre-therapy)

T: Tell me something about your family.

D: This there /lə/… the last man…the the …/lei…/the latest is come in for the…of…of a…/dufɛt/…all the…we will…actually to /seiz/ what…all what we had done with the /silz/ the…and the /pleizin/ on…As a matter of fact when we see what happens…the…the…/blu/…/du/…/du/…of the balance…he was at the… er… /dijɔɪzɪz/…/ ɪzmʌstəvə/ the/wɔnəvə/…/kliz/ as they seen everything up there and they…/su/ it and they send everything up there.

T: About your family… do you have a daughter?

D: …/və/…/dɔdɪd/ …vəʊlɪn/ …/səʊwɔn/ in there…all in the…/dəʊtə/

T: What is she called?

D: …the doctor's name? …/dəʊ…dɔ/…actually all/sɪn/ in there…and /dɔ/ … and the /deim/ in the …/wɪkʊdz/…/dei/…

APPENDIX 3.3

Examples of semantic categorisation tasks

Co-ordinate based

stick	wicket	volley	racquet	half
corner	wing	bowler	strings	service
bat	penalty	four	ace	stumps
HOCKEY		*CRICKET*		*TENNIS*

Attribute based

sunshine	steam	ice cream	frost	fire
fridge	winter	oven	Antarctic	radiator
HOT			*COLD*	

Concept based

hot	European	safari	malaria	sterling
raining	Nairobi	John Major	African	Tescos
KENYA			*ENGLAND*	

APPENDIX 3.4

Therapy task using word selection to elements of composite picture

PEOPLE	ACTIONS	OBJECTS
man	drinking	menu
girl	collecting	notepad
waiter	stirring	coffee
chef	writing	water
waitress	reading	table
boy	putting down	food
woman	eating	eggs

(from Certner Smith and Morganstein, 1988)

APPENDIX 3.5

Examples of repetition of single words (post therapy)

Target	*Repetition*
comb	/wəʊm/
mountain	/məʊn.../
screw	/ru/
glove	+
belt	/lɛts/
cow	/lɛʊ/
fork	/lɔks/
chair	/lɛə/
bread	/lɛp/
shoe	/lju/
elephant	/ləekɪt/
bird	/bɜ/
brush	/laik/
thumb	/lʌm/
scissors	/leisɪs/
toaster	/ləʊks/
watch	+
dog	/lɔk/
foot	/vʊk/
knife	/laits/

APPENDIX 3.6

Examples of conversational speech (post-therapy)

T: Tell me something about your family.

D: What do you want me to say? … Well I've got only…five…I've got very small…better…a very small /bɛkə/ and…I've got only two people in three in my house. First of all there's me…and I've got my…brother…and I've got my…I've got…/ɛs/…I've got /ɛs/…I've got /ɛs/…couldn't name of the time of it…my…[points to name of his wife in communication book].

T: You mean your wife?

D: Yes, my brother…my brother and then I've got my…daughter, yes, daughter…So it's just two of them. And from there…and I have got my…my brother there [points to name in communication book] and after that, I have got…very big one…a very big one.

T: A big family?

D: Yes, a…/dɔl/. And at the moment, here the moment, maybe you really want to know, I've got many brothers…[points to list of names] That's…1…2…3…4…5…Yes, I've got 5 brothers.

APPENDIX 3.7

Pre- and post-therapy rating scales

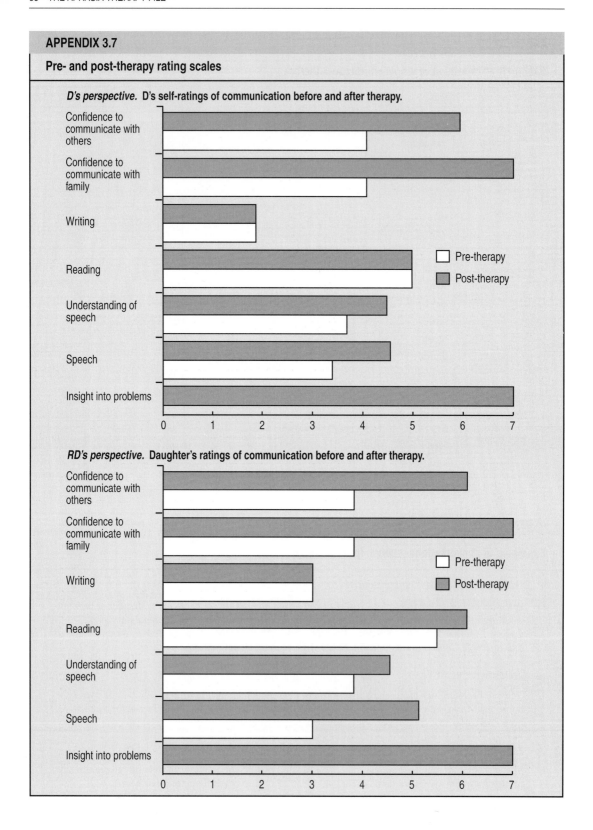

D's perspective. D's self-ratings of communication before and after therapy.

RD's perspective. Daughter's ratings of communication before and after therapy.

APPENDIX 3.8

FAM form showing pre- and post-therapy scores on communication, cognitive, and psychosocial adjustment

Communication	Initial	Goals	Review	Review	Review	Docm	Comments
17. Comprehension (SLT/RN)	2	3				4	Better with gestures and pictures
18. Expression Spoken (SLT/RN)	1	–				2	
18. Expression Spoken (SLT/RN)	1	–				2	
Non-verbal (SLT/RN)	2	4				3	
19. Reading (SLT/OT)	3	5				3	
20. Writing (SLT/OT)	2	3				2	
21. Speech intelligibility (SLT/RN)	6	–				6	
Psychosocial adjustment							
22. Social interaction (RN/SW/CP)	7					7	
23. Emotional (all)	7					6	
24. Adjustment to limitations (all)	6	–				6	
25. Employability (OT/CP/SW)	1	3				3	
Cognitive function							
26. Problem solving (OT/SLT/CP)	5	–				6	Language difficulties make difficult to score
27. Memory (OT/SLT/CP)	7	–					
28. Orientation (OT/SLT/CP)	7	–					
29. Attention (OT/SLT/CP	7	–					
30. Safety judgement (all)	7	–					

SLT = speech and language therapist; RN = nursing staff; CP = clinical psychologists; PT = physiotherapist; OT = occupational therapist.

(Adapted from Forer, 1990).

4

Drawing on the semantic system: The use of drawing as a therapy medium

Jon Hunt

BACKGROUND

Joan was a 64-year-old housewife living at home with her retired husband when she suffered a left cerebro vascular accident (CVA). She was admitted to hospital where she remained for the next 4 months. She was seen by a speech and language therapist 5 days after her admission. Auditory comprehension was described as "very poor". She produced no voice and was diagnosed as having a severe oral and articulatory apraxia.

After 4 weeks her auditory comprehension was said to have improved and some spontaneous vocalisation was heard. A week later she could vocalise on command. She was then able to repeat vowels in isolation and produce approximations to consonant-vowel (CV) words in closure tasks (no data available).

No assessments of reading or writing ability are reported until 6 weeks post onset when she wrote correctly four words to dictation (using her non-preferred hand) before beginning to perseverate. She is reported to have read and shown signs of understanding a power of attorney letter after 5 weeks. There are no reports of her having used writing spontaneously, nor gesture, nor pointing, nor any other form of non-verbal communication.

During her stay in hospital, Joan was seen by the speech and language therapist two to three times weekly. Input during this time consisted of: (1) articulatory drills involving repetition and imitation of articulatory gestures, (2) work on gesture by imitation, (3) provision of a communication chart, and (4) provision of a "Canon" communicator.

By the time of her discharge from hospital 5 months later, the speech and language therapist felt there had been "No improvement" in her spontaneous output. She continued to produce no intelligible speech beyond an occasional yes and no. She did not use the communication chart, nor the Canon communicator. Her failure to use the latter was attributed to poor spelling. Prior to her discharge she was tested on a word-picture matching task from the PALPA (Kay, Lesser, & Coltheart, 1992) and scored 38/40 in both written and spoken versions (two close semantic distractors).

Following her discharge home she was seen by a different therapist as an outpatient twice weekly for 8 weeks. The goal of therapy was to develop a communication book with written words divided into sections such as family and friends, shopping, and time. Joan is reported to have used the book "very occasionally".

ASSESSMENT

First meeting and initial assessment

I first met Joan and her husband Tony approximately 9 months post onset of the CVA. She was tearful on arrival and on many occasions throughout the session. However, her husband explained that she often reacted this way when she met strangers, and subsequent experience bore this out.

Joan gave the impression of having little or no difficulty following what was said during the meeting, and indicated that she did not feel understanding to be a problem. Tony added that on occasions she would seem to be thrown by a sudden change of topic, but agreed that understanding was not a significant problem.

Joan's only spoken output was /dəs/ for "yes" and /dəʊ/ for "no". Production of these words was usually effortful and preceded by some struggle. She did not produce any automatic phrases. Her yes/no responses would at times contradict her head gesture which she did not self-correct. She was facially expressive but made no use of gesture except for pointing. She had not brought the communication book which she had been given, and Tony reported that she had not been using it at

home. Through facial expression she indicated a lack of enthusiasm for the book.

Although /dəs/ and /dəʊ/ were her only successful spoken output, it was striking that Joan would persist in trying to speak. When she did attempt anything other than yes or no, the result was generally the same: her vocal folds would adduct and apparently seize in that position for the duration of her attempt to speak. Her lips would come together and part, but no voice would emerge. On some occasions voice was produced, the resulting syllable /b/ then being repeated several times. These attempts seemed to cost her great effort, and gave rise to much tension in her neck.

Since I had read reports of her having some written ability, I handed her the pen and asked her some questions. She continued to attempt spoken answers, and needed reminding to try writing.

Question	Written response
"How many children do you have?"	ONE
"Boy or a girl?"	(no response)
(I wrote the two words and asked her to choose)	GIRE
"How old is she?"	Thity
"Thirty?"	8
"Thirty eight?"	(nodded yes)
"Where does she live?	NEWER
	(attempt abandoned)

(Having established that her daughter lived in the UK, I drew a map of the British Isles and she pointed to Norfolk.)

"Does she come and see you?"	(nodded yes)
"How often?"	ONCY (attempt abandoned)

She had conveyed two pieces of information (without help) through writing, and two more with help from the map and written words. In addition she made spontaneous use of drawing on one occasion. I had drawn a stick figure to represent her daughter, and Joan added a smaller stick figure by its side (see Fig. 4.1). She confirmed that this indicated that her daughter had a child.

It seemed, then, that pen and paper offered some potential as a medium for expression beyond the yes/no response.

Indicating that her daughter has a child.

Investigations of access to phonology

For the moment I was keen to find out how much phonological information she had available to her when she attempted to speak. Of course there would be no way of knowing what was happening during her attempts at spontaneous speech, but by comparing her attempts at oral picture naming with rhyme judgements I felt I might get some idea of any discrepancy between internal phonology and output.

However, I was cautious at this early stage about trying picture naming because I expected nothing more than the blocking seen in spontaneous speech and in a question and answer session. In order to minimise her sense of failure I decided to give her the option of a spoken or written response. I chose 40 high-frequency targets with simple CV structures to minimise articulatory demands (all but four were CVC or CV).

I included a high proportion of targets with initial bilabials as I felt this would increase her chances of success and perhaps boost her confidence.

In most cases she attempted the target orally first. To my surprise in 23 out of 40 cases she achieved, albeit in the midst of much struggling, an approximation to the target phonology in that the vowel was correct as were some consonants within what seemed to be a severely reduced phonological system. Word initial consonants were [b] (or slightly aspirated [p]) or [d], or a combination of the two [bd], or slight phonetic variations on these. Word final consonants showed a little more variety (but not necessarily accuracy) including /s/ /z/ /n/ and /t/, e.g. gun—/bn/; hat—/pd et/; queen—/pdid/.

In those cases where she did not achieve the target phonology, she seemed to benefit from both semantic facilitation and closure cues. In some cases her attempts at repeating targets once I had spoken them were better than her previous attempts, but in most cases they were not, and were limited to the same reduced range of sounds as her other attempts. She went on to write 23 of the targets correctly, although in some of these cases she had by that time been given help to achieve oral output. Again, however, she appeared to benefit from semantic facilitation and from closure cues (both written and spoken).

Interestingly, her written attempts were clearly more accurate once she had heard me say the target word. This could be interpreted as evidence that her internal representation of the target phonology was deficient, since otherwise hearing me say the word would presumably have made no difference to her success in written naming. Possibly by providing the phonology her grasp of the semantics was consolidated, which in turn drove phonology better. Unfortunately, no "pure" measure of written picture naming was taken at this stage.

At the same time it seemed possible that she might have more phonological information available than she was able to realise articulatorily (the discrepancy which would typically be labelled as articulatory apraxia). While Joan's struggle behaviour was very suggestive of apraxia, in view of other evidence of deficient phonological knowledge (e.g. improvement in oral picture naming as a result of semantic facilitation, improvement in written picture naming when given the phonology), I did not feel justified in embarking on an apraxia therapy programme.

One reservation here is that if we believe in two-way interactions between levels of processing (such as those proposed in connectionist models, e.g. Dell & O'Seaghdha, 1992) then we must allow for the possibility that articulatory apraxia could have some impact on phonological representations (and presumably also have an effect on the stability of semantic representations).

It certainly seemed plausible that the apraxia could be a contributory factor, but not that it was the sole explanation, since we could not then explain the discrepancy between her spontaneous oral output and her oral picture naming. Furthermore, severe apraxia exists in some (rare) patients with little or no apparent effect on the availability of phonological knowledge for internal judgement tasks. The final deciding factor was the knowledge that Joan had received extensive treatment for her (presumed) apraxia during the previous 8 months with no apparent improvement in her oral output.

I decided, therefore, to pursue the hypothesis that Joan's attempts at oral output were based on reduced phonological information. The next question was whether this reduction was due to "loss" of information or failure to access it. The discrepancy between her spontaneous output and oral picture naming, together with her response to cueing, certainly supported the latter hypothesis. Could this be attributed to an inadequate "drive" from semantics, i.e. although she had semantic information available, the level of activation was insufficient to drive a phonological response/access to phonology?

Investigations of semantics

Joan had made only two close semantic errors in the word-picture matching task in both modalities. In a similar but tougher test involving target plus three intra-category semantic co-ordinates, she scored 29/31 (auditory version). When presented with a picture of an object and a list of written words of which (on average) 10 were related to the target

and 6 were unrelated, she selected 98/100 targets and only four "distractors". Responses were on the whole fairly swift.

However, it is questionable how much such input judgement tasks can tell us about an aphasic person's ability to assemble semantic representations for output in the absence of help from pictures and spoken or written words, since our understanding of the processing involved in accessing semantic information (for input or output) is as yet very primitive.

Alternative forms of output

One medium of expression which does not (ostensibly at least) require access to linguistic form for output is drawing. I was unsure how to assess this. The obvious way seemed to be to name an object and ask Joan to draw it. The results are shown in Fig. 4.2.

The drawings are well specified and it is clear that under these conditions she was able (with one exception, "flower", for which she required semantic facilitation) to access the necessary semantic information, at least concerning visual attributes. It will become clear later how this assessment was misleading in a way particularly relevant to Joan's case.

Another non-verbal medium of expression is gesture, which was assessed in two ways. First she was presented with a photograph of somebody doing something and was asked to convey through gesture what they were doing. By carefully studying the positions of limbs and fingers she was able to reproduce fairly

FIGURE 4.2

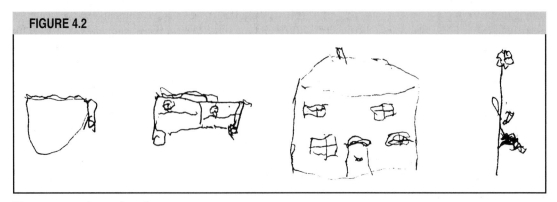

"Draw a cup; car; house; flower."

accurately the static postures of the people in the photographs, but was unable to produce the relevant movements. This could be interpreted as meaning either that she had difficulty inferring the movements entailed, or that she had difficulty producing them, or both.

Second, she was asked to imagine that she had a bad cold and had a number of requests of her husband—she wanted paper tissues, lozenges, the central heating turned up, to go to bed, for him to phone their daughter. Again she was asked to convey these requests (presented one at a time in written and spoken form) through gesture. Examples were given. This request seemed to throw Joan completely. She perseverated on one (inappropriate) hand configuration.

This task was, I realise in retrospect, inherently more difficult than the drawing task ("draw a named object") since in the latter the required response was highly constrained whereas in the gesture task there were a number of possible responses. It subsequently emerged that in more constrained gesture tasks she was able to produce appropriate responses, albeit with rather gross configurations and movements.

Conclusions from investigations so far

These investigations had been very haphazard, with too many variables between tasks. The result was that at this stage I failed to recognise that evidence was emerging that degree of constraint was a significant variable in determining Joan's ability to output not only spoken and written language but also gesture and drawing. At the time, I remained puzzled by the discrepancy between her spoken output in picture naming tasks and that in her attempts at spontaneous speech. I wondered if a sentence processing deficit could be responsible, but further investigation and high levels of success on sentence processing tasks suggested this area was not a fruitful one to target at this stage and was not obviously related to her severe spontaneous output impairment.

Other activities and investigations

By this stage I had been seeing Joan for 8 weeks, three times a week. During this time our sessions had featured various other activities:

- attempts to enable Joan to express her feelings about her circumstances
- work on gesture
- investigations of variables affecting her success with written output and with drawing (see later)
- observations of her attempts to express herself outside structured activities.

Joan continued to be facially expressive and to make use of some vocalisation, and still continued to attempt spoken language without success (except for yes/no). I had been encouraging her to use pen and paper but had to do so repeatedly as she never attempted use of this medium spontaneously.

The investigations of variables affecting her success with written output and drawing had been yielding some insights. She was certainly not dependent on a picture stimulus to access orthography, since her written naming to definition of common objects was comparable to her written picture naming. However, when she was asked to name items within a category she had great difficulty—she was unable to name any garden tools or items of furniture. It seemed that under conditions of less constraint she was unable to assemble a semantic representation strong enough to enable her to access orthography. When asked to draw items within these categories she was very hesitant and the resulting drawings were poorly specified by her standards (see Fig. 4.3). She was, however, able to label the garden tool as a "hee" (hoe?). She was unable to name the item of furniture.

When she was asked to draw a part of the human body, she hesitated at great length and finally indicated that she could not do this. I suggested she look at me and draw part of me. She began to draw my arm, but looking intently at it as she did so. She included the rest of my upper body (i.e. all that was visible) in her picture (see Fig 4.4a).

Next she was asked to draw something you could put in a sandwich. She drew a sandwich and carefully drew a filling inside it. I asked her to draw the filling separately. Again she seemed hesitant and drew something unrecognisable (see Fig 4.4b).

In these last two examples it seemed that Joan had difficulty segmenting concepts into their

FIGURE 4.3

Drawing items within a category: "a garden tool, an item of furniture, a musical instrument."

FIGURE 4.4

(a) "Part of the human body",
(b) "something you can put in a sandwich".

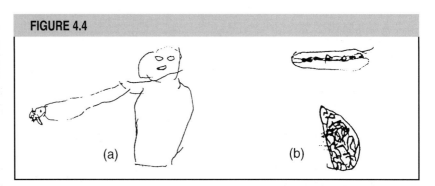

(a)   (b)

component parts (arm from body, filling from sandwich).

CONCLUSIONS AND IMPLICATIONS FOR THERAPY

It was looking increasingly as if Joan's difficulties were not purely linguistic, and that a sentence processing deficit, which had previously been hypothesised to account for the discrepancy between her picture naming and her spontaneous output, could not account for the previous observations.

It was instead hypothesised that Joan's difficulties with spontaneous output were rooted in a difficulty assembling semantic representations under conditions of low constraint, such as would certainly exist in conversation. It also seemed feasible that this could be intertwined with a difficulty segmenting concepts for the purposes of output.

What implications did this hypothesis have for therapy? Since she had performed input semantic judgements swiftly and accurately was I to conclude that such judgements could not be effective as therapy? Or were the input judgements simply not demanding in the right kind of ways? At the time I did not know how to make them more demanding, so I felt I had no option but to take an approach that required her to access semantics for output, through whatever medium.

THERAPY

The media which had shown most potential so far (at least in constrained tasks) were writing and drawing. Whereas the written medium has the advantage of allowing the expression of abstract concepts, drawing promised to enable Joan to express concepts (at least imageable ones) which were only half-formed and inadequate to provide access to orthography. It was also felt that expressing concepts through drawing might facilitate access to orthography under less constrained conditions. Finally it seemed possible that drawing could develop as a useful means of expression for Joan should her ability to output language not improve.

Since Joan was having most difficulty producing output under conditions of low constraint, the obvious approach seemed to be to begin with relatively constrained tasks and gradually move on to less constrained ones. (Some time later a colleague suggested the opposite approach, beginning with a totally unconstrained task, e.g. free drawing. This task was subsequently introduced with interesting results, described later.) The next question was how the constraint hierarchy should be arranged.

At the highest level of constraint seemed to be the tasks in which Joan had already shown relatively good ability even to the extent that she could access the written form, for example, in picture naming and naming to definition. On a similar level would be more "general knowledge" questions with a specific answer such as "What instrument does Nigel Kennedy play?" or "What animal do you associate with Lester Piggot (a jockey in the UK)?" (In the latter two examples she would, however, need to separate the object from the person.)

At the lowest level of constraint, I felt, would be tasks requiring her to convey novel information ("Any news?", "What did you do at the weekend?") since they would require her not only to formulate a message but also to think of a way to represent that message in picturable form. The challenge was to find and grade intermediate levels, since I had no idea what aspects of constraint were helpful to Joan. Possible candidates for intermediate levels were:

1. drawing items within a specific category (e.g. transport, food, tools)
2. drawing items within a broader semantic field (e.g. "things you might find in a kitchen", "things you might see on a walk in the country")
3. drawing items associated with particular activities (e.g. knitting, making tea) or with

more abstract concepts (e.g. professions, hobbies).

However, it seemed possible within each of these categories to vary the constraint a great deal. For example "transport" could be constrained to "something you might see driving in a town"; the activities in category (3) could be of high constraint ("chopping down a tree") or low ("relaxing"). It seemed therefore that the constraint would have to be individually gauged for each task.

The next question was what intervention should be provided when she was struggling. Possibilities were:

1. provide extra constraint to guide her towards a particular target
2. encourage her to draw poorly specified items again in more detail, or where there was more than one component part to the drawing encourage her to draw the parts separately.

There did, however, seem to be a danger that an approach based on drawing would be geared primarily towards representing "objects" and would neglect the realm of expressing predicative concepts.

Example 1. Joan was asked to draw something you might find in a kitchen. She drew a figure holding an object (Fig. 4.5a). She drew the figure first. She was then asked to draw the object separately and in more detail. She drew a square with vertical lines across it but was unable to add more detail.

I asked yes/no questions about its functions and attributes (Is it involved in cooking? Is it made of wood?). She answered these questions with a look of uncertainty, which gave the impression that she wasn't quite sure what she had drawn. The "20 Questions" approach led to its identification as a grill pan, although I did not name it as such.

Following further discussion of its attributes and functions (I commented how awkward it would be to use without a handle, which she then added) and a closure cue "put the bread under the _____" (no phonemic cue given) she was able to label the drawing.

Example 2. Joan was asked to draw a weapon of any kind. She hesitated at length and finally indicated that she could not do this. It was felt unlikely that she had failed to understand the word "weapon" since in my experience she would always request clarification (through facial expression) when she did not understand something.

I constrained her to "a weapon used in a duel" and she immediately drew a sword, which, like the grill pan, was minus handle until this was pointed out (Fig. 4.5b). She was unable to label it until given the phonological form. (I had been unable to think of ways to cue for it semantically!)

Example 3. (Week 2 of drawing programme.) Joan was asked to draw something she might give her husband for Christmas. Again she hesitated. I assured her it didn't matter how daft it was or whether he'd be likely to like it. But she remained unable to think of anything.

Eventually I offered "How about something to wear?" She drew a pullover and labelled it without further help. She went on to draw a shirt, tie, and trousers which she again labelled with minimal help (Fig 4.6).

Example 4: (Week 2.) Joan was asked to draw things you might see at the seaside. Again she was unable without constraint, such as "you can see some children playing—what are they playing with?", upon which she drew a ball. With further constraint she drew the items in Fig 4.7 and labelled them without help.

Impressions of therapy so far

I was encouraged by these results and it was clear that Joan was too. Even though she continued to require constraint it seemed that drawing enabled her to consolidate her hold on a concept even to the extent that she was able then to access the written

FIGURE 4.5

(a) "Something you might find in the kitchen",
(b) "A weapon of some sort (used in a duel)".

FIGURE 4.6

"A Christmas present for Tony (something to wear)."

FIGURE 4.7

"Things you might see at the seaside."

form in many cases. I had now been seeing Joan for 7 weeks and we were 2 weeks into the drawing programme having three sessions per week.

Was there any generalisation to functional communication at this stage? She still had to be invited to draw, as she continued to attempt speech whenever she wanted to express something. When asked what she and Tony had bought in their Christmas shopping trip she was able to draw the presents with little difficulty, but then this task was relatively constrained.

When such constraint was not provided, she remained on the whole unable to produce anything to convey novel information. There had been two exceptions: once, when asked what she had done at the weekend, she drew a female figure (Fig 4.8a) which she was unable to label. However, after some 5 minutes of hesitation and my asking questions as to the person's identity, she finally wrote "mother". (Tony confirmed that they had visited Joan's mother the day before.) As often became the case with writing after much struggle she then scrutinised the

word as if she had little idea whether or not it represented her intention.

The other exception was the drawing shown in Fig 4.8b. She produced this drawing at the beginning of a session following one in which I had explained rather briefly what a stroke was. Joan confirmed that she was indicating that she wanted to know more.

Beyond semantic co-ordinates

Joan's ability to draw items within a category was still variable. It seemed she had relatively little difficulty generating semantic co-ordinates (as in the "clothes" task above) but struggled with activities such as the "at the seaside" task in which fewer semantic co-ordinates were available as targets. If left to her own devices in such tasks (a homework book was given), she would often draw the same item repeatedly (e.g. for "things you might see on a walk in the country" she drew nothing but trees). I felt more tasks were needed that required her to access semantic associates other than co-ordinates.

Example 5. Joan was asked to draw items she would associate with various occupations. For "postman" she drew a figure holding a poorly defined object. When asked to draw the object separately it remained underspecified until I insisted on more detail (Fig 4.9).

I told her that from now on human figures were prohibited in this exercise. She looked worried! However, with much encouragement she drew a jug for "milkman" and a spade for "gardener", but for pilot she resorted to drawing a face wearing goggles. Despite much cueing she took several minutes to arrive at drawing an aeroplane. She had

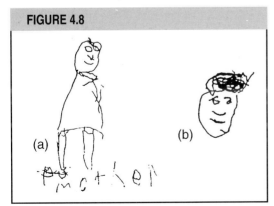

FIGURE 4.8

(a) "What did you do at the weekend?", (b) wanting to know more about stroke."

FIGURE 4.9

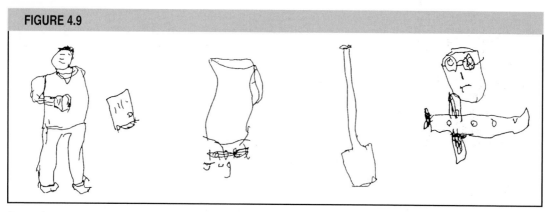

Occupations—postman, milkman, gardener, pilot.

similar difficulty arriving at a drawing of a boat as an associate for "sailor". I asked Joan to draw something to indicate what her daughter did for a living. After some hesitation she drew a vacuum cleaner (her daughter does cleaning work).

Example 6. I asked Joan to imagine she was organising a children's birthday party and to draw items which she would feel to be necessary. Perhaps her experience of organising such events stood her in good stead, because with no cueing (beyond "what else?") she drew and then labelled the items in Fig. 4.10.

This choice certainly seemed to show some ability to shift from semantic co-ordinates. I then asked hopefully "What else would you do at this party?" She immediately wrote "play games", without drawing a picture. This was the first time I had seen Joan use sentence structure. She rounded off the activity by drawing and labelling the final essential—the lavatory!

In general, however, there remained a tendency to become stuck in a category. When asked (a week later) to think of things she might see on a farm, she wrote (without help and without drawing them first) "cattle, sheep, chicken, horse, pig". When asked "What else apart from animals?" she drew a bird which she labelled "starting", and then wrote "rabbit, fox", which showed only a partial shift (to wild animals). It seemed that increasingly Joan was becoming able to write without going via drawing. One problem, however, was that on those (still

FIGURE 4.10

Items needed for a children's birthday party.

frequent) occasions when her written attempt was unsuccessful it would seldom occur to her that she had the option to switch back to drawing.

At this stage we began to have sessions in which drawing exercises grew (with varying degrees of contrivedness!) out of "conversation" (cf. Lyon, 1992). I felt that in this way we could start to bridge the gap between structured tasks and more functional communication. The following is an extended example of a therapy interaction intended to convey the flavour of a therapy session and to exemplify my attempts to facilitate Joan's contribution to the conversation:

Example 7:
Jon: Are you doing anything at the weekend?
Joan: (attempted writing without success. Drew a figure. Labelled it "Doris")
Jon: You're going out with Doris? (yes) Where to?
Joan: (wrote "Weymout")
Jon: Weymouth (yes) when?
Joan: (wrote "SATDAY")
Jon: Saturday. What do you hope to do?
Joan: (wrote "out on")
Jon: "Out on..."
Joan: (wrote "sunyy")
Jon: Out in the sun? Where?
Joan: Out on the
Jon: Out on the...
Joan: (wrote fonth)
Jon: On the sea front? (yes) OK imagine you're there now. Can you think of something you might see on the beach?
Joan: (long delay. Drew a figure holding something and labelled it "shells".)
Jon: What else might you see?
Joan: (drew a pair of legs in shorts! Much laughter)
Jon: Whose legs are they?!
Joan: (wrote her husband's name)
Jon: What else?
Joan: (drew a stone, but couldn't label it)
Jon: What would you use it for?
Joan: (wrote "fling away")
Jon: Fling away?
Joan: (wrote "over the...")
Jon: Fling away over the...
Joan: (wrote "water" with some help)

This example again shows how some sentence structure was becoming possible for Joan. She often seemed to benefit from having those words she had written so far read aloud. This seemed to act as a "closure" type of cue.

Where was Joan now as a communicator? Although she was clearly producing more substantial output, the process was, on the whole, painfully slow. Production of single words or short phrases was generally punctuated by lengthy pauses. Although Tony had reported instances of her having used pen and paper to communicate at home, it was clear that use of the "20 questions" approach still predominated. This was hardly surprising as Tony was so good at it. He would begin with "Is it something to do with..." (offering various topic fields such as themselves, friends, going out, their daughter) and gradually narrow the field down. On balance this method generally yielded results far more quickly than the pen and paper method, which held the added inconvenience of requiring the materials and a work surface.

I had initially held hopes that improved semantic access (which I felt we were achieving) might be reflected in improved spoken as well as written output, but this had not been the case. I still did not feel that "dyspraxia" work was appropriate, because it continued to be the case that when Joan was struggling to access the written form of a word she was greatly helped by hearing me say the word, suggesting that her phonological representation (or semantic representation, or both) of the target was deficient.

The pen and paper approach had, I felt, provided a useful medium for therapy. But as a functional means of communication it was clearly very slow as well as inconvenient. I began to question whether I had been wise to leave aside the alternatives of gesture and the communication book. Gesture can be quick and obviates the need for materials. At the beginning we had spent some time working on gesture but a number of problems had become evident:

1. The hand configurations and movements that Joan produced were very gross.
2. She had great difficulty thinking of appropriate gestures to convey information.

3. Joan made it clear she did not like gesture as a medium and always looked awkward attempting it.

It was striking that Joan never used spontaneously any form of gesture other than pointing.

Implementation of a communication book had been the main thrust of therapy prior to our encounter. I felt it was important to consider why she had not taken to this approach. Joan herself was unable to express anything more than a general distaste. Intuitively it seems that the ability to use such a book is likely to be dependent on the ability to formulate a message and hold on to it while a search is made for a suitable symbol or written word to convey that message. My feeling was that if Joan had a message formulated to this degree she would be able to express it on paper anyway, either through drawing or writing, in which case the communication book would offer no advantages (beyond the convenience of not requiring a pen) but would impose limitations (e.g. the number of symbols or words available).

We discussed the options. It was clear that as things stood speech was not even approaching becoming a viable one and Joan acknowledged this, tearfully. The remaining three options (gesture, communication book, pen and paper) were discussed. I tried to summarise the pros and cons of each as I saw them, but Joan looked rather bewildered. She indicated that she was not able to make a choice between them. My impression was that her model of my role was "therapist knows best".

Yet another option, of course, was to pursue more than one approach. I was reluctant to do this because Joan had demonstrated great difficulty switching from one modality to another. For example, when the required response involved a number (e.g. in answer to the question "how many weeks holiday does your granddaughter have?"), Joan would always need reminding of the option of counting on her fingers, even when the method had been used only minutes before. Similarly, as mentioned earlier, she had difficulty remembering to switch from writing to drawing when the former failed her. Tony was clear that he favoured the pen and paper approach, as it offered a broader range of

possibilities, and even though it was slow he felt it could get quicker. Joan seemed to agree with this conclusion and we decided to continue as we had been.

At this point Joan went down with 'flu and missed two sessions, the first she had missed in five months. When she returned she was off form. Her handwriting was less clear, her spelling of single words was noticeably poorer and she produced no sentence structure. Initially I imagined she was suffering the after-effects of the 'flu, but as the weeks passed and she did not return to form, I started to wonder if she had had a small stroke during her illness. To add to the problem we were short staffed and had to cut down on outpatient therapy, with the result that some weeks Joan and I were able to meet once only or not at all.

Even though this was an unhappy time during which little or no progress was apparent, Joan seemed not to lose her determination. We continued with exercises based on the same rationale: Joan was given a topic or a category and asked to draw or write appropriate items. In view of the difficulty she was having with writing, she was heavily encouraged to draw first and then label if possible.

"Free" drawing therapy

For some weeks, however, she had difficulty generating ideas even through drawing. A colleague suggested trying free drawing. This was an idea which had not occurred to me at all, and was effectively the antithesis of the approach to date. It promised to afford Joan a medium through which she could assemble semantic representations for output without them having to meet required specifications. If this were successful, constraint could gradually be reintroduced. The rationale felt vague but the idea was exciting and I felt we could only learn from the experience.

Joan was asked to "draw anything". Despite encouragement she was unable to produce anything at all. I suggested she just start moving the pen and see what comes out. The movements that ensued evolved into a map which she labelled "Itay" (Italy) (Fig. 4.11). This was rather perseverative since minutes earlier I had asked Joan to draw a map to show where she had been at the weekend.

Subsequent attempts continued to show perseveration, but when asked to produce more variety she was able to.

She was asked to continue this activity for homework, filling one page of an exercise book each day with different drawings. Some drawings she labelled spontaneously—see "Lamons saked" (Lamont sacked, a reference to a UK politician) in Fig. 4.11, the first two-word phrase since her illness 8 weeks earlier. Some weird and wonderful drawings emerged through this activity!

After three weeks, constraint was reintroduced. Topics included (some had been used before): professions/jobs, things to do with farming, things at the seaside, things you might buy when you go out shopping, transport/ways of getting about, dangerous pastimes, relaxing pastimes, things to do with gardening, things to do with school, things that run on electricity, and things you might see in a busy High Street. Again she was asked to produce a drawing first and then label it if possible. What was striking about the results was the increase in diversity in that she seemed to have developed a new potential to shift from semantic co-ordinates. In addition her dependence on drawing human figures seemed to have diminished (see examples in Fig. 4.12).

This period certainly marked Joan's return to form. She was asked to keep a diary at home documenting "one thing you've done today" and "one thing in the news" (Fig. 4.13). This was a great challenge as it required Joan to think of a drawing to convey an event. Her success was variable. Sometimes she would produce only a human figure with some unsuccessful writing; at other times she would produce clear drawings which truly captured the event (Fig. 4.14).

Other more constrained exercises included drawing something to convey specified historical events; drawing advertisements for specified organisations (Fig. 4.15); things you'd like to take to a desert island (Fig. 4.16); items which would be required for particular jobs (e.g. build a fire, clean your shoes, knit a jumper) or in particular circumstances (you have a headache, it's raining) (Fig. 4.17); and "problems and solutions" (Fig. 4.18). There was also some attempt to introduce predication in the form of "change of state" into the exercises:

1. Joan was presented with a picture of a tree and an axe and asked to draw the outcome of the probable event. In some cases this exercise elicited a written verb.

FIGURE 4.11

Examples of free drawing.

FIGURE 4.12

Professions, things to do with farming.

FIGURE 4.13

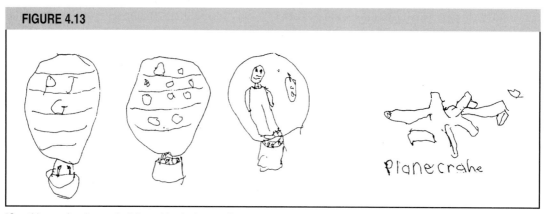

"One thing you've done today", "one thing in the news".

2. Joan was asked to draw something to represent the consequence of an event (e.g. you eat three cream buns a day for six weeks; you park your car on double yellow lines).
3. She was asked to draw somebody doing something with various objects (e.g. paintbrush, spade, accordion).
3. She was presented with a picture of an agent (e.g. a woman) followed by a written verb (e.g. "push") and a space in which she was asked to draw or write a feasible theme.

Joan was also given specific messages to convey through drawing only. The complexity varied from simple (e.g. you've decided to have a new shower fitted in your bathroom) to complex (e.g. Sarah is coming to stay but she's phoned to say the car's broken down and she won't be able to come until Saturday). Not surprisingly the longer messages caused enormous problems, since they required Joan to decide which information was crucial to conveying the message and eliminate the remainder. I felt that this exercise probably came nearer than any other we had done to simulating the processing load involved in spontaneous output. She tended to need much guidance in extracting the essence of the message.

Joan has returned to writing short phrases and sentences regularly. For example, in a recent session, when asked what she and Tony did on a trip to Weston-Super-Mare, she wrote "We had relly good luche (really good lunch)", and when asked how she came to know a friend they had visited she wrote "I went to shool with her". The

FIGURE 4.14

Events.

FIGURE 4.15

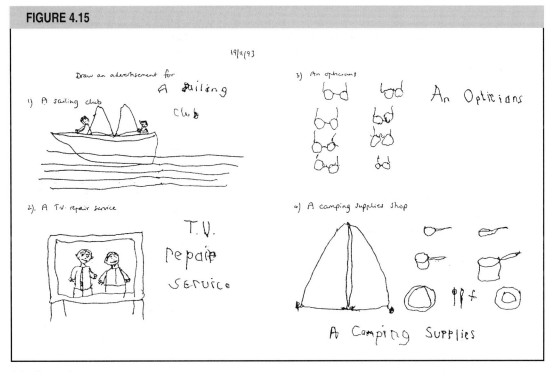

Advertisements.

production of such sentences remains laborious in that it is generally necessary with the addition of each new word to read aloud what she has written so far. In this way she recently wrote the Cookie Theft description (Fig. 4.19a) shown in the appendix. The help given invalidates comparison with the version (Fig. 4.19b) produced six months earlier, in which she produced single words only.

EVALUATION OF THERAPY AND CONCLUSIONS

The data in this study have been almost entirely anecdotal. In retrospect it was foolish not to have at least attempted to devise some kind of objective measure of Joan's ability to express herself through drawing and writing. Ideally this should have involved the communication of specified messages to naive listeners (or viewers, in this case) since it seems likely that my increased familiarity with Joan, her background, and her individual strengths

and weaknesses (as well as hers with mine!) will have influenced the ease with which we communicate (although when Joan spent a session with a student who did not know her there was no obvious diminution in her ability to express herself).

I did not feel that picture naming could be considered a useful measure since this was the condition of highest constraint and her performance in this task would say nothing about her ability to output under conditions of low constraint. This measure, therefore, was not repeated.

Any conclusions, then, have to be based on a subjective comparison of her spontaneous output before and after therapy. There can be little doubt that the quality of her drawing has improved (Joan swears she had done no drawing since she was at school). It is also clear that sentence structure began to appear in her written output only after a substantial period of therapy. It is open to question whether the sentence processing therapy (which had been discontinued some 3 months previously) might have played a part in this development.

FIGURE 4.16

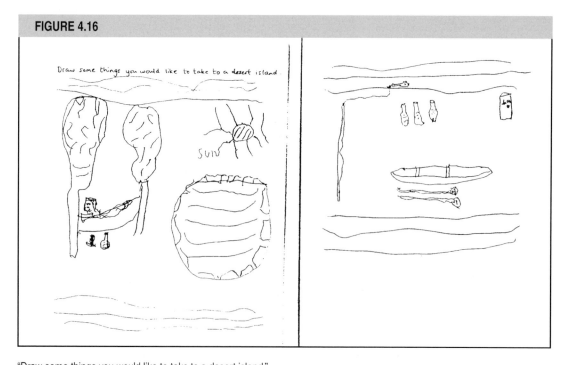

"Draw some things you would like to take to a desert island."

FIGURE 4.17

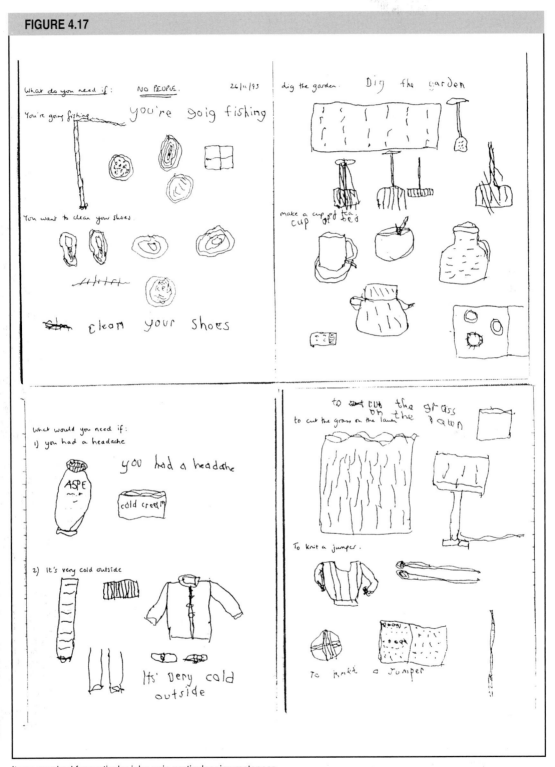

Items required for particular jobs or in particular circumstances.

FIGURE 4.18

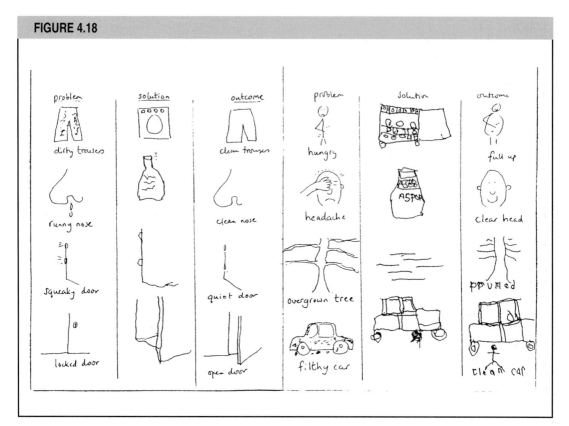

Problems and solutions.

FIGURE 4.19

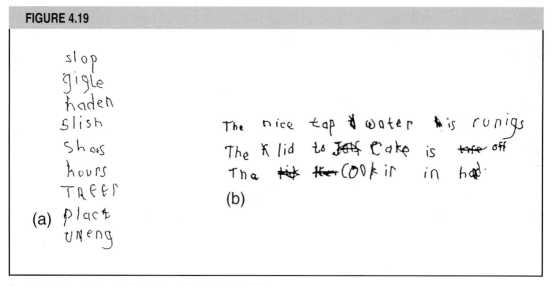

Cookie theft description, (a) September 1993, (b) March 1994.

When working with Joan it is striking how drawing boosts access to orthography. It seems plausible that this is due to increased semantic access which occurs during the process of the drawing. Drawing appears to have afforded Joan a means of assembling and holding onto semantic representations that the written medium alone did not. One of the many unanswered questions I have about Joan's therapy programme concerns the relative potency of the two opposite approaches, taken at different times, one beginning with maximum constraint and gradually reducing it, the other (free drawing) beginning with minimum constraint and gradually increasing it. Whatever the answer, it might have implications for the treatment of other forms of non-verbal (and possibly verbal) expressive deficits.

EMOTIONAL AND PSYCHOSOCIAL ASPECTS

Tony. Tony has always maintained (outwardly at least) a cheerful and positive attitude to his and Joan's situation. In the early days following her stroke he pushed hard for the maximum amount of input from physiotherapy, occupational therapy, and speech and language therapy. At home, however, he has cared for Joan (who remains severely hemiplegic) without help, and does not feel he wants any.

He feels that he and Joan communicate well given the circumstances. He insists that Joan does use pen and paper effectively at home and elsewhere, but when we meet all communication between them is through yes/no questions, and I suspect this is representative of the majority of the communication that takes place both between them and between Joan and friends and other family members.

Joan. From the time of our first encounter it was clear that Joan had been, and remained, devastated by her stroke. During the first few weeks she would cry for long periods during the sessions. I did not discourage this, although I often wondered if she would rather I had. Her crying was most often precipitated by any acknowledgement of her disabilities, physical or cognitive, so it was not possible to attribute it entirely to lability. Although I saw this means of expressing her grief as positive, I also felt I should try to help her express her feelings in more specific ways. Clearly this is not easy with somebody so limited in their expressive language.

One possible method is to ask yes/no questions. I asked Joan questions such as "Do people ever talk to you as if you are stupid?" (yes), "Do you feel angry with them for that?" (yes), and "Are you able to show them that it makes you angry?" (no). Although Joan indicated that she found this approach useful it was clearly unsatisfactory in that I was imposing on her my own perceptions of her circumstances.

An approach that gave Joan a little more control involved presenting her with a series of 46 drawings of different facial expressions, each labelled with a corresponding adjective describing the feeling portrayed. Joan was asked to choose those that conveyed how she felt. Both positive and negative feelings were included. Joan immediately chose "angry", then "disgusted", "idiotic", "frustrated", "sad", and "withdrawn". It was then possible to ask her, where appropriate, to whom these feelings were directed, although again it was necessary to suggest possibilities to her. Joan was very positive about this approach. At the beginning of a session I would offer her a choice between this and language work, and for several sessions she chose to discuss feelings.

It is highly questionable the extent to which Joan, now 2 years post onset, has accepted her new life and identity. Although she seldom appears distressed now, and consistently displays a wonderful sense of humour, there are strong indications that she continues to grieve greatly for her loss. Recently I wrote in her homework book "Draw some ideas for your idea of heaven". At our next meeting she placed the book on the table and began to cry. She had drawn just one item, a female figure standing up. It was clear that this represented herself before her stroke.

ACKNOWLEDGEMENTS

Thanks to Joan and Tony for agreeing to being "written up". Thanks also to Eirian Jones, Shula Chiat, and Lynne and to Jan Dorling, Wenna White Thompson, and Janet at Southmead for encouragement and useful discussions; and to Chris, Caroline, and Jane for much-needed help with word-processing.

REFERENCES

Dell, G.S., & O'Seaghdha, P.G. (1992). Stages of lexical access in language production. *Cognition, 42,* 287–314.

Kay, J., Lesser, R., & Coltheart, M. (1992). PALPA: Psycholinguistic Assessments of Language Processing in Aphasia. Hove: Lawrence Erlbaum Associates Ltd.

Lyon, J.G. (1992). Communication use and participation in life for adults with aphasia in natural settings: The scope of the problem. *American Journal of Speech-Language Pathology, 3,* 7–14.

5

Increasing effective communication using a total communication approach

Richard Lawson and Maggie Fawcus

INTRODUCTION

This is the case study of a 58-year-old man, TS, who, functionally, had no understanding of the spoken word and whose sole verbal utterance was an expletive. He had a few poorly developed communication strategies, and presented as depressed, negative, and often angry.

This study will describe the total communication approach to therapy, which gradually enabled him to become an increasingly effective communicator.

PREVIOUS SPEECH AND LANGUAGE THERAPY

TS had a CVA which left him with a right hemiplegia and global aphasia. He demonstrated almost no functional understanding of the spoken word and no verbal or written output (apart from recurrent utterance of a single swear word). In addition, he showed a neglect of his right side, and perceptual problems that led to the inappropriate use of objects. His wife wrote later to say that when he came out of hospital, he was a very angry and bitter man. "He swore at me and wiped the floor with me for months. I cried every day because I thought I'd never be able to cope. He didn't understand a spoken word or gesture given to him."

He was referred to a Rehabilitation Centre 4 months post onset. By the time he was discharged from the Centre 3 months later he could walk unaided, and was able to walk outside on his own. He made a bus journey and a shopping excursion with an escort, all indicating that mobility was not a problem. There had also been a decrease in his outbursts of temper and emotional lability. During the 6-week period at the Centre there was some improvement in his ability to communicate, but his severe dysphasia persisted. The speech and language therapist reported that he had a marked receptive loss which was evident even for simple, personally relevant conversation. He was unable to identify the names of body parts, or to select an object by name from a group of three or more objects. There had been some improvement on identifying one out of two of a series of unrelated object pictures—on admission he scored 14/20 (hardly better than chance level) and on discharge his score was 19/20.

There was some impairment of visual perceptual skills, with difficulty in matching real objects to line drawings, and matching pictures of objects associated by function. He was able to recognise highly familiar material, such as his name and address. He tended to match single written words to one or two pictures with more accuracy than for the spoken word—his score on admission was 16/20 and on discharge 19/20. (See Table 5.1 for a summary of performance on specific tasks.) On discharge he recognised concrete, common written words quite well. Functionally, this meant that he could recognise public signs, advertised TV programmes, and menu cards.

His severe impairment of speech had persisted, with recurrent utterance of the single swear word already mentioned. There was some repetition of sounds (e.g. /a/ and /m/) but he was unable to repeat sounds or words. He was considered to have a severe articulatory dyspraxia.

On admission to the Rehabilitation Centre he had no writing ability. At the completion of his therapy there he could write his own name and occasional family names. Despite his emotional outbursts, he had been consistently hard-working and co-operative. The following were the aims of therapy:

TABLE 5.1

Initial assessments (Rehabilitation Centre), 4 months post onset

Test	Description	Results
1. Biber test	Word to picture matching. 3 pictures: target related and unrelated pictures (e.g. moon, star, chair).	
	Spoken presentation	0/10. Pictures seemed difficult to recognise.
	Visual presentations	Did not understand task requirement.
2. Pyramids and Palm trees	Picture to picture matching task on the basis of semantic association	Scored just above chance level, but numerous errors and loss of idea of the task.
3. Auditory discrimination	Real words: Same/different judgement	Unable to respond.
4. Word to picture matching	2 unrelated object pictures to one word.	
	Spoken word	14/20
	Written word	16/20
5. Object to Gesture Matching	Choice of 10 objects	0/10
	Choice of 3 objects	6/12
6. Copying Gestures and Pantomime	Imitating therapist (e.g. phoning)	10/15
	Imitating action photographs	6/12
7. Tool Use— demonstrating	Real objects	7/7 (actually holding them)
	Pictured objects	1/7

1. Comprehension and use of both natural gesture and Amer-Ind signals.
2. Improving reading skills.
3. Encouraging drawing and writing as a means of communication.
4. Making him more aware of his recurrent swearing, in the hope of reducing its occurrence.

Both he and his wife were given explanation about the nature of the communication impairments and advice on how to deal with them. By the time of his discharge from the Centre, he showed more awareness that speech was no longer a communication option, and was beginning to use more pointing gesture and drawing, and was even attempting to use writing in order to convey his message. Nevertheless, his communication problems remained severe. As his therapist commented, his outbursts of anger and misery were understandable, but were often hard for the family to cope with.

He had had some group experience during this period, which he apparently enjoyed and from which he seemed to benefit. He was therefore placed on the waiting list for more long-term and intensive group work.

SOCIAL HISTORY

TS had been a skilled manual worker, working as a messenger at the time of his CVA. His hobbies included fishing, gardening, and motor bikes. He enjoyed reading and playing cards. Following his CVA his wife commented that the only things that "stimulated his mind" were visual things like places, faces, and parts of London when seen on television.

So far as his pre-morbid personality was concerned he was described as "terribly kind and generous", and although he could be very bad-tempered he got over his anger very quickly.

He lived with his wife, son, and daughter, and his wife always seemed interested and involved in his care. He appeared to belong to quite a close family, who visited quite regularly. Following his CVA he no longer went fishing. He attended a day centre where he received occupational therapy.

GROUP THERAPY

He commenced attendance for intensive group therapy 1 year post onset. At that time his communication skills were observed to be as follows: His comprehension of the spoken word was functionally and formally almost non-existent. He had no verbal output, apart from recurrent utterance of his one swear word. He had no written vocabulary, except his name, and demonstrated few communication strategies. His one strength appeared to be his understanding of a single salient written word.

He presented as depressed, quick to anger, and essentially negative about communication. This was hardly surprising, in view of the frustration he must have experienced, and the virtual isolation he had experienced for the preceeding year. He gave the impression that he regarded himself as beyond help. It appeared that he had made no progress since being discharged from the Rehabilitation Centre, and, indeed he seemed to have lost some of the gains he had made there.

TS was placed in a "closed" experimental group of eight patients who all commenced therapy simultaneously. The group met twice weekly (10.30–12.30 and 1.30–3.00 pm) for a total therapy period of 8 months spread over 1 year. All members of the group presented with non-fluent aphasia and were seriously handicapped by their communication deficits. They were, however, very much less handicapped than TS in their understanding of the spoken word.

Despite his negative approach to therapy, he was essentially a supportive group member, and demonstrated by unequivocal non-verbal behaviour, such as hand-gripping and hugging, that he appreciated the efforts made to help him. Some non-verbal behaviour (e.g. facial expression) was not impaired. His severe comprehension deficit made management in the group setting quite difficult, but adjustments were made to accommodate his auditory difficulties by presenting him with the written word, or other visual clues wherever possible. Since his receptive difficulties meant that TS obtained most social meaning from visual sources (e.g. other people's actions, gestures and facial expression), he consequently often appeared to misread situations, or have problems in understanding the underlying structures of tasks or activities. His ability to make links was severely limited (e.g. making associations between tasks and drawing inferences from what he had seen). However, once he began to understand what was demanded of him—mostly through observing others in the group—he soon found that he could use facial expression and drawing to good effect.

From the initial stages of therapy, emphasis was placed on encouraging a total communication approach to communication (gesture, mime, drawing, and writing) with the idea of optimising on any available communication channel. There appeared to be a significant latency period before any real progress was observed, partly because of the severity of his problems, but also because of his lack of confidence and essentially negative attitude to communication. He had also become very passive, to the extent that his wife had to wash and bathe him. It seemed that his role as a verbally non-communicating individual had been thrust on him suddenly and completely, changing his identity and role fundamentally. It took a long time for him to become aware of his full potential as communicator and to "adopt" his new role.

At the time of his admission for intensive group therapy, TS was 12 months post onset, and it seemed that no spontaneous recovery had taken place, certainly not in the 6 months since he was discharged from the Rehabilitation Centre. On admission, he was assessed on the Huskins Non-Verbal Apraxia Screening Test (1986) and on TROG (Bishop, 1983) and he was re-assessed on the same tests 12 months later. The Boston Naming Test was used with the other members of the group, but not formally with TS. Some items were given, however, in order to examine his communication strategies. He demonstrated some spontaneous use of gesture, drawing, and writing the first letter of the target word.

RATIONALE FOR THERAPY

The following was the rationale for a total communication approach:

1. All members of the group had little or no verbal communication. All were at least a year post-onset, and in view of this it seemed that improvement in verbal output might be an unrealistic goal.
2. It was considered important that group members should have the chance to explore and exploit all possible channels of communication.
3. We wanted to give the group the opportunity for successful communication as soon as possible, and this seemed best achieved by an approach that allowed the use of any modality that could be employed effectively.
4. The small group setting seemed appropriate in order to encourage total communication skills. TS was the most severely impaired member of the group.

TREATMENT STRATEGIES

Details of the treatment strategies will now be described and discussed.

Gesture and sign

The initial signing programme was Amer-Ind based (Skelly, 1979), taught in association with speech. However, there was gradual move towards encouraging more spontaneous gesture and mime. It was felt that group members might be more likely to remember and to use signs that they had been involved in creating.

Examples of activities:

1. Each group member was presented with a word (e.g. beer, newspaper) on card. S/he was then required to sign what was written on the card to the rest of the group, who rated performance on a scale of 1–5. The words chosen moved from those with fixed signs

(e.g. man, woman) to those that needed a more creative approach to signing (e.g. whisky, fat).

2. An object with a well-defined shape was placed in a bag. One group member felt the object and then gestured its shape to the rest of the group.

3. Using PACE pictures (Edelman, 1986), each group member gave as much information as possible from the picture to the rest of the group. TS achieved particularly well on PACE activities, since he had a good eye for detail.

Mime

Perhaps the distinction between mime and gesture is rather an artificial one, but by mime, we meant the ability to go beyond signs learned to the gesturing of sequential activities, and vocabulary items not associated with previously learned signs. Duffy & Duffy (1981) defined pantomime as "the deliberate use of bodily or manual movement to convey a meaning". This was an important step with TS who had so little in the way of communicative confidence. He gained markedly from the modelling that was done both by other group members and the therapist. Mime allowed him to explore ways of expressing more complex ideas.

Examples of activities:

1. The name of a game or sport was written on a card, which had to be mimed by the rest of the group.

2. Members were requested to mime a familiar "domestic" activity—again written down or in picture form (e.g. pouring out a cup of tea; putting in two lumps of sugar).

In all these activities considerable emphasis was put on the monitoring of performance by other group members, as well as the turn-taking element of the task. This was an important step in ensuring that sign and mime did not become an empty academic exercise, but was valued from the beginning for its communicative purposes.

Drawing

We had to accept that drawing was the least preferred mode of communication with most group members. For TS, however, drawing proved to be an important strategy to communicate his ideas. Comparison of early and recent drawings (Fig. 5.1, and 5.2) indicate how much his performance improved with practice. Drawing activities were included in each session and TS's eye for detail no doubt contributed to the marked improvement in his ability to convey information through this channel. Considerable emphasis was placed on features which distinguished items from the same semantic field (e.g. fruit, vegetables, clothing).

Examples of activities:

1. Members were asked to convey information through drawing (e.g. What did you have for breakfast? What is your favourite hobby?) In the case of TS it was not always easy to explain a task of this kind, but examples carried out by other members of the group, and the use of simplified written instructions (e.g. Breakfast?) enabled him to be successfully involved.

2. Group members were requested to draw four fruit—having done this, discussion (or in TS's case, demonstration) of the essential distinguishing features took place (How can a strawberry be differentiated from a plum, or an apple from an orange, or lemon?).

3. All group members were asked to draw the same thing (e.g. an elephant) and the drawings were then compared and rated.

Reading and writing

Considerable emphasis was placed on developing basic reading and writing skills. Although TS showed almost no writing ability, his strength lay in the recognition of many written words. It was therefore felt—in view of his total absence of speech—that every effort should be made to encourage the written word. The fact that nearly all the important message-conveying words used by the group were written for TS's benefit undoubtedly helped develop his written lexicon.

Examples of activities:

1. *Semantic field task.* A topic was written on the board, e.g. HOLIDAY. Group members

FIGURE 5.1

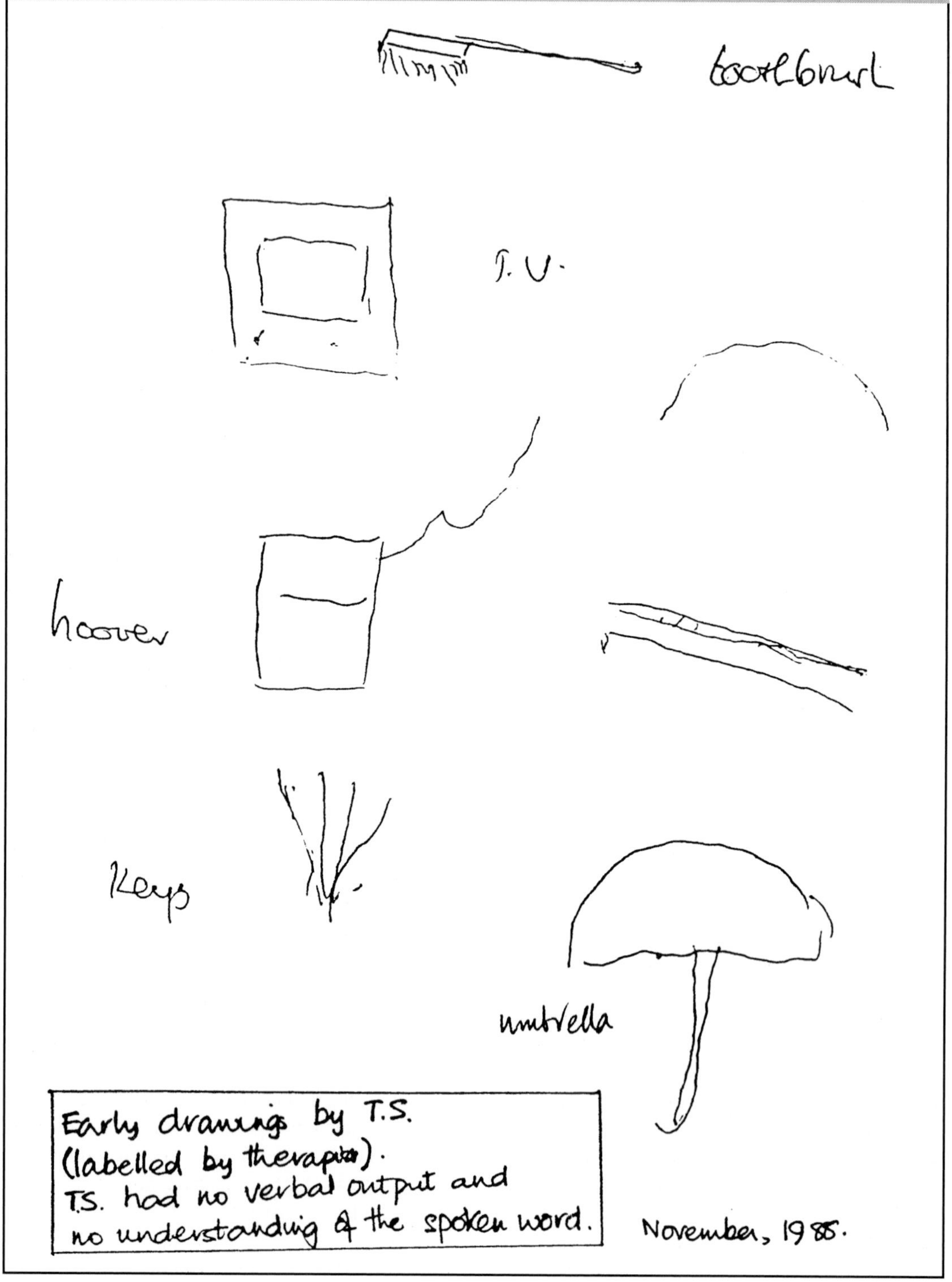

Early drawings by TS (labelled by therapist), November 1985.

FIGURE 5.2

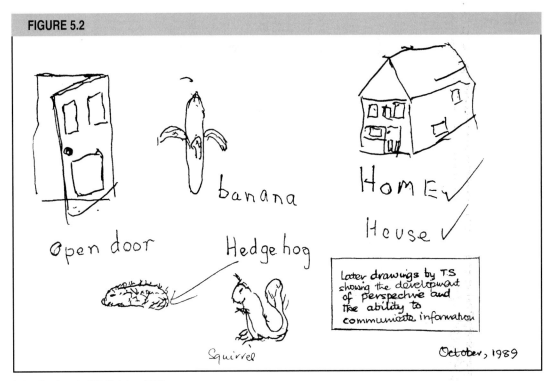

Open door

banana

Hedge hog

Squirrel

HOME ✓

House ✓

Later drawings by TS showing the development of perspective and the ability to communicate information

October, 1989

Later drawings by TS, October 1989.

were then encouraged to produce semantically related activities.

2. *Categorisation task.* Each member was given a written list of items from three categories, which were written on the board (e.g. drinks, cars, sports). The items were then assigned to the appropriate categories.

3. *PACE-type activities.* (Davis & Wilcox, 1985).

From the beginning, it was made clear that any attempt to communicate was acceptable. Although it was accepted that speech was the desired goal for most group members, the aim for the group was effective communication through any available channel. In TS's case speech did not appear to be a viable option, and every effort was made to reinforce any communication attempt he made.

After 6 months of group therapy, TS's wife was asked to give an account of any communication strategies used at home (Table 5.2). An analysis of these showed that he was using gesture, mime, pointing, and drawing, and had begun to use writing. It was clear that the burden of communication still rested quite heavily on his partner, but it also demonstrated that he was becoming quite resourceful and persevering (e.g. the Columbia Road episode).

The experimental group was concluded after 9 months but all members of the group were offered the opportunity to continue as members of a regular thrice-weekly dysphasic group. TS' attendance continued for a further 18 months.

The second stage of therapy added two elements to the therapy programme:

1. To encourage him to "read" signing as well as the written word, which would obviously be a quicker method of conveying information to him. It would, we hoped, also underline the efficacy of signing to him.

2. To place a greater emphasis on encouraging him to listen to and use the spoken word. He has great difficulty in initiating words, which appeared to be dyspraxic in nature (although, unlike the typical dyspraxic person, he does

---

TABLE 5.2

Communication strategies documented by TS' wife 6 months into therapy

- I came in after breakfast. T held up 3 fingers. I thought he'd seen 3 birds, but no. He drew I realised he'd seen 3 people viewing house for sale, back of us.

- T led me by the hand into lounge and pointed to garden—I asked what he had seen—In the air he wrote R, and stroked his breast—I knew he'd seen a robin.

- T asked for a cigarette by pretending to smoke with his mouth and fingers.

- I came in from work. T picked up half an onion and put it to his mouth. Got angry because I couldn't understand. He then got out the sliced bread and I realised he wanted onion in his cheese sandwich in future not cucumber.

- T's brother called one evening with his wife. T pointed at them both and wrote the word CABBIE. None of us could understand. He then pointed to the plants in the garden and got out street guide. He found COLUMBIA Road on map and we realised he wanted them to drive him to the flower market.

- T has started having an occasional cigarette and my sister asked him why he wasn't using his old Tommy lighter. He drew a maple leaf on piece of paper which signified he still had it. The lighter had a leaf and the word CANADA written on it.

"Things like this help me so much, and when T gets a message across to someone it makes him feel he is achieving something."

---

not normally even attempt speech). There was a continuing problem here: When he did produce a word—often with some clarity—it had no meaning for him (e.g. tea, money, car). This seemed to mirror the difficulty he had in understanding other people. However, he began to say "hallo" spontaneously and to recognise "tea" when he produced it—again with some degree of spontaneity. Currently, a small lexicon of spoken words is beginning to be produced with increasing ease. The word "hallo" was recently used at home. He has become less resistant to attempting speech, but care has to be taken not to put too much emphasis on this aspect of treatment since he can get frustrated and angry when he fails to initiate a word.

OUTCOMES

TS now gets the gist of what is said to him, providing verbal presentation remains simple and slow. A blank look and a shrug of the shoulders clearly indicates when he has not understood. TS is one of the few members of his group who actively uses drawing to communicate his ideas and messages, and he does this quite skilfully (Fig. 5.3). He is also clearly aware of its potential and, most importantly, uses it as spontaneous mode of communication.

We would suggest that aphasic people, as a general rule, select the alternative mode of communication which is most effective and most comfortable for them, and they do this with a considerable degree of consistency (Fawcus, 1990). We would agree with Disimoni (1986) when he notes that the best approach for an individual is the one that facilitates communication to the greater degree.

Kraat (1990, p.329) has suggested that clinicians interested in functional communication have concentrated on behaviours that evolve from the client, "among them the use of non-verbal behaviours, self devised symbolic gestures, pointing to objects and action in the immediate environment, drawing, pantomime, written attempts or residual speech and intonation". Allowing TS to make and exploit his own

FIGURE 5.3

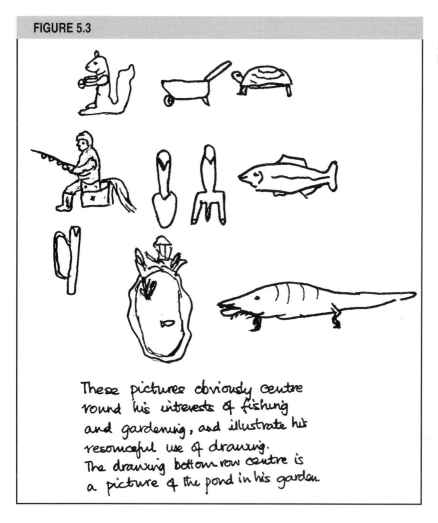

Drawings by TS to convey his interests.

These pictures obviously centre round his interests of fishing and gardening, and illustrate his resourceful use of drawing. The drawing bottom row centre is a picture of the pond in his garden.

communication choices has been the general philosophy behind our approach.

TS now appreciates that signs have meanings and is becoming increasingly successful in understanding both a single word and "strings" of signs. He does not use gesture as spontaneously as he uses drawing and writing, but is making increasing use of skywriting. Through these various modes of communication, it is now possible to have simple "conversational" interactions with TS. Table 5.3 gives some examples of recent two-way interactions with his wife—showing not only his attempts at communication but also the adjustments she has made in communicating with him. He is making more use of skywriting, which reflects the improvement in his written word production. These words frequently show spelling errors, but none the less are normally recognisable for the target word. His written output, and his active use of it, has increased steadily over the months. Where he cannot find the written word, he will resort to drawing. Although sign and mime are not used to the same extent as writing and drawing, he makes frequent and effective use of other non-verbal behaviour—indicating clearly when he needs more time, is feeling dissatisfied with his therapist, or is feeling pleased with his performance. His facial expression is used to great effect to question, reprimand, show surprise, pleasure, and approval.

He is developing into a successful and increasingly confident communicator, despite the absence of speech. It remains to be seen whether the

TABLE 5.3

Communication strategies documented by TS' wife 18 months after therapy started

- When T does an M in the air he is telling me something about Maria at the Day Centre.
- When I draw a letter R with my finger he knows its Richard (his therapist). He now writes in the air GILL & LES which helps.
- When I point to a plant which L's girlfriend bought me—he knows I mean Jackie.
- If I pretend my arm really hurts—he knows I mean my Sister in Law on the kidney machine.
- He had the sense to break a stick roughly 12" in length and one 4" he was able to plant his allysum around the garden at equal intervals.
- T awoke me early and pointed to a heron in the sky and said a few swear words—One ate all my sister's fish out of her pond.
- My friend M looked after T at a party recently, he draw a shape in the air like this she thought he wanted a drum stick—no not that—he then put piece of paper—she got him a piece of quiche—that was wrong—third time lucky, he wanted triangular sandwiches.
- When T flutters all his fingers to the ground it's raining. A big letter C means—damn cats have scratched up garden.
- When T draws this, bluetits are in and out of the nesting box.
- T pulls a piece of hair and pretends to cut it with scissors that means haircut is in order.
- He said "Hello" to my friend T on Sunday and she was so pleased.
- T wanted to take 5 fish to the handicapped school. He wriggled his hand like a fish—put up 5 fingers and wrote a capital "M"—I phoned Maria and arranged it.

spoken word will eventually play a part in his communication.

It has become increasingly clear that, if TS is indeed dyspraxic, this is not the only reason for his lack of speech. He demonstrates an essentially "all or none" level of success in speech attempts. He shows little of the groping behaviour typical of dyspraxia. Most significant of all is the extreme difficulty he has always experienced in recognising the words he succeeds in producing. Only as words have become greatly "over-learned" has he been able to produce them with any degree of confidence and spontaneity.

One of the problems we have encountered in working on speech has been TS's own attitude: He has often been singularly unwilling to attempt speech, particularly in the group. When requested to attempt the target word, he would frequently put his finger to his lips, and put on his unblinking look, indicating that any further attempts at persuasion were doomed to failure. He has, however, recently been much more responsive with a particularly persuasive student. He has been willing to drill on an increasing list of core words with a level of success that has reinforced his efforts.

With hindsight, we should perhaps have worked on auditory discrimination (e.g. minimal pair work). If, however, he had been unable to see the relevance of such an approach (and it is difficult to know how we could have explained this to him!), it is doubtful that he would have been prepared to collaborate. Now that he has reached a stage where he is actually interested in trying to produce "tea" and "key" appropriately, it might well be that continued work on auditory discrimination and speech might be effective.

The use of his expletive is much rarer and, when it is used, it is produced more appropriately. We assume this is because he now has alternative ways in which to express himself. TS is a "creature of habit", and makes his displeasure clear when any changes are made in the group venue, or in the seating arrangements. This may have been a pre-morbid trait, but it may be some unconscious attempt to make some order out of a chaotic "noisy" world. He finds noise very trying, and will show disapproval of other group members who distract him. Although he has a rather low tolerance threshold, he is emotionally much more stable in the group.

The change in TS as person has been the most rewarding aspect of his progress—he is no longer the passive, negative, and depressed man who commenced intensive therapy 2 years ago. His wife can have the final word:

His drawings are very good and his actions tell me a lot. He comes home and is doing splendidly. Without help T practises his words. Everybody thinks he or myself would have ended up in Barley Lane! (Reference to a local psychiatric institution)

ACKNOWLEDGEMENTS

We would like to thank Sarah Ross, Speech and Language Therapist, whose initial assessments and report are included in this case study and Jane Marshall for her re-assessment and observations. We are grateful to TS's wife, who took the trouble to give us such useful feedback on his performance at home. Finally, we would like to say how much we enjoyed working with TS and wish to place on record how impressed we were with his perseverance and resourcefulness in the face of apparently insuperable difficulties. Sadly, TS died shortly after the completion of this study.

REFERENCES

Bishop, D.V.M. (1983). *Test for reception of grammar (TROG)*, University of Newcastle-Upon-Tyne, UK.

Davis, G.A., & Wilcox, J.M. (1985). Adult aphasia rehabilitation. *Applied Pragmatics*. Windsor, Berks: NFER-Nelson.

Disimoni, F.G. (1986). Therapies which utilate alternative or augmentative communication systems. In R. Chapey (Ed.), *Language intervention strategies in adult aphasia*. Baltimore, Williams & Wilkins.

Duffy, R.J., & Duffy, J.R. (1981). Three studies of deficits in pantomimic expression and pantomimic recognition in aphasia. *Journal of Speech and Hearing Research, 24,* 70–84.

Edelman, G. (1986). PACE (promoting aphasics' communicative effectiveness) photographs. Bicester, UK: Wilmslow Press.

Fawcus, M. (1990). *Communication choices*. Paper presented at British Aphasiology Society study day, London.

Huskins, S. (1986). *Working with dyspraxics—a practical guide to therapy for dyspraxia*. Bicester, UK: Winslow Press.

Kraat, A.W. (1990). Augmentative and alternative communication: Does it have a future in aphasia rehabilitation? *Aphasiology, 4*(4), 321–338.

Skelly, M. (1979). *Amer-Ind gestural code based on universal American talk*. New York: Elsevier.

Part 2

Word retrieval therapies

6

Introduction to Part 2:Therapies for word finding utilising orthographic relay strategies

Although the aphasic individuals described in these three case studies differ considerably both in biographical information and the nature of their processing strengths and impairments, a range of interesting similarities emerge regarding the nature of the therapeutic process, the clients' response to the therapy, and the questions which these outcomes pose.

In each case the chapters present a clear analysis of the proposed level of psycholinguistic break-down, backed up by pre-therapy clinical assessment. The key impairments of concern are: accessing graphic motor patterns and additionally processing problems associated with the graphemic output buffer resulting in an inability to write words (MF; Chapter 7); accessing phonology from relatively well-preserved semantics resulting in a marked impairment in spoken naming (BC; Chapter 8); converting graphemic to phonemic information when attempting to read function words resulting in impaired ability to read sentence and paragraph length material (PH; Chapter 9).

STRENGTHS AND STRATEGIES

In each case the aphasic person also exhibits striking pre-therapy abilities which lead the therapist to devise a strategy based around maximising these preserved processing abilities. MF demonstrates markedly superior oral than written spelling; BC demonstrates significantly better written than spoken naming; PH is considerably more able to read aloud content words than function words. Wisely each therapist attempts to lessen the functional impact of the aphasic person's impairments by building bridges combining confidence and language founded on these obvious strengths.

Another interesting similarity between the chapters is the importance each therapy places on the stage-wise development and internalisation of the selected strategy. In Chapter 7 Mortley presents some interesting reflections on the processing cost of performing a task, e.g. spelling aloud, whilst simultaneously juggling with the demands of recall and implementation of the three part strategy—spell a word aloud, name, and write to dictation each letter, all this in the context of inconsistent ability to recall individual graphic motor patterns. In Chapter 9 Sheridan identifies one of the problems with PH's strategy as an inconsistent ability to relate a chosen key word with its initial phoneme (little—small), highlighting the importance both of establishing and breaking some more automatic patterns. White-Thomson in Chapter 8 describes a five-part hierarchy of tasks which have the key focus of encouraging BC to internalise the self-cueing orthographic visualisation strategy. Although not an explicit aim of the therapy, both BC and MF appear to derive additional benefits from the cognitive demands of strategy acquisition and application. In MF's case this relates to improved mental stamina/concentration and an enhanced understanding of the need to pace himself according to fatiguability. With BC the work on matching spoken to written words, a foundation task for improving awareness of phoneme/grapheme correspondences appears to have contributed to the additional post-therapy benefit of improved self-monitoring ability.

The authors do not refer explicitly to the prerequisite cognitive skills for successful acquisition of fairly laborious and demanding strategies. One might reflect that the success of the clients in applying their chosen strategy so effectively lies partly in their cognitive readiness and partly in the way their preserved language processing abilities support and guide them down an intuitively well-directioned path.

OUTCOMES/FUNCTIONAL CHANGE/GENERALISATION

Improvements relating to the therapeutic intervention in each of the three cases is unequivocal. The length of time post onset of the clients—9 months, 12 months, and 18 months—and in the cases of MF and PH the reported stability in the targeted areas (written spelling and reading function words) suggest spontaneous recovery does not play a significant (if any) role in post-therapy

results. BC is perhaps less stable at the time of intervention but the lack of change on picture naming and reading aloud control measures clearly illustrates the specific gains on spoken naming. The authors are also each able to describe clients using a strategy (in therapeutic tasks and other informal communicative contexts) that they have acquired through the therapy and did not have at their functional disposal before therapy began.

Theoretically driven and carefully focused impairment-based programmes of the type described have sometimes been accused of their limited functional utility, setting up the false dichotomy of either cognitive neuropsychological or functional approaches to therapy. It is pleasing therefore to note the authors' anecdotal accounts of direct and significant generalisation of the effects of therapy on communication and lifestyle. The naming therapy for BC resulted in improvements in production and monitoring of spoken output. For MF, the ability to identify and write initial letters led to the ability to use a dictionary and, one would imagine, a computer spell-check facility. For PH improved ability to read function words dramatically reduced the amount of time spent reading a passage and enabled him to re-access his preferred leisure option of reading history books.

TEASING OUT STRANDS OF THERAPY AND CHANGE

One of the questions that these, as many other therapy studies, leave unanswered is which tasks or series of tasks most contribute and most efficaciously contribute to the gains noted after therapy? In the case of BC, for example, the range of input- and output-based tasks might be working at a number of different levels selectively and/or simultaneously. The input task requiring matching a written word to auditory stimulus is not dissimilar to tasks used by Harding and Pound (Chapter 3) and also Morris, Franklin, Ellis, Turner, and Bailey (1996). Although used specifically to encourage BC's ability to match spoken sounds to their graphemic correspondences, such a task clearly makes demands on early auditory processing of input and may be directly responsible for the improved self-monitoring of speech noted post therapy.

The issue of how many areas of impairment to address in any one therapeutic intervention is also raised by White-Thomson when she questions post hoc whether she might also have incorporated a semantic component into her therapy tasks. This is a question clinicians frequently face when treating clients with multiple language impairments whilst simultaneously juggling with timing, resources, needs, and effectiveness. Clinical reality often dictates that therapy programmes are less rigorously controlled than, for example, research studies where baselines are painstakingly collected and control measures carefully selected, hopefully enabling a coherent analysis of the specific effects of a particular therapy. As White-Thompson shows in her summary, however, clinical reality does not abnegate the need for focus and reflection on anticipated, actual, and putative outcomes relating to differential patterns of therapeutic input. The complexities of the ways in which similarly presenting patients respond in different ways to apparently similar therapeutic programmes is perhaps most clearly demonstrated in the recent series of papers by Nickels and Best (1996).

The more isolated, less "messy" level of underlying impairment in MF and PH make the selection of area of focus less contentious. There are still, however, different ways to address a single problem. The elegance of the study by Sheridan (Chapter 9) is in demonstrating that, although both therapies work, the second therapy, with its wider generalisation effect to function words untreated in therapy, works better. In this case reorganisation triumphs over restoration.

In Mortley's chapter (Chapter 7) there is again room for debate as to which elements of the therapy most, least, or in combination pack the therapeutic punch—the focus on recall/recognition of graphic motor patterns, the focus on spelling aloud to support lexically retrieved information, or the process of converting spoken letter names to written graphemes. The qualitative description of the therapist/client exchanges also highlights the as yet non-explicit processes and imponderables of therapeutic interaction. How does the decision making of the therapist regarding stimuli, facilitation, and feedback interact with the response of the client—not just in terms of their psycholinguistic but also their cognitive and emotional response to the therapist and therapy? For more on the role of interactions in therapy see Byng (1995) and Horton and Byng (submitted).

INTENSITY OF THERAPY

Finally, an interesting feature of each of the cases was the relatively small amount of therapy time required to produce a significant change in the aphasic person's abilities. BC received only 14 sessions of therapy, whereas PH received 12 sessions of therapy, on each of the two therapy programmes. The amount of therapy received by MF is not specified but of interest here is the ease with which the therapy programme could be supported by non-therapist directed computer work or practical exercises with his wife. The systematic approach to strategy use for both PH and BC suggest a potential role for proxy therapists in the delivery of the therapy programmes. Clearly this does not imply that any non-SLT delivered therapy does not require close supervision, monitoring, and direction. However, given the routine and repetitive nature of the tasks and feedback (adequately undertaken by a computer in MF's case) and the constraints on face-to-face therapist–client time reported by many aphasia therapists, the potential for high quality and appropriate therapy, given greater intensity and duration by therapist directed but non-therapist delivered support work is an important issue to consider. Less specific or less focused therapy programmes have the disadvantage of being less explicit both to the aphasic person and to any other possible therapeutic helpers.

REFERENCES

Byng, S. (1995). What is aphasia therapy? In C. Code & D. Muller (Eds.), *Treatment of aphasia: From theory to practice.* (pp. 3–17). London: Whurr Publishers Ltd.

Horton, S., & Byng, S. (submitted). Of cues, feedback and interaction — what is the how of language therapy in the 1990s.

Morris, J., Franklin, S., Ellis, A. Turner, J., & Bailey, P. (1996). Remediating a speech perception deficit in an aphasic patient. *Aphasiology, 10*(2), 137–158.

Nickels, L., & Best, W. (1996). Therapy for naming disorders (Part I): Principles, puzzles and progress. *Aphasiology, 10*(1), 21–48.

Nickels, L., & Best, W. (1996). Therapy for naming disorders (Part II): Specifics, surprises and suggestions. *Aphasiology, 10*(2), 109–136.

7

An intensive strategy-based therapy programme for impaired spelling

Jane Mortley

BACKGROUND TO THE SINGLE CASE STUDY OF MF

MF is a 67-year-old gentleman who lives with his wife. He has four grown-up children and six grandchildren. He is a retired civil servant. He is very involved with family life, having regular contact with his children. Prior to his stroke he was an active member of a club for retired civil servants.

MF has a history of left carotid bruit. He was on the waiting list for an endarterectomy when he suffered two CVAs within 8 weeks. His first stroke caused mainly left-sided weakness. According to the medical notes his speech was slightly dysarthric, but this resolved itself within 2 weeks. His second stroke, however, was much more severe. He was described in the medical notes as having:

> a right sided weakness of the face, arm, and leg with speech problems and dribbling. Right arm stiff and shaky but can move it. He was able to rise unaided from a chair and walk unaided. Marked problems with expressive dysphasia.

A CT scan confirmed "multiple infarcts in the left hemisphere. Not possible to say whether CVA embolic or thrombotic". His carotid artery had occluded and he was removed from the list for an endarterectomy as a result.

Initially MF presented with a right hemiplegia, severe dysarthria, and a mild to moderate dysphasia affecting written output more than spoken output. Therapy within the first year focused on the speech difficulties caused by the dysarthria.

ASSESSMENT

At a review appointment (1 year post onset) MF reported that his speech improvement had been maintained. He no longer felt that he needed to focus on this area of his communication. He was, however, concerned about his writing as this did not appear to be improving. The inability to spell made him feel "disabled" as he had taken pride in his spelling prior to his stroke. Since MF had responded so well to the previous episode of care offered, it was decided to assess MF on his spelling difficulties and determine whether it was appropriate to offer therapy.

Assessment on the Shortened Schuell (Schuell, 1965) and the Aachen Aphasia Test (AAT); Huber, Poeck, Wehigar, & Willmes, (1983) showed that MF was able to copy symbols and letters but had difficulty writing letters to dictation. He was still unable to write any words down from dictation. His response to this task was either no response or what appeared to be a random selection of letters. What was of interest was that he found composing words, i.e. spelling words using Scrabble-type tiles, a little easier, suggesting that he still had a representation of the word available. This had implications for therapy, which will be discussed later.

These assessments clearly confirmed that MF had a severe spelling deficit, and that it had not improved since being assessed 9 months earlier, but the origin of this deficit needed clarification, however. Assessments based on cognitive neuropsychological models of language processing were therefore administered, in order to hypothesise where in the writing process the impairment was arising (Table 7.1).

Summary of spelling abilities

1. MF can copy letters and words well.
2. MF can cross case match at the letter and word level.
3. MF can sometimes spell a word out aloud that he cannot write down.
4. MF's writing attempts are mainly single letters or no response.
5. MF's spelling is assisted by Scrabble letters

An hypothesis of the area of breakdown

In the situation where MF can spell a word out aloud but is unable to write, and is assisted by the use of Scrabble letters, the impairment is likely to be at a peripheral, post-graphemic buffer level where graphic motor patterns are accessed and realised (see model in Fig. 7.1). A patient IDT, whom it had been hypothesised had an impairment at the graphic motor pattern, has been cited in the literature by Baxter and Warrington (1986). He was able to spell words out aloud normally, yet was totally unable to write even common three-letter words correctly. His writing, like MF, was limited to single letters, and he was also good at copying.

This hypothesis would not explain the situation where MF is unable to spell a word out aloud, is not assisted by Scrabble letters, and gives a non-response to a spelling to dictation task. In this

---

TABLE 7.1

Summary of pre-therapy assessment results on PALPA (Kay, Lesser, & Coltheart, 1992)

Assessment	Sub-set	Pre-therapy
PALPA 18	Mirror reversal task	100%
PALPA 19	Upper/lower case matching	100%
PALPA 22	Letter naming	77%
	Letter sounding	62%
PALPA 23	Spoken letter–written letter matching	86%
PALPA 39	Letter length spelling	0%
PALPA 44	Regularity and spelling	0%
PALPA 53	Spelling picture names	0%
PALPA 45	Non-word spelling	0%

Model of the processes
involved in the spelling to
dictation.

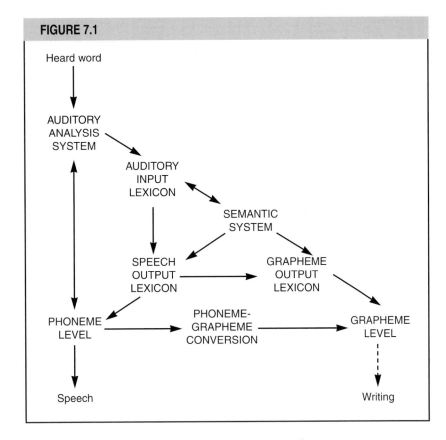

FIGURE 7.1

Heard word

AUDITORY
ANALYSIS
SYSTEM

AUDITORY
INPUT
LEXICON

SEMANTIC
SYSTEM

SPEECH
OUTPUT
LEXICON

GRAPHEME
OUTPUT
LEXICON

PHONEME
LEVEL

PHONEME-
GRAPHEME
CONVERSION

GRAPHEME
LEVEL

Speech

Writing

situation, the impairment is likely to be more central in nature arising at a lexical or output buffer level.

In conclusion, it is hypothesised that MF has an impairment at both a graphemic (and/or lexical retrieval) level, and at a graphic motor level resulting in his very limited written output. Therapy therefore targeted these two levels of impairment.

The aim was to develop a strategy that made use of his (then inconsistent) ability to spell a word out aloud letter by letter, and his ability to write a single letter down from dictation. The goal was that this strategy could be applied to any word and thus therapy would generalise to untreated items. This would obviously have the greatest functional benefits to MF.

The specific strategy to be developed was:

- say the word out aloud
- spell the word out aloud letter by letter
- write the word letter by letter.

The writing sections of the shortened Schuell, AAT, and PALPA assessments would be administered post therapy to evaluate the efficacy of the therapy.

THE STAGES IN THERAPY

The therapy administered was based on small incremental stages, in which the objectives were clearly defined. It was important to the success of this therapy for MF to gain a clear understanding of the goals of each stage, and how each stage related to the long-term objective of improving his writing. Only when MF fully understood the goals of each stage, would the therapy commence.

It was necessary to develop certain skills prior to the full strategy being introduced. These formed the basis of stages 1 and 2. It was proposed that a computer would be used to supplement therapy and provide intensive practice. MF had never used a computer before, so he had to become familiar with the keyboard, which formed the basis of stage 3 in therapy. The strategy was then introduced in stage 4, being applied to single words only. MF was taught how to use a dictionary in stage 5, and finally the strategy was applied to sentence-level tasks with stage 6.

Stage 1: To improve MF's ability to write down a letter from dictation

Goal 1
To improve the identification of a written letter from the spoken letter

Materials. Alphabet chart

Task "A" description
1. Therapist vocalised a letter at random. MF points to the letter on the alphabet chart. Therapist provides feedback.
2. Therapist/client role reversal of the above task. First MF then therapist provide the feedback.

Goal 2
To improve the accuracy of written response to a spoken letter.

Materials. Paper and pen

Task "B" description
1. Therapist vocalised a letter that MF writes down.
1. Therapist and client reverse roles, i.e. MF says a letter which the therapist writes down.

Response to stage 1
It was found that MF's performance on this task was greatly influenced by fatigue. Therefore, incorporated into this task was feedback to MF of how to recognise this and take a short break. MF was encouraged to indicate to the therapist when this was happening.

Stage 2: To improve MF's ability to spell a word out aloud letter by letter

MF was not aware of his ability to vocalise the letters of a word that he could not write down. Since this is crucial to the successful use of the strategy being developed in therapy, MF was encouraged to do this with tasks C and D.

Task C

Materials. None.

Description. Practise using three-letter words.
1. Therapist said a three-letter word.
2. MF was encouraged to spell it out aloud letter by letter.
3. Therapist prompted by giving the next letter in the situation where MF appeared to block.
4. Four- and five-letter words were introduced in the same task.
5. His wife was encouraged to play these spelling games, little and often during the day.

Task D

Materials. None.

Description
1. Therapist would start to spell a word letter by letter out aloud.
2. MF was encouraged to try to identify the word before completion and say it aloud.
3. MF was then encouraged to spell the word out aloud letter by letter, to complete the word.

Response to stage 2
MF showed an increased ability to spell aloud during this task. The number of occasions when his mind blanked reduced. He became accurate at indicating the first letter of the words attempted. The word games that MF played with his wife had also been successful. MF proudly reported that he had managed to spell some local place names aloud. He was clearly getting a lot of satisfaction from his improvement.

He was not able to spell aloud all words he attempted, however, but what was of significance was that a much higher proportion of the first few letters were now correct. MF's performance on this task was again affected by fatigue, with the effect that his mind would go blank. It helped MF greatly to have a short break and come back to the word, at which time he had a much higher chance of success.

Stage 3: Familiarisation with the computer keyboard

In order for the strategy to be generalised, it would need to be well established. A computer in MF's home was used to supplement therapy and provide intensive, repetitive practice of using the strategy. MF had never used a computer before and was unable to use the "qwerty" keyboard. Tasks were therefore administered aimed to familiarise MF with the standard computer keyboard (task E).

Task E

Materials

- A BBC computer.
- Concept keyboard with an overlay containing eight letters of the alphabet in the same position as the "qwerty" keyboard.
- "From pictures to words" software (see Appendix).

Description

1. A letter appeared on the computer screen, which MF was encouraged to say out aloud.
2. MF then matched the letter by pressing the same letter on the concept keyboard.
3. The computer provided feedback by indicating the letter if an incorrect response was made.
4. More letters were gradually added to the overlay and the same task used to reinforce the position of the letters.
5. Concept keyboard removed and same task administered using the standard computer keyboard.

Response to stage 3

MF experienced the following difficulties using the computer:

1. He found it confusing when all 26 letters were displayed, reporting that he would prefer to have used a normal alphabetic ordered keyboard. It was explained to him why it was preferable to use the "standard" keyboard (because very little software supports the concept keyboard). MF, was however, given the same task with an alphabetically ordered overlay but found that he had become familiar with the "qwerty" keyboard overlay, and was happy to proceed with it, and made the transition to the normal computer keyboard easily.

2. Due to limitations of the software, the letters appearing on screen were lower case whereas those on the overlay were uppercase (the same as the standard "qwerty" keyboard). MF reported that this was confusing for him, and he had too many things to think about. MF scored 100% on PALPA 19, an isolated cross case matching task. It was, therefore, felt that his difficulties were likely to be due to processing overload. It was necessary, if the therapy was to be functionally beneficial, that MF would have to cope with different situations. MF was therefore encouraged to keep with the same conditions and the task was recognised as providing additional case matching practice.

Stage 4: Develop the strategy in full

The aim of this stage in therapy was to combine the progress made in the first two stages for MF to develop the full strategy. Since MF was confident at using the computer, it was possible to introduce further computer tasks at this stage, in order to provide intensive practice.

Task F

Materials. Paper and pen.

Description

1. Therapist spells a word letter by letter.
2. MF writes down the letters as they are spoken.
3. MF was asked to say the word as soon as he identified what it was.
4. MF was asked to try to complete the word by spelling the whole word letter by letter and writing down the remaining letters.

Response. MF did well at this stage. He was very accurate at writing down the spoken letter. He was able to identify the word before the end, and on about 50% of occasions could complete the word.

Task G

Materials. Paper and pen.

Description

1. Therapist spoke a three-letter word for MF to write down.
2. MF was encouraged to spell the word aloud and then write down each letter to spell the whole word.
3. The therapist intervened by providing the next letter if MF blocked.

Task H

Materials

- BBC computer.
- Concept keyboard.
- Overlays used in task C.
- "From pictures to words" software.

Description

1. A line drawing picture representing a three-letter word was shown on the computer screen.
2. MF was required to use the full strategy (as in task G) in order to spell the word letter by letter using the concept keyboard.
3. The computer would only accept correct responses and would provide the letter if three errors in a row were made.
4. The task was built up to include gradually more letters on the overlay, and words containing four, five, or six letters.

Task I

Materials

- BBC computer
- "Gapfiller" software (see Appendix).

Description

1. A definition was shown on the screen.
2. MF was required to think of the word.
3. MF then applied the full strategy to spell the word using the standard computer keyboard.
4. The software provided feedback and gave the next letter if an error was made.

Response to stage 4

MF continued to respond well to the therapy. He was able to apply the strategy to words such as "computer, castle, animal". It became apparent, however, that MF had an additional problem not identified in the original analysis—a timing problem. Sometimes, MF spelt a word aloud correctly but found that he was unable to write the letters down quickly enough. This led to transposition-type errors, or in some instances becoming confused so that he was unable to complete the strategy of writing the word down letter by letter. MF was usually helped on these occasions by slowing the pace and by going through the strategy step by step. These difficulties were discussed with MF, and it was felt that with practice, and his ability to self monitor, that they would be overcome.

An informal assessment was developed in order to investigate the efficacy of using this strategy for three-, four- and five-letter words. The assessment aimed to monitor whether generalisation was taking place to untreated items. The results were very encouraging. He had reached ceiling on the computer-practised words and had shown evidence of generalisation. His writing attempts were much closer to the target, which made it possible to review the original hypothesis. See later for discussion on MF's emerging spelling abilities.

Stage 5: Develop ability to use a dictionary

As already reported, MF was using the strategy well. On those occasions when he could not spell the whole word he was showing a pattern of being able consistently to give the first couple of letters. It was therefore felt that he should be able to use a dictionary. This would obviously have great functional benefits.

Task J

Materials

- Paper and pen.
- The "Oxford" Junior Dictionary.

Description

1. Therapist gave MF a five- or six- letter word.
2. MF was encouraged to write the word using the strategy.

3. If MF could not write the whole word and had first few letters he was encouraged to look the word up in the dictionary.
4. He was taught to look at the alphabet at the top of the page in order to locate the correct area in the dictionary.
5. When he had found the word, he then copied the remaining letters from the dictionary.

Task K (Computer tasks)

Similar to previous tasks, but MF was encouraged to use his dictionary to assist his writing.

Response to stage 5

MF rapidly learned how to use the dictionary. He appeared to enjoy using it and reading the definitions. The ability to use a dictionary contributed towards his independence in writing and appeared to increase his self-esteem.

Stage 6: Use of the strategy at the sentence level

MF was using the strategy well at the single-word level, and was able to use a dictionary. It was therefore felt appropriate to apply the strategy at sentence-level tasks.

Task L

Materials

- Paper and pen.
- Dictionary.

Description

1. Therapist said a short sentence.
2. MF was required to write the sentence down using the strategy already developed.

Response to stage 6

At the time of writing, stage 6 represents the current ongoing phase of therapy. MF's response to stage 6 therapy thus far is as follows. MF has not been automatically able to apply the strategy to sentence-level tasks.

The following difficulties have been experienced, but through task modification and feedback, these difficulties are becoming less significant.

1. Sometimes it was difficult initially for MF to isolate the individual words in the sentence necessary in order to apply the strategy. I would intervene by encouraging MF to focus on one word. I would write a line on the paper for each word, which MF would point to while being encouraged to say the sentence slowly. This feedback has had the positive effect of MF being able to focus on individual words.
2. Initially, it appeared that MF had too many things to think about at the sentence level and had difficulty remembering the strategy. I therefore talked MF through the strategy in the early stage of applying it to the sentence level.
1. MF's performance was influenced by fatigue. Initially MF was not able to complete a sentence without having a break in the middle. He was encouraged to self-monitor his levels of concentration and have short breaks. It is noticeable how much his concentration has improved with practice.

Stage 7: Computer-based sentence-level tasks

As MF's performance improved on stage 6, it became a concern that he was relying heavily on me for prompting. I felt that MF did have the ability to use the strategy in sentences, but was under-confident of his ability. Computer sentence-level tasks were therefore introduced. Although the computer would provide feedback and intervention, MF would need to apply the strategy, and through success would hopefully gain the confidence necessary to apply the strategy in everyday situations.

Task I

Materials

- BBC computer.
- "Phraseflash" software (see Appendix).

Description

1. A sentence was displayed on the screen for a set period of time (clinician controlled).

2. When it disappeared MF was required to type the sentence back into the computer using the "qwerty" keyboard.
3. The computer provided feedback by showing the sentence again if MF forgot it, and giving the letter if several errors were made.

Response to sentence-level computer tasks

MF found these difficult initially and his performance was very variable. Structured tasks were administered based on a hierarchy, increasing in difficulty by:

● the number of words in the sentence
● the complexity of the individual words.

At the time of writing, MF is progressing through the hierarchy well and has increased in confidence in both using the strategy, and also in his ability to self-monitor. The next stage in therapy will be the introduction of an adaptive word processor.

THE THERAPY OUTCOME

The written sections of the Shortened Schuell and AAT were readministered three and a half months post therapy. The results are presented in Table 7.2.

The results show a significant spelling improvement, not only for single words, but sentence and paragraph level tasks. Results from the PALPA assessments show that word length has an effect on MF's spelling. Regularity and grammatical class does not have an effect.

THE THERAPY PROCESS

The stages described previously for developing the strategy do not give a complete picture of the therapy administered. In order to gain an understanding of the therapy process it is also necessary to include:

a description of the therapeutic interactions, that is how the therapist responded to the

patient in relation to the type of response made by the patient (Byng, 1993, p.126)

Tables 7.3 and 7.4 illustrate in more detail the actual interchanges which took place between the therapist (JM) and client (MF). Table 7.3 shows the therapist–patient interaction of MF trying to spell the word "magazine" in the sentence "The magazine is on the table". Table 7.4 shows the therapist–patient interaction when MF attempts to spell the word "table" in the same sentence.

The following summarises what has taken place during this interaction, in terms of the spelling abilities that MF is able to demonstrate, as well as those areas he has difficulties with:

Positive factors

1. MF is able to spell "the" spontaneously without using the strategy.
2. He was able to use the strategy for the word "on" and "table",
3. He is aware of his errors.
4. He is able to look up words in the dictionary.
5. He is able to copy from the dictionary.
6. He gave positive facial expression that although it was considerably hard work and he required much prompting, he did enjoy the task and felt pleased with himself.

Difficulties

1. MF requires considerable prompting throughout the task.
2. He is sometimes unable to follow the strategy through despite successfully saying the letters out aloud, e.g. "mag".
3. He needs prompting of when to leave a word and come back to it.
4. He needs prompting of when to look a word up in the dictionary.
5. He sometimes needed prompting to help focus on the word within the sentence framework.

It became apparent that as progress was made, MF still relied on me to prompt him. But JM felt that the strategy had become well enough established for MF not to need this level of prompting. It was at this stage that computer sentence-level tasks

TABLE 7.2

Summary of pre- and post-therapy assessment results

	Pre-therapy	Post-therapy
Shortened Schuell—Section D		
1. Copying Greek letters	5	5
2. Writing numbers to 20	5	5
3. Reproducing letters	5	5
4. Writing letters to dictation	5	5
5. Written spelling	0	4
6. Producing written sentences	0	5
7. Writing sentences to dictation	0	4
8. Writing a paragraph	0	4
Possible (max. 40)	**18(45%)**	**37(93%)**
Aachen Aphasia Test—written section		
Written language: Reading aloud	100%	100%
Composing words to dictation	50%	90%
Writing to dictation	0%	87%
Total	**50%**	**92%**
Cognitive Neuropsychological Assessment		
PALPA: 18. Mirror reversal task	100%	100%
19. Upper/lower case matching	100%	100%
22. Letter naming	77%	100%
Letter sounding	62%	72%
23. Spoken letter–written letter matching	86%	100%
39. Letter length spelling	0%	81%
44. Regularity and spelling	0%	86%
(Dictionary use)	–	100%
53. Spelling picture names	0%	75%
(Dictionary use)	–	100%
45. Non-word spelling	0%	10%

were introduced, so that MF could practise intensively and independently (see task M for details).

DISCUSSION

What has therapy achieved?

1. MF has developed a strategy that he has been able to generalise to sentence-level tasks.

2. MF is showing an increasing ability to be able to spell shorter words spontaneously, without resorting to the strategy.

3. MF is able to use a dictionary to look up words that he is unable to spell using the strategy.

4. MF is able to use a computer independently using the standard keyboard.

5. MF is learning to recognise the effects of fatigue on his writing ability and is able to deal with it constructively.

6. MF has a high success rate of correcting his spelling errors.

TABLE 7.3

Therapist–patient interaction to spell "magazine"

	MF	Spoken	Written	Non-verbal	Comments
1.	MF	maga		looks to therapist	
2.	JM	can you say it letter by letter			prompt to use the spell aloud strategy
3.	MF	no			
4.	JM	say the word			going through the strategy step by step
5.	MF	magazine			
6.	JM	spell it letter by letter			step 2 of the strategy
7.	MF	m a g m a g		looks at therapist	requests further prompting
8.	JM	no response			trying to encourage independence
9.	MF	m a g no			remains unable to proceed requests further prompt
10.	JM	okay we will leave it and come back to it			

7. His concentration levels for writing have improved considerably over the period of therapy.

Future intervention

Although MF has made remarkable progress with this writing therapy, there remain the following obstacles to significant functional gains:

1. It remains very hard work.
2. It is very time consuming.
3. MF has to rely heavily on a dictionary for longer words.
4. MF does not like the look of his writing.
5. There is still a significant fatigue factor on his performance. Functionally this means that MF would need to start a letter and keep adding to it in small bursts. At the moment of writing this is still a daunting task for MF.

Future intervention will include the introduction of an adaptive word processor. This is a word processor that has been specifically developed to speed up the process of writing. When a word is typed into the keyboard, a list appears of words beginning with that letter. As more letters are typed the selection becomes more specific. The intended word is retrieved from the computer by pressing the associated number. MF has the necessary skills to use this tool:

1. He is accurate at indicating at least the first letter of a word.
2. He is able to identify words from a word list.
3. He is much better at breaking a sentence up into individual words.

The introduction of the adaptive word processor aims to:

- speed up MF's writing
- provide an on-line dictionary
- enable a print-out to improve the presentation of his written attempts
- enable MF to start a particular document, and add to it and have the satisfaction of seeing a well presented written text emerge.

The influence of technology on the therapy programme

The role of the computer in the initial stages. The computer was used initially as a means of providing

TABLE 7.4

Therapist–patient interaction to spell "table"

	MF	Spoken	Written	Non-verbal	Comments
1.	MF	table			
		tab	t a b		spoke "l" but wrote "e" and
		ll	e		vice versa
		e	l	looks towards	
		no that's wrong		therapist	
2.	JM	can you correct it?			
3.	MF	the table		looks at written word	?MF has lost focus
4.	JM	okay say the word			attempt to refocus MF on word
5.	MF	say the word spell it			shows he knows the strategy
6.	JM	so the word is			2nd attempt to refocus MF
7.	MF	table			
8.	JM	can you spell it letter by letter			encourages strategy use
9.	MF	t a b l e			successful oral correction
10.	JM	good			
11.	MF		table		corrects written spelling
		yeah			mistake
12.	JM	well done			

intensive repetitive practice of the strategy being developed. The particular aspects felt to be important were:

1. Unlike a paper and pen homework task, the computer provided constant feedback to MF as to whether his response was correct or not. This stopped incorrect responses being reinforced.
2. The software also gave intervention to assist if, as was inevitable in some cases, MF was unable to proceed with a word.
3. All the software used was "content free". This enabled the clinician to input to the computer-based task those words relevant to MF at each stage of therapy. As MF progressed the computer tasks were modified.

4. The computer was useful in teaching MF to pace himself. As mentioned, fatigue factors had a major influence on MF's performance. Practically, MF would turn the computer on, do a short burst of practice, have a break and return to the computer later.
5. The computer results that were automatically recorded played an important part in MF's motivation. He had access to these results and could see the effects of his work.
6. These results were also very important to the therapist, to review MF's progress on the computer tasks and modify the tasks accordingly.
7. MF was motivated to use the computer. Although the tasks were very basic he felt that they had "hi-tech" status when administered by the computer.

8. MF did not mind the repetitive nature of practising the strategy on the computer.

The role of the computer in sentence-level tasks. As well as providing intensive practice applying the strategy to sentence-level tasks, the computer played an important role in the following:

1. As mentioned in the therapist–patient interaction process, MF required much prompting from the therapist. As he continued to improve, however, the therapist felt that MF was too quick to rely on this, and that in fact he often had the necessary skills to solve the problem himself. When working at the computer independently, MF had to rely on generating the strategy himself, deciding when leave a word and come back to it, or when to use the dictionary.

2. His self-pacing was crucial at these tasks because his performance was affected even more by fatigue than during single word tasks. Initially MF would tend to give up on these tasks and make random selections. When he saw the effect that this had on his stored results, however, he tended to break off and return a few moments later when he had a greater chance of succeeding.

The anticipated role of the computer in the future. So far in this therapy MF has become familiar with using the standard "qwerty" computer keyboard, and has experienced writing sentences. With the introduction of an adaptive word processor with an on-line dictionary, the computer is likely to continue to be a major influence on MF's writing.

Was the original hypothesis correct?

Evidence from MF's emerging spelling ability, and spelling errors includes the following:

1. When MF was first assessed his writing errors were either no response, or single letters not related to the target.

2. After stages 1 and 2 in therapy it was noticeable that MF was much more accurate at writing the initial letter of a word.

3. When the full strategy was being developed during stage 4 of therapy, it became apparent that MF's spelling ability was emerging. The errors arising were mainly substitutions (e.g. horse—HOSTE, shoe—SHOW), transpositions (e.g. meat—MAET, duck—DUKC), and omissions (tree—TEE, jumper—JUMERS).

It has been observed that MF is sometimes able to spell spontaneously without using the strategy. The reduction of the incidence of no response or single letters, and the increased number of errors of substitution, omissions, and transpositions requires the original hypothesis to be reviewed.

In the original hypothesis, it was proposed that the impairment was arising at the graphic motor level. MF presented similar to IDT (Baxter & Warrington, 1986). Unlike IDT, however, MF was proposed to also have an impairment at the graphemic level.

Graphic motor-level impairment. MF no longer presents like IDT. His errors have changed from no response and single letters to substitutions, additions, and transpositions within words.

How can this change in presentation be accounted for?

1. Could it be that therapy has directly targeted the graphic motor level, and this is no longer impaired?

2. Could it be that the strategy that MF has developed enables the impaired graphic motor level to be bypassed, by verbalising a letter before writing it down?

3. The ability for MF to write some words spontaneously suggests that the graphic motor level is unlikely to be bypassed unless MF has learned how to internalise the strategy.

4. Could it be that the impairment was not at this level?

Graphemic-level impairment. The incidence of substitutions, omissions, and additions in his spelling suggests an impairment at the graphemic level. MF now presents similarly to a patient, FV, described by Caramazza, Miceli, Villa, and Romani (1987), who it is proposed had an impairment at the graphemic output buffer level. His spelling errors were additions, substitutions, and transpositions of letters. The original hypothesis did propose an impairment at the graphemic level. It is suggested that MF did not present like FV initially because of the additional impairment at the graphic motor-level and the possibility of additional lexical retrieval difficulties.

MF has increased his ability to spell aloud a word letter by letter. This suggests that the impairment at the graphemic level is reducing. How can this be accounted for?

1. Could it be that therapy has directly targeted the impaired process?
2. Could it be that this process was not as impaired as first thought and that therapy has increased MF's confidence of spelling a word out aloud?
3. Transposition errors made when a word is correctly spelled aloud but written incorrectly would suggest an impairment at the allophonic level. These errors could, however, be accounted for in terms of a timing problem which is not taken account of in these models of spelling.

The reader is referred to Lesser (1990) and Pound (1996) for alternative interpretations of superior oral to written spelling abilities and processes in dysgraphic clients.

Phoneme–grapheme conversion route. The therapy administered has been based on letter names not phonemes, because MF found the sounds of letters difficult to write down. Furthermore when he spelt a letter aloud, it was always using the letter names and not sounds. The post-therapy assessment shows little improvement in non-word spelling. This result suggests that the improvement made was a direct effect from the

therapy administered, which emphasised lexical retrieval and semantics (e.g. dictionary, sentence-level work) as a by-product of the direct strategy work.

To summarise, the response to therapy does support the original hypothesis made. MF is likely to have had an impairment at both the graphemic output and graphic motor levels. Initially the graphic motor-level impairment had the greatest influence on spelling. As he progressed from the therapy, however, the graphic motor-level appeared to be less of an influence and MF presented more like a patient with an impairment at the graphemic, and allophonic level.

CONCLUSIONS

The study evaluates the efficacy of intensive therapy for the treatment of a man with a spelling deficit. Results of pre- and post-therapy standardised assessments show that significant improvement was made. The therapy involved developing a strategy aimed at targeting an impairment at the graphemic and graphic motor levels of the spelling process. A computer was used successfully to supplement therapy and provide intensive practice of using the strategy. The specific role of technology has been discussed, as well as whether the original hypothesis was correct in the light of MF's spelling errors that emerged during the therapy. The future intervention is discussed and the introduction of an adaptive word processor in order for MF to gain maximum functional benefits from the therapy.

ACKNOWLEDGEMENTS

I would like to thank MF for his participation in this therapy study. His determination and motivation is much admired. I would also like to thank my husband, Peter for his support in writing this paper.

REFERENCES

Baxter, D.M., & Warrington, E.K. (1986). Ideational agraphia: A single case study. *Journal of Neurology, Neurosurgery and Psychiatry, 49,* 369–374

Byng, S. (1993). Hypothesis testing and aphasia therapy. In A. Holland and M. Forbes (Eds.), *Aphasia treatment: World perspectives.* London: Chapman & Hall.

Caramazza, A., Miceli, G., Villa, G., & Romani, C. (1987). The role of the graphemic buffer in spelling: Evidence from a case of acquired dysgraphia. *Cognition, 26,* 59–85

Huber, W., Poeck, K., Wehigar, D., & Willmes, K. (1983). *Der Aphasie Test* (AAT). Gottingen: Hogrefe Verlag.

Kay, J., Lesser, R., & Coltheart, M. (1992). PALPA: Psycholinguistic Assessments of Language Processing in Aphasia. Hove: Lawrence Erlbaum Associates Ltd.

Lesser, R. (1990). Superior oral to written spelling: Evidence for separate buffers? *Cognitive Neurosurgery, 7,* 347–366

Pound, C. (1996). Writing remediation using preserved oral spelling: A case for separate output buffers. *Aphasiology, 10,* 283–296.

Schuell, H. (1965). *Minnesota Test for Differential Diagnosis of Aphasia.* Minneapolis: University of Minnesota Press.

APPENDIX: SOFTWARE RESOURCES

From Pictures to Words
Widgit Software
102 Radford Road
Leamington Spa CV31 1LF
£35 plus VAT

Gapfiller (£35 plus VAT) and Phraseflash (£25 plus VAT)
Aphasia Computer Team
Speech Therapy Research Unit
Frenchay Hospital
Bristol BS16 1LE
Tel: 0117 9186529

8

Naming therapy for an aphasic person with fluent empty speech

Morwenna White-Thomson

BACKGROUND

BC is a 55-year-old woman who is married with three grown-up children and has been employed as a cleaner all her working life. She collapsed and was admitted to hospital. A CT scan carried out 2 days later revealed "An extensive haemorrhagic infarct with surrounding oedema, displacing the midline structure to the right. There was some pooling anteriorly in the sylvian fissure after contrast". A left middle cerebral artery aneurysm was diagnosed and an operation was performed to clip the aneurysm and to remove the clot in the left temporal parietal region.

INITIAL OBSERVATIONS AND ASSESSMENTS

On initial presentation BC appeared alert and quite well orientated. Her speech was fluent and empty. Islands of correct automatic social speech remained but her main output consisted of paragrammatic jargon, perseveration (especially on the word "Matthew"), and neologisms. Although auditory comprehension was fair at a functional level, severe auditory comprehension problems became apparent in specific tasks. She was very poor at monitoring her own output and showed little insight into her output difficulties. She was unable to repeat except at an echolalic, non-volitional level.

A cookie theft picture description (Appendix 1) is an example of BC's speech taken 9 months post onset. BC's use of her own high frequency words is particularly striking, e.g. "Celia" and "Matthew" (members of her family), "wool" (she enjoys knitting) and "garden" (her husband is a gardener).

Over a period of months, during which BC had regular speech therapy, certain patterns began to emerge which influenced the decision taken about therapy. For the purposes of this chapter I am only going to describe one particular treatment programme. BC's performance on a number of specific tasks suggested some particular deficits.

Auditory input

BC's ability to do auditory lexical decision was assessed using 78 word/non-word items controlled for syntactic category. All the non-words were created by changing either voice or place of articulation. She scored 42/78 and 29 of those errors were on the non-words. BC's ability to judge whether two words were the same or different was assessed using 30 minimal pair words controlled for distinctive feature difference and syllable length. As in the lexical decision task BC's performance was severely impaired and she scored 14/30. Finally, BC's ability to do phonological segmentation was assessed. She was presented with three Scrabble tiles which made up a CVC word. She was then given another CVC word auditorily and asked to identify where in the written word the sound had changed. BC was totally unable to do this. However, several weeks later, when assessed on her ability to judge if words rhymed or not, she performed well, scoring 41/44. This might suggest that the demands on phonological input processing are different, even when the tasks appear quite similar.

Semantic processing

In addition, her comprehension of semantically related items was tested using the Pyramids and Palm Trees test (Howard & Patterson, 1992) and the picture word matching test from the PALPA (Kay, Lesser, & Coltheart, 1992). The Pyramids and Palm Trees test required BC to judge which of two pictures was semantically related to the target picture. She scored 47/52 on this test which is only just outside the normal limits (49/52). The picture word matching test required BC to choose the correct picture in response to an auditory or written stimulus from four distractor pictures: a close semantic, a distant semantic, a visually related, and an unrelated distractor. She scored 31/39 on the auditory version, producing eight semantic errors and 38/40 on the written version. BC showed impaired performance on the auditory version but her performance with the written stimuli was within normal limits.

BC also did some informal tasks such as sorting pictures and written labels into appropriate categories, identifying the odd one out with pictures and written stimuli and matching semantically related pictures. She performed well on all these tasks. It would therefore seem that BC had reasonably good semantic processing of pictures and written words, but less good ability to comprehend heard words accurately.

Oral and written naming

From observation there seemed to be a discrepancy between her ability to say and write words, so her written and oral naming were compared by asking her to name 40 pictures. Half the pictures were of highly frequently occurring names and half were of infrequently occurring names. In oral naming she was able to name only three of the highly frequent items correctly and none of the less frequent items and her errors consisted primarily of perseverations with occasional semantic errors (Appendix 2). Her written naming was, however, considerably better. She named correctly 16 of the highly frequent and 16 of the less frequent items. Her errors in writing the high frequency words were bread—LOAR, heart—HERATS, desk—OFFING, and glass—CLASS and on the low frequency words they were kite—VEN, thumb—TUMB, flute—TUBA, and drum—BUI DRASS. These responses can be classified into different types of errors, for example semantic, e.g. TUBA and possibly OFFING (based on "office"), visual or phonological, e.g. CLASS and TUMB. and incorrectly ordered letters, e.g. HERATS.

Conclusions from assessment

I hypothesised that although BC did show the occasional semantic error in written tests, she generally performed very well in both written comprehension and written naming. I took this to indicate that she had adequate semantic knowledge of the words required. Informal tests also showed that BC had good abilities in classification and categorisation of pictures and written words and she scored satisfactorily on the Pyramid and Palm Trees test. I therefore speculated that BC's semantic store was, although vulnerable, relatively intact and BC's errors on auditory input were largely due to poor access or drive from the auditory input lexicon. BC showed a similar pattern to PC (Jones, 1989) who also presented with relatively preserved semantics in the presence of impaired auditory input. His total inability to respond to auditory lexical decision tests suggested an inability to deal with single word auditory input alone. Given BC's difficulties in processing auditory input, she performed better on auditory semantic comprehension tasks than might be expected. Perhaps, like PC, she is able to use top-down processing to assist her.

Because of PC's poor performance in interpreting incoming phonology, as evidenced by her minimal pairs judgement and lexical decision and her apparently poor access to phonology for output, I hypothesised that BC had a deficit in accessing information from both the auditory input lexicon and phonological output lexicon. This would explain BC's poor spoken naming and repetition and poor monitoring. However, she seemed to be able to process written and pictorial information more adequately, suggesting a comparatively intact orthographic route and semantic system.

THERAPY

BC's verbal output was the area most severely affected and the area that she was most keen to work on. My aim in therapy was, therefore, to improve BC's verbal naming and her ability to self-monitor by concentrating on two main areas. First, the aim was to re-establish a link between phonology and orthography via both input and output tasks and, in so doing, use BC's intact written route to aid her

verbal naming. Second, the aim was to improve her self-monitoring by incorporating auditory input tasks into the therapy.

Design of the therapy—9 months post stroke

Thirty pictures of predominantly single syllable CV words were given to BC to be named orally. She named 10 of these correctly (due to having had some work on them prior to the design of this particular therapy programme) and 20 incorrectly (Appendix 3). Four of these 20 she named correctly given extra time. I took these 20 pictures and divided them into two groups, A and B. The pictures were divided into the two groups on the basis of their initial sound. Group A words began with the following sounds: [b, s, t, ʃ] and Group B words with [p, n, k, d, aɪ]. Although the division was random concerning these initial sounds the rationale was that, following therapy on the initial sounds, there might be carry-over to other words beginning with the same initial letter. I therefore wanted to ensure that the two groups did not include the same initial sounds.

Group A was treated first for a total of three and a half hours representing five sessions over one and a half weeks. I had been seeing BC intensively (three times a week) prior to beginning this therapy programme and felt it was appropriate to continue with this regime. Having reassessed Group A, Group B pictures were introduced for therapy. Although BC, when reassessed, performed very well on Group A, I was concerned about the stability of her improvement and I therefore continued to work on Group A at the same time as working on Group B, although I concentrated more on the new therapy items. Therapy continued for 5 hours representing nine sessions.

Two additional measures were used as a control for the effects of the therapy. BC named another set of 40 pictured items, none of which was included in the therapy sets (Appendix 2). She was also asked to read aloud 20 frequent and highly imageable words (Appendix 4). Both these measures consisted, in the main, of more complex consonant vowel structures than the therapy items. The intention was to use them as additional controls, but on reflection they were probably not the best controls to use given the nature of the

TABLE 8.1

Pre-therapy scores

Group A	Group B	Picture naming control	Reading aloud control
20%	20%	7.5%	0%
*(2/10)	*(2/10)	(3/40)	(0/20)

*Items correct when BC given extra time.

therapy tasks implemented. The results are given in Table 8.1.

It is interesting to note BC's poor performance in reading aloud, given her apparently good comprehension of written words. Many of her errors are clearly like her spoken naming, i.e. perseverative, but there are also possible visual or phonologically similar errors and one example of a semantic error which BC was not happy with. The similarities between her reading aloud and spoken naming provide support for the hypothesis that one of her deficits is in accessing phonological forms for output.

The therapy tasks

Introductory task
BC had to write the correct word in response to the picture. This was done to ensure that she was able to find the correct lexical item and write out the graphemic form accurately. She was able to do this and it acted as a preliminary task before commencing therapy, capitalising on an existing observed strength.

Tasks that did not require a spoken response
These tasks are not provided in any hierarchical order but represent the kinds of tasks undertaken.

A *Choose the written word to an auditory stimulus.* BC had to identify the correct written word in response to an auditory stimulus from a choice of two written therapy items then three, then four, increasing up to 10. The aim was to help BC establish a relationship between a sound and

its graphemic form in preparation for the use of grapheme/phoneme conversion to assist verbal naming. Also the aim of this task was to encourage BC to attend to sounds on input in order to improve self-monitoring.

B *Write the word to dictation.* The aims of this task were similar to those of task A, but were more demanding as BC was required to generate the written form herself from the phonological form provided, instead of just matching.

C *Identify individual letters to dictation.* BC had to identify the correct letter in response to an auditory stimulus from a choice of two, three, and then four letters taken from the initial letters of the therapy items. Once again the aim was to establish a relationship between the sound and the graphemic form, and improve self-monitoring.

D *Draw a picture of the word to auditory stimulus.* Although this seemed like a good idea at the time and BC enjoyed the task its link with the overall hypothesis is somewhat tenuous. It required BC to comprehend the spoken word, but did not specifically work on any aspects of phonology.

Tasks that required a verbal response
One of the aims of therapy was to use BC's intact writing ability to aid her verbal output. Many of the output tasks, therefore, concentrated on re-establishing a relationship between the graphemic form and the phonological form. For example:

A BC was encouraged to sound out the initial letters of the therapy items in isolation, in response to a picture.

B She was asked to read aloud the therapy items which were grouped together according to their initial letter.
C She was asked to read aloud the therapy items presented in a random order.
D In order to encourage BC to target the correct initial phoneme when converting from orthography to phonology she was encouraged to extract and sound out the initial phoneme from the whole written word.

Tape recordings of BC's speech were often used in the tasks where she had to produce verbal output. She was asked to judge whether her output was correct and if she judged that she had made an error, was then encouraged to self-correct. BC found this very difficult but the tape recordings had the advantage of enabling her to compare her output with the target letter or word several times before making a judgement.

Tasks to encourage internalising of strategy
A In response to a picture, BC was asked to trace the *written word* on the table with her finger and then name the picture verbally.
B In response to a picture, BC was asked to trace the *initial letter* on the table with her finger and then name the picture verbally.
C In response to a picture, BC was asked to imagine the written form in her mind and then verbally name it.

D BC was encouraged to name the picture in response to a simple question. Although BC might trace the written word out on the table, once again she was encouraged to internalise the strategy and imagine the written form in her mind.
E BC was asked to describe a composite picture which included many of the therapy items, using the internalising strategy.

Evaluation of therapy

The results shown in Table 8.2 indicate that BC's improvement in verbal naming was in response to the treatment tasks and that this improvement was maintained over a period of 1 month without therapy. The improvement is primarily confined to the treated items but there is some evidence of generalisation to untreated items. For example, out of the five correct in the reading aloud control following therapy on Group A, four (out of a possible six) began with an initial letter worked on in therapy. In general, however, BC did not appear to be able to generalise the strategy she used with the therapy items to the controls. The controls were, however, made up of more complex consonant vowel structures and this might have affected her performance.

Although generalisation was not measured on the assessment tasks it was evident in her spontaneous language. BC began to be aware that she was often not saying what she intended and she began to stop her flow of speech when attempting

---

TABLE 8.2

Pre- and post-therapy scores on treated word groups and naming and reading aloud controls

Pre	Group A	Group B	Picture naming control	Reading aloud control
Pre-therapy	20% (2/10)	20% (2/10)	7.5% (3/40)	0% (0/20)
Post-therapy on Group A	100% (10/10)	10% (1/10)	17.5% (7/40)	25% (5/20)
Post-therapy on Groups A and B	100% (10/10)	90% (9/10)	20% (8/40)	15% (3/20)
Reassessment after one month without therapy	100% (10/10)	100% (10/10)	Not assessed	Not assessed

to find a specific word. Instead of substituting her own high frequency words in the place of content words, she began to search for the correct target and would regularly use the strategy of tracing the written form of the word on the table with her finger in order to cue herself in verbally.

SUMMARY

On reflection, having considered the therapy in detail retrospectively, there are a number of things that I would now do differently. In my original hypothesis, I proposed that BC had relatively intact semantics. I would now, however, interpret the few semantic errors she made in output, and her score of eight semantic errors on the picture word matching test, as more significant. Although I believe that BC had a deficit at the phonological level on both input and output, I also feel her performance revealed impairment at the semantic level which the therapy did not address adequately.

Also, I do not feel I had a very clear hierarchy for the tasks I chose and more thought could have been given to exactly what each task demanded.

I have tried to think out retrospectively which of the therapy tasks were the most effective. It could be argued that some tasks, e.g. drawing a word to auditory stimulus and producing the word in response to a simple question, also tapped her semantics even if they did not meet my original criteria for the purpose of the therapy. I felt that BC primarily benefited from the grapheme/phoneme conversion work, which focused her attention on the initial sound, and also the tasks which encouraged her to internalise the strategy.

On reflection, I would also have chosen different controls. It might have been interesting to have a control where I would have expected generalisation, e.g. CV words beginning with the same initial letters as the therapy items, and a control where I would not have expected to see improvement, e.g. simple calculation. Finally, it would have been useful to have taken a sample of BC's spontaneous conversation or picture description before and after therapy, so that her improvement in spontaneous language could have been formally documented.

For the purposes of this chapter, I have tried to describe one particular aspect of therapy with BC. Following the completion of the treatment programme, she continued to attend therapy, but details of this would be another story!

REFERENCES

Howard, D., & Patterson, K. (1992). *Pyramids and palm trees*. Bury St Edmunds, UK: Thames Valley Test Company.

Jones, E. (1989). A year in the life of PC and EVJ. In E.V. Jones (Ed.), *Advances in the clinical setting:* Proceedings of the Cambridge Symposium on Aphasia Therapy. London: British Aphasiology Society, 3–58.

Kay, J., Lesser, R., & Coltheart, M. (1992). *Psycholinguistic assessments of language processing in aphasia*. Hove, UK: Lawrence Erlbaum Associates Ltd.

APPENDICES

APPENDIX 8.1

Boston cookie theft description—pre-therapy

Two there is children. Little girl and boy going u' …up the wool (STOOL)* to get in the garden (CUPBOARD) and…for the Matthew (BISCUITS) i'…in the garden 'n he shouldn't. Pretty. And…climbed up and he felled up on the Matthew then. 'Is Dad (MUM) was so busy with the dinner time…picking (PLATES) up for dinner time again and the water for (?) dinner time making wet.. picked up all the dinner /taɪ/…goose…goose? Celia (CUPS) and dinner time (SAUCERS) as well picked up again. All pretty very Matthews here…'e just did'll wonder what 'e do er pic in look at the garden and theres er lovely pictures. There's pictures, water, garden… pictures again, another garden. Wool (TREE) in the garden, nice pictures looking through them. Climb up the dinner time for the… wool. Um… 1, 2, 3, 4, 5.. Matthews (CUPBOARDS) here and getting all wet, horrible. Dad (MUM) with 'is water dinner time.. and the children (?) all these waters is about all things I can think of.

Note. Words in brackets indicate target, e.g. while pointing to the stool BC said "wool".

APPENDIX 8.2

Spoken picture naming, control group

High frequency		Low frequency	
ball	/bud/ …	drum	bed b.r.u.w.
desk	/med/	snail	matthew—thats the wrong one
chair	raid	leaf	/b ɪ l/
boat	big	dagger	snap beg
dress	dinner	spoon	Good
glass	cup	thumb	din…matthew, matthew
fire	picture	duck	cat…no not dog
bread	lunch	glove	bed
book	✓	kite	cat
wheel	lunch	mouse	cat c.a.t.
horse	dinner	spade	dinner time…lunch…dinner
coat	picture	goat	(unintellible)
knife	picture	frog	ah, he squeak up don't he…/fendə dʒɪn dʒɪnə/
train	raid	sock	cut
heart	dinner…thats wrong again boy	stool	tea
snake	cat…gone again /z/	nail	picture
nose	(pointed to it)	doll	plate
hair	dinner	pear	here we go again, dinner
girl	boy	flute	I don't know anyway, whatever its called
foot	/ru/	clown	/raʊn/

SCORE.   High frequency 3/20; low frequency 0/20.

APPENDIX 8.3

Spoken picture naming, pre-therapy baseline

four	four ✓
pea	pick—pea
shoe	toe
tea	/wɛtəf/…pic…/weɪt/ washing
baby	boy book walk
eye	/kik/ /ɛə/
tear	boy—no—mean picture—crying—pic. picture
toe	toe ✓
cat	toy
pie	cup—wrong—on—pie—pipe—pea cup of tea, pie
two	two ✓
pear	pear ✓
beer	put—pub—picture—cup—pug—jar—drink—beer
boy	boy ✓
deer	pick—pea—christmassy chris—chris—chris don't know
knee	toy—cup
nose	cup—cup wrong one
door	boy cup
tie	kite /kaɪ/ /tʃ3/ cup of tea
sea	boy picture /ʃi ʃi ʃitə/ cup of tea
cow	c.o.w. /kəʊ/ cup—no
bee	picture—bee—buzz—bee—buzz—buzz
key	key ✓
car	toy t.a.w. toy
d	/t/… /di/ ✓
bow	t.a.w. toy—no pic—pic—picture
bear	bear ✓
saw	c.a.w. bore bore bore—book—no
Becky	Becky ✓
Sheila	Sheila ✓

APPENDIX 8.4

Reading aloud of high imagery and high frequency words

ball	rose
boat	dolly doll
book	doll
coat	doll
desk	/dɛp/
fire	dial cup of tea
foot	/kɔit/ cup of tea
hair	doll
girl	bill
nose	coat
bread	read
chair	tea
dress	dread
heart	cup of tea, ah
horse	car
glass	lass
knife	tea cup of tea
snake	/preɪn/…s…s dog cat
train	brain
wheel	/pri/

9

A treatment programme for an impairment in reading function words

Jenny Sheridan

PH, a right-handed 40-year-old security guard, was admitted to hospital following sudden onset of right hemiplegia and aphasia. CT scans showed extensive areas of low density in the left frontal, temporal, and parietal lobes, probably as a result of mid cerebral artery infarction. Tunnel vision was noted in the left visual field of the left eye. PH subsequently had epileptic fits and severe headaches, for which no neurological cause was established and which he continues to have. He was hospitalised for 4 weeks and then admitted to a rehabilitation unit as an inpatient for 3 months. He continued for twice-weekly outpatient therapy after this period, which was reduced to one session a week during this study, which took place approximately 18 months after his stroke.

LANGUAGE INVESTIGATIONS

Comprehension of spoken language

At the time this therapy was designed comprehension of spoken language was excellent, both in conversation about abstract subjects and on the Boston Diagnostic Aphasia Examination (Goodglass & Kaplan, 1972).

Production of spoken language

Spoken language was slightly hesitant and effortful but syntactically correct with pauses for word finding. The following represents his attempt to describe the Cookie Theft picture:

There's a woman washing up and the sink is…overflowing by her. There's a boy on a …stool and it's wobbling, but he's trying to reach a cookie jar. He's got some cookies and he's handing them down to a girl. Out the window I can see some bushes and a tree …and the corner of a house. The kitchen is …um…nicely planned.

He could repeat complex words and phrases, but had some difficulty in repeating low-probability sentences. He scored 61/65 on the Boston Naming Test.

Production of written language

PH made many errors in spelling. Regular words were not spelt better than irregular words, but there was evidence that words that occur frequently were more often spelled correctly. Analysis of PH's spelling errors showed that the first few letters of words were usually correct but additional letters were inserted or substituted, e.g. fresh—freard, circuit—curriment. He could judge whether a word he had written was correct or not, but could not correct it. In connected writing he often substituted one function word for another.

Oral reading and comprehension of written language

In reading aloud single words 10% of the errors PH made were semantic errors, e.g. married was read as "wed", counter as "shop" (initially a far greater proportion of his errors were of this nature); visual errors, e.g. accordion was read as "accordingly"; and morphologically related errors, e.g. walked read as walks. He also made function word substitutions, e.g. were—was, for—from. The meaning he derived from written words was that of his paralexic error not that of the printed word, e.g. sequel—"stable, that's for horses". He made fewer errors with words that were concrete (93% correct) than with words which were abstract (50% correct).

He was unable to read aloud any unfamiliar words or non-words. His main difficulty in effective reading arose from his inability to read function words. Seventy per cent of his errors in reading connected prose were function word errors so that he was unable to comprehend any connected prose. In a list of function and content words matched for frequency of occurrence and length he read 18/20 content words correctly and 8/20 function words correctly. He could therefore be described as having a phonological dyslexia.

Pre-morbidly, PH had been a devoted family man whose only hobbies were car maintenance and reading, especially history. After the stroke his marriage broke up and his hemiplegia left him unable to work on his car. His deficit in reading function words was the main obstacle to effective reading at the time this therapy began, and was the reason why this was selected as an appropriate area for therapy.

THERAPY 1

Aim. To retrain PH to read a set of function words by improving recognition and comprehension of specific function words.

Approach. Restoration of function, i.e. learn to read a set of specific function words again through the normal word recognition system.

Hypothesis. As PH is learning only about a specific set of words, improvement will only be evident in that set of words, and will not generalise to untreated words.

Selection of words for treatment. A total of 46 function words were chosen at random for PH to read aloud. Four baseline tests were obtained over a 1-month period. No spontaneous improvement was measured over this time. Words failed on one or more occasions were selected and divided into a Treatment and a Control group, each containing 17 words. Each group was matched for the number of words failed.

Therapy method. PH was seen twice weekly for 1 hour for a total of 12 sessions, with homework provided between sessions. The homework comprised the same tasks as had been worked through in the previous therapy sessions. He was given a sentence with blank spaces to complete and a choice of two or three "semantically related" function words from the Treatment set to select two from to complete the sentence, for example:

> John asked the foreigner ____ he came ____.   for where from

He was then given a sentence containing each of the three words to read aloud. The meaning of each of the words was discussed. When the three words seemed to be well established, another set of three words was provided, and the procedure was repeated. The Control words were not treated at all.

Results. Four post-treatment tests were carried out. Aggregating the test results, PH read 48/68 of the treated words correctly after the treatment, compared to 27/68 pre-therapy. However only 29/68 of the untreated, control words were read correctly after the therapy, compared to 22/68 pre-therapy. A Wilcoxon test showed that control words did not differ from baseline, whereas treated words had improved significantly ($P< .005$).

THERAPY 2

Aim. To encourage PH to use letter to sound conversion rules to assist his oral reading.

Approach. Reorganisation of function, i.e. carry out a task using an alternative method of doing the task from that usually used.

Hypothesis. As PH is learning a strategy that can be applied to any word, improvement should not be confined to the words used in therapy but should generalise from treated to untreated words.

Procedure. Ten words from the Control set in therapy 1, which had been failed at least once in the post-treatment measures, were used as the treatment set in therapy 2. A second control set of

10 words was introduced. Two baseline measures were taken over a period of 3 weeks. All words were low imageability, high frequency functors. PH read three words in each set correctly on the first baseline and four different ones correctly on the second baseline.

Method. PH attended 12 sessions over a 5-month period and was given homework between sessions. It had been noticed that when PH was unable to read a word aloud he could be assisted by thinking of a word beginning with the same letter. The therapy method was devised to capitalise on this already apparent ability. It is loosely based on the therapy strategy described by de Partz (1986).

A mnemonic alphabet was created using PH's own choice of words. PH would choose one word to represent a letter, e.g. fish for "f". He would see a word he could not read, e.g. from, and would say "fish, /f/". This would either immediately cue him into the rest of the word, or he would go on to sound out the other letters of the word, e.g. "rabbit /r/, orange /o/, man /m/— from". He rarely had to go through this whole process, often just the first letter was sufficient to allow him to produce the whole word, so after a few sessions the first and last letters only were used as cues.

Results. Two measures were taken after the therapy finished of both the treated and untreated words. He had improved in his ability to read both sets. Combining scores on both sets, he read 35% correctly pretherapy and 68% correctly post therapy, reading seven out of 10 correctly in both the treated and untreated groups. This improvement is statistically significant (McNemar $P < .005$). It was evident in therapy sessions that PH was using this strategy to read many words, not just function words, that were unfamiliar or difficult to read.

In retrospect, it was unwise to allow PH to devise his own mnemonic alphabet as he chose some less familiar words, which he then found hard to memorise. These words also induced paralexias, for example his mnemonic for 'l' was "little", but when trying to use the strategy to read a word such as "like", he had difficulty as he was trying to read it with the cue "s" from "small"!

SUMMARY

The first therapy aimed to restore specific lexical items and resulted in improvement on those items that were treated but not on untreated items. The second therapy aimed to teach a strategy that could be applied to any word, and this resulted in improvement to treated and untreated words. The cross-over design of the therapy suggests that the improvements measured were attributable to the therapy and not to spontaneous recovery because words which had shown no improvement in the first phase of the therapy were subsequently shown to improve after therapy aimed to improve them.

PH's relatively intact skills were used in devising the therapy. Therapy 1 could only have been attempted by a patient with relatively good content word reading and therapy two capitalised on developing further a strategy that PH was already attempting to implement.

By the end of the therapy period, PH could read a 100-word passage in $3\frac{1}{2}$ minutes, in contrast to taking 10 minutes pre therapy. At the outset of the therapy PH could only read newspaper headlines. After therapy he is slowly, and not without difficulty, managing to read a demanding book on naval history. The therapy was carried out within normal clinical practice and was neither time consuming nor intensive.

REFERENCES

De Partz, M. (1986). Re-education of a deep dyslexic patient: Rationale of the method and results. *Cognitive Neuropsychology, 3,* 149–177.

Goodglass, H., & Kaplan E. (1972). *The assessment of aphasia and related disorders* (2nd edition). Philadelphia: Lea & Febiger.

Part 3

"Beyond the single word" therapies

10

Introduction to Part 3: Therapies addressing impairments in processing verbs and sentences

All four studies in this part concern therapies aimed at enhancing production and/or comprehension of structured utterances. Despite having a different overall aim, there is much commonality between the studies here and some of the other studies in this volume. For example, the therapies address, amongst other things, the semantics of single words, circumventory strategies, and the relationship of psychological state to the use of newly acquired communication skills.

There is a similarity in the spoken language of each of the four people described in these studies: They are all relatively non-fluent, reflecting a recent interest in the literature with these kinds of language impairments (cf. Berndt, 1991, Byng & Lesser, 1993, Marshall, 1995). There is some variability in the underlying nature of their impairment however, ranging from hypotheses about verb impairments (Greenwood in Chapter 12, and Marshall in Chapter 11), difficulties in integrating sentence form and sentence meaning in both input and output (Greenwood in Chapter 12, Marshall in Chapter 13,

and Swinburn in Chapter 14) to a more unusual but compelling account of an impairment (Marshall, Chapter 11) at the "Message Level" of Garrett's (1980) model of sentence processing (see also Schwartz, 1987). Few aphasic people with impairments at this level have been described, but the account of the underlying nature of the problem and the therapy addressing it has a ring of authenticity to it, corresponding with clinical intuition, such that it feels to be addressing an issue that may be critical for many people with aphasia, or at least for a greater number than have so far been described.

The focus of three of the studies in Chapters 12, 13, and 14, is on facilitating clarification of how the basic structural relations of "who is doing what to whom" are represented in sentences in both input and output. What is interesting to see in each case is how quickly improvements were achieved after even small amounts of therapy, and even when the therapeutic task was well within the capability of the aphasic person. The clarifications seemed to be helpful even for people who already had a basic understanding of the sentence. This suggests that enabling conscious thought about a component of language processing can provide some basic support in tackling sentence interpretation and production (Byng & Black, 1996).

Taking the issue of conscious processing of language through therapy further, Greenwood describes working well within the capabilities of IG, commenting on the lack of traditional "therapy task struggle" (Chapter 12). This is an intriguing perspective, raising the issue that therapy can be creative and productive even when the aphasic person "knows the answer". This suggests that working through a task which is not in itself difficult or challenging can still be educative if the person is learning some principle about how language works which can be extrapolated (consciously or unconsciously) from the task, understood, and applied of itself.

Even though the therapies were devised to address specific language impairments, some had functional goals as well. The language and communication skills underpinning those functional goals were the target of intervention, and the remaining and new language skills of the aphasic people were used to devise alternative communication strategies. The relationship between functional communication and therapy studies addressing sentence-level impairments can often be obscure. Performing syntactic gram-maticality tasks appears to be a far cry from both understanding and producing language in context and day-to-day communication needs. It could be argued that for many people with aphasia, particularly those with reasonably good single word input and retrieval skills, communication via single words is quite effective, so the purpose of working on producing longer utterances with more structure can at best seem irrelevant and at worst just to be satisfying the intellectual curiosity of the therapist, neglecting the needs of the aphasic person. Is working at the sentence-level (or event/message-level as in Chapter 11) an effective use of therapy resources?

Judging by the response of the aphasic people who are described in these studies it seems to be the case that these therapies are clarifying underlying concepts about language, providing foundations on to which other communication strategies can be built, as exemplified by MW (Marshall, Chapter 11), IG (Greenwood, Chapter 12), and EM (Marshall, Chapter 13). Sentence therapies that are clarifying underlying concepts about language or the relationship between language and the intended conceptual message seem to serve to enhance both input and output of structured language (e.g. Chapters 11 and 13). For example, in the case of MW the therapy was effective, serving both to improve comprehension of incoming language and to reduce confusions of output, allowing MW to describe quite complex transactions. Single words might serve the purpose of some functional communication, e.g. getting a simple message across, but it is difficult to see how MW could have communicated the buying and selling of properties as he needed to without being able to convey who was doing what to whom, even if it was not all through language, but using gesture and drawing as well to convey meaning.

Therefore, working on "sentences" does not need to involve working on language—in this case the clarification of how to represent who was doing what to whom helped MW to convey these concepts accurately through both language and gesture. Likewise, EM's therapy focused on clarifying the message and improved her ability to convey propositions through a variety of media. This is an important point because there seems often to be an assumption that sentence work and non-verbal communication are at opposite ends of the therapeutic spectrum—one being highly functional, the other being rather abstruse and an intellectual exercise rather than a therapy technique. These therapies demonstrate the critical interrelationship between the concept behind the therapy, the means of conveying that concept, and the variety of forms of demonstration of the implementation of that concept.

The relevance of working at this level is further underlined by the response of the aphasic people. IG, who in a prior therapy had been having direct work for her "articulatory dyspraxia", appeared to gain enormously in confidence through a therapy that took the focus off her speech and on to her underlying language processing. Would this increase in confidence have happened as a result of any other therapy input? It is not clear but there is a sense of this therapy "hitting the spot"—addressing a real need to clarify some issues about language. Comparing the reaction of IG and EM to therapy provides a contrast between the lack of confidence and distress caused by what seemed to have been prior, inappropriate, therapy as in IG's case, and the anxiety and distress caused by clinical depression, as in EM's case.

Both Marshall and Greenwood (and also, to some extent, Swinburn) use an evaluation method that relates to the functional relevance of these therapies. In each case they ask naive raters to judge the informativeness of language samples produced by EM and IG respectively, pre and post therapy, to assess whether, as a result of the therapy, they are more "communicative". In each case they are able to convey more to the listener, even when the listener is not used to listening to aphasic speech and when they do not know which was the "before" and which the "after" sample. They also use the aphasic person's own perception as an additional outcome measure.

In all these studies, which seem to be addressing fundamental issues about how language "works", there is a sense of pleasure and relief for the aphasic people in undertaking some of these tasks. It is as if some of the underlying confusion that they were perhaps feeling about their language impairments (Parr, Byng, & Gilpin, 1997) is lifted through the clarity of these tasks. None of these aphasic people had any particular interest in language prior to becoming aphasic nor were particularly academic. These therapies seem to a certain extent to be playing the same function as word puzzle books do for many non-aphasic people—providing accessible intellectual stimulation, but which, in their case, crucially also allows them to further develop their language and communication skills. PC, reported by Eirian Jones at a British Aphasiology Society symposium (1989) and referred to in Chapter 11 of this volume, described his language therapy as providing him with the opportunity for further education that he had never had.

A commonality between all the studies is that in every case the therapy tasks have been generated

from observing strategies already used by the aphasic person in question. The therapists observed an aspect of performance during formal and informal assessment and then proceeded to adapt this into the basis of a task that could be used in therapy to address the hypothesised underlying impairment. The tasks were then extended and adapted during the therapy in response to the aphasic person's needs.

Interestingly although the aim of each therapy was to improve language output, each of the therapies involved predominantly comprehension and judgement tasks to bring about those changes. Judging by the outcome, working on input to facilitate output is an effective strategy, when the underlying hypothesis can relate the difficulties in output to impairments in input.

The studies in Chapters 13 and 14, although on a smaller scale than the others, are included because they reflect a similar focus of therapy with similar kinds of outcomes. This is an example of how the *Aphasia Therapy File* will be used—studies which on their own might not be published in a journal can find a place here in order to reinforce what seems to be a significant trend in the effects of a therapy and to give other clinicians more ideas about how to present and modify a type of therapy. In this way collections of single cases can be assembled to give more validity to claims about effectiveness and outcome.

REFERENCES

Berndt, R.S. (1991). Sentence processing in aphasia. In M.T. Sarno (Ed.), *Acquired aphasia*, (pp.223–270), 2nd Edition. London: Academic Press.

Byng, S., & Black, M. (1996). What makes a therapy? Some parameters of therapeutic intervention in aphasia. *European Journal of Disorders of Communication, 30,* 303–316.

Byng, S., & Lesser, R. (1993). A review of therapy at the level of the sentence in aphasia. In M. Paradis (Ed.), *Foundations of aphasia rehabilitation.* Oxford: Basil Blackwell.

Garrett, M. (1980). Levels of processing in sentence production. In B. Butterworth (Ed.), *Language production.* Vol. 1, (pp. 177–219). New York: Academic Press.

Jones, E.V. (1989). A year in the life of PC and EVJ. In E.V. Jones (Ed.), *Advances in aphasia therapy in the clinical setting: Proceedings of the Cambridge symposium on aphasia therapy*, (pp. 3–58). London: British Aphasiology Society.

Marshall, J. (1995). The mapping hypothesis and aphasia therapy. *Aphasiology, 9, 6,* 517–539.

Parr, S., Byng, S., & Gilpin, S. (1997). Talking about aphasia: *Living with loss of language after stroke.* Milton Keynes: Open University Press.

Schwartz, M. (1987). Patterns of speech production deficit within and across aphasia syndromes: applications of a psycholinguistic model. In M. Coltheart, G. Sartori, & R. Job (Eds.), *The Cognitive Neuropsychology of Language,* (pp. 163–199). Hove, UK: Lawrence Erlbaum Associates Ltd.

11

Doing something about a verb impairment: Two therapy approaches

Jane Marshall

INTRODUCTION

EM experienced a left CVA when she was 52. Her stroke resulted in severe aphasia and a hemiplegia, which rapidly resolved. At the time she was working as a receptionist in a local sports centre. Prior to that she had held various secretarial posts. She has three adult children who all live near her. During this study she also acquired a grandchild. She was originally from Wales and came to England when she was 18. She is a monolingual English speaker.

Little information is available about EM's presentation and management immediately following her stroke. A reported Boston Diagnostic Aphasia Examination 1 month post onset suggested a Broca's profile, with reduced phrase length, dyspraxia, and relatively spared comprehension.

Following her CVA she received twice-weekly outpatient speech and language therapy at her local hospital for approximately 1 year. She was admitted to the City Dysphasic Group in London (CDG) 18 months after her stroke. At the onset of this study she was attending 2 days a week.

Informal observations

When EM first joined CDG her participation in group therapy was limited. She tended to sit back from the table and rarely initiated communication. When pressed to contribute she often aborted her speech attempts and peppered them with comments about her inadequacies. EM reported that she also felt very unconfident about communicating with her family, except on a one-to-one basis. Her priority for therapy was speech.

Her conversation was almost entirely limited to single words and phrases. Word finding problems were evident, particularly with low frequency targets, such as "parsnip" and "pot-pourri". The naming difficulties seemed to incur semantic errors, such as "swede" for parsnip, "perfume" for pot-pourri and "New Year" for Boxing Day.

JM: How was your Christmas?
EM: Fine fine fine fine … um New Year and Christmas … um Daren
JM: Did he come to you?
EM: No (gestures away from self) … yes
JM: You went to him. How long did you stay with him?
EM: Well … its um Christmas and um New Year no … um /bə/ Boxing Day
JM: Were there any others there?
EM: Oh no very … um mother and father and brother and nan and Beverley and Paul
JM: What did you have?
EM: turkey and stuffing … potatoes /kə/ cauliflower sprouts carrots … swede … no (draws shape on table)
JM: Parsnip?
EM: Yes
JM: What about the presents?
EM: Perfume (gestures to table) … no
JM: Its something to do with perfume?
EM: yes … but its room … air
JM: Pot-pourri?
EM: Yes .. um nightdress … I don't know
JM: What presents did you give?
EM: um Beverley its jumper and trousers and its um Paul its um CD

However, these errors were rapidly self corrected and, in the case of perfume, followed by clarifying circumlocution. This suggested that her errors did not arise from a semantic deficit *per se*. The phonological "groping" seen in the sample indicated that EM's naming difficulties might be at the level of phonological retrieval. It was hypothesised that the semantic approximations may reflect blocked targets at this level (Caramazza & Hillis, 1990) and might have been produced as a strategy for directing the listener to the target.

Striking in the sample is the lack of any verbs. Verb information is either conveyed by completing

a predicate in the question or through "it's" phrases, e.g. "Paul its um CD" (target: I gave Paul a CD). Despite her word finding problems EM accessed 28 content nouns in the sample (including family terms and proper names) in comparison with no verbs. Although EM's verb production was poor she seemed to understand verb information. For example, she responded correctly to "reversible" questions such as "did he come to you?" and "what presents did you give?"

From these observations it was hypothesised that the chief obstacle to communication was a verb retrieval deficit, although EM's apparently good comprehension suggested that her knowledge about verbs was relatively spared.

SPONTANEOUS SPEECH ANALYSIS

A fairy tale sample was elicited using the methodology recommended by Saffran, Berndt, and Schwartz (1989).[1] Analysis confirmed the reduced verb production. The proportion of nouns:verbs was abnormally low (3:46) and the majority of her utterances were single noun phrases (72%) (Byng & Black, 1989; see Table 11.1). Twelve utterances apparently contained a verb (26%). However, this score may be generous since the status of some of these verbs ("bite", "cooking") was ambiguous. Only four utterances contained verb argument structure, and, as suggested in parentheses, this may also be overestimated:

TABLE 11.1

Number of utterances in each structural category produced in the spontaneous speech samples

Structure	No. of Utterances
Noun phrase	33
Verb only	8
Verb + arguments	4
Combined phrases minus verb	1
Total number of utterances analysed	46

"She's prettied up"

"The queen is changed as the wicked witch"

"Knock on the door" (this may have been a noun phrase)

"One man is work" (this utterance may have omitted the main verb e.g. "one man is going to work".)

Although EM's syntax is often anomalous her few sentences do show some ability to realise verb phrase morphology—indeed, her "Aux Score" (a measure of the syntactic/morphological complexity of the verb phrase, Saffran et al., 1989), was within the unimpaired range.

The sample also displayed phonological error (e.g. /dʒraɪm/ for rhyme and /draʊ/ for dwarves). These further supported the hypothesis that EM's naming difficulties were at the level of phonological retrieval.

VERB AND NOUN PRODUCTION

Spoken naming

Noun/verb photos (Byng, 1988)
This task uses noun/verb pairs which share phonological forms. For example, the noun member of a pair shows a bicycle pump, and the verb member someone pumping up a tyre. With the action pictures the subject is encouraged to produce just the name of the verb. EM scored 38/42 with the noun pictures (90%) and 25/42 (59%) with the verb pictures, which was significantly worse (chi square = 9.143, $P < .01$). Despite the instructions, 18 of EM's correct verbs were produced within a complete sentence, for example:

"The man's putting the belt on"

"The baby no … the lady's changing the baby"

As in her spontaneous samples these responses showed an ability to retrieve function words and inflections. There were other promising signs of verb knowledge (such as the correct argument structure with "put").

Errors with the verb pictures were various. Six showed verb omission in the presence of relevant noun retrieval, for example:

"The lady's … the hoover" (hoovering)

Five responses employed inappropriate verbs, or in one case a "pseudo" verb, for example:

"The woman's helping the books and the case" (boxing books)

"Booking the books on the shelf" (shelving books)

Three responses included related verbs, although in all three EM was aware of the errors, for example:

"The lady's mowing the lawn … its er dig no" (hoeing)

Three responses were aborted at the point were the verb was required, for example:

"The lady is …".

One included "phonological groping" for the verb:

"/ləɪ/ .. /dəɪ/" (dialling).

Interestingly, EM had achieved "dial" quite easily with the noun picture. This last example offered further evidence that EM was having difficulty at the level of the phonology of verbs. This was also suggested by some of her other errors. For example, "mow" is both a semantic and phonological error for the "hoe" and "booking the books on the shelf" seems an attempt to employ "put" which has been taken over by the more dominant noun phonology.

Naming from definitions
This task required EM to produce either a single noun or verb in response to a definition. The 33 noun and verb targets were matched for frequency and syllabic structure (taken from Zingeser & Berndt, 1990). Examples:

What men have to do if they don't want a beard   (shave)

A leather strap used to keep your trousers
up   (belt)

Results. Nouns 29/33 (88%); verbs 16/33 (48%). As in the picture naming task, noun access was significantly better than verb access (chi square = 10.06, $P < .01$). Furthermore, EM's verb errors showed the noun bias observed with the pictures, for example:

"instructor"   (teach)
"fire"   (melt)
"menu"   (eat)

Written naming

This was tested using the Byng verb and noun photos. With the nouns EM scored 38/42, which was identical to her spoken performance (although her error items were different). With the verbs EM scored 35/42 which was significantly better than her spoken performance (25/42 vs 35/42; McNemar chi square = 7.143, $P < .01$). In all but one of her correct verb responses EM attempted to write a complete sentence. Fourteen of these were entirely correct and interestingly used a range of verb morphology, for example:

"The lady whisks the eggs"

"The man has washed his hair"

Despite her good written performance, EM made surprisingly little use of this modality. It seemed that therapy might help her exploit writing more effectively.

Summary

In spoken language EM could access nouns more easily than verbs, even when they shared the same root phonology or were matched for frequency. EM's written verb production was significantly better than her speech. Observation during the task suggested that once EM had written the verb she could often read it aloud. She rarely spoke the verb before writing it.

Why was EM failing to produce spoken verbs? A number of hypotheses were entertained:

EM might have a deficit in the "message-level" processes (Garrett, 1982) that extract the semantic *properties of events.* EM's good written verb production seemed to discount this hypothesis. Furthermore she subsequently performed well on non-verbal tasks which required her to make judgements about events.

EM might have a category specific impairment in the semantic lexicon affecting verbs (McCarthy & Warrington, 1985). Again EM's good written production seemed to disqualify this explanation. In addition, a number of comprehension tasks revealed good semantic knowledge of verbs: (1) she could reliably reject inappropriate names for action pictures, even when those names were closely related to the target (picture of a man eating, question "is this drinking?"); (2) she could comprehend reverse role verbs, such as "buy" and "sell". The latter were tested by showing her a picture of a transaction, such as a woman selling a car to a man, and asking her to point to the person who was buying or selling; (3) she could detect and correct verb argument anomalies in a sentence judgement task; (4) she was well above chance in comprehending reversible active and passive sentences. This latter test, however, seemed to indicate some difficulty with more "abstract" verbs that express sensory experiences, although in a subsequent sentence completion task involving these verbs, she performed surprisingly well (20/22), for example:

Dark streets … women
(lurk, frighten, dread, bore)

The parents were … by the crying baby
(grizzled, admired, comforted, exhausted)

The input tests suggested that EM was recovering considerable semantic information from verbs, including the thematic information which is problematic for many aphasic people (Marshall, 1995). There seemed little evidence that her verb production impairment was due to a semantic disorder.

EM might have a deficit in the processes that retrieve the phonological representation of the verb from semantics. The presence of phonological errors, the written>spoken effect, and the good semantic performance encouraged this view. Of interest here was EM's apparent ability to read verbs aloud. This was "confirmed" by a task in which she was asked to read aloud the noun and verb targets used in the definition naming test ("bow" and its noun partner were omitted due to its ambiguous status). Her performance is shown in Table 11.2, with comparative naming data.

EM's reading of verbs was virtually faultless. It was also significantly better than her verb naming (chi square = 14.67, $P < .001$). How was EM accessing the phonology of written verbs? She may have been using sub-lexical letter to sound rules. Yet EM read the irregular verbs as well as the regular ones. Also her non-word reading, which depends entirely on sub-lexical conversion, was quite poor (7/24).

Two other routes access phonology from the written word. One passes through semantics. This is identical to the naming route. Therefore its sole use would anticipate an equal naming and reading performance. The fact that EM read significantly better than she named suggested that she was engaging an additional route to phonology. The second lexical reading route accesses phonology directly from the visual input lexicon. By elimination EM must have been using this route. Of course her good written comprehension (see earlier) indicated that she could access semantics from the written word. It is only when the task demanded production that she called upon the direct reading route.

Conclusion

The reading aloud assessment confirmed that the phonological representations of verbs were available to EM, provided they were accessed from the written word. I concluded that this access was principally achieved by the direct reading route. This indicated that her naming disorder lay in the processes which link phonology and semantics. Her good object naming demonstrated that these processes were largely intact for nouns. It seemed that EM's deficit was specific to the connections between the semantic and phonological representations of verbs.

Investigations so far already offered useful indications for therapy. The main obstacle to EM's spoken production seemed to be her inability to retrieve verbs. Verbs which *were* produced, e.g. in the picture naming task, tended to appear within complete sentences. Comprehension tasks confirmed that EM was aware of the semantic and structural properties of verbs. Therefore it was perhaps unsurprising that once a verb was accessed she was able to use it in a sentence. This offered a strong therapy prediction. If treatment could improve verb access, more structured output should result. This prediction was tested in a final cueing assessment.

Cued production

In this task EM was asked to generate spoken sentences from provided written verbs and nouns. The stimuli were the 64 frequency matched nouns and verbs used in the definition naming and reading aloud tests. EM produced 11 correct sentences from the 32 noun cues. Two of these exploited a low frequency verb partner and should arguably be excluded, for example:

"The man was belting the trousers" (belt)

"The school ... teach is ... caning the boy" (cane)

Verb cues stimulated 27 sentences, which was significantly better than the performance with nouns (27/32 vs. 11/32, chi square = 14.57, $P < .001$). Furthermore EM used a range of forms with the provided verbs, for example:

"The little boy is bleeding" (NP + V)

"The judge hanged the murderer" (NP + V + NP)

"The man is sitting down" (NP + V + PP)

TABLE 11.2		
Definition naming test		
	Naming to definition	*Reading aloud*
Nouns	28/32	32/32
Verbs	15/32	30/32

"The girl was drowned in the pool"

(NP + V + Non Arg)

"The girl ripped the trousers in the tree"

(NP + V + NP + Non Arg)

Summary and discussion of investigations

EM's ability to produce verbs and verb structures was impaired. Most spontaneous utterances were single noun phrases, and spoken naming tasks showed that verbs were significantly more impaired than nouns. Despite the poor verb production EM's knowledge about verbs was good. She made few errors in comprehension tests, even when tasks required appreciation of the grammatical properties of verbs.

Given EM's semantic abilities I hypothesised that her production deficit lay at the level of phonology. This was supported by evidence of comparatively unimpaired written verb production and the observation of phonological errors. Reading aloud was virtually faultless, which suggested that the phonological representations of verbs were retained. It was concluded that EM had a specific deficit affecting the route between verbs' semantic and phonological representations.

EM's deficit was apparently very focal, with much of her production system still intact. Yet there was little evidence of this in her output. It seemed that her verb deficit generated a more widespread structural impairment. This view was supported by the results of the cued production task. This showed that simply providing the verb form dramatically improved the quality of EM's speech, presumably because this supplied the phonological information which was unavailable spontaneously. This was also an important prognosticator for therapy. If treatment could make verb forms more available to EM her output should be markedly improved.

THE DESIGN OF THE THERAPY STUDY

It seemed that EM's sentence structure was impaired principally by her inability to retrieve verbs' phonologies. This hypothesis motivated the first therapy programme, which aimed to improve her access to and retrieval of a group of 35 verbs. If therapy was successful it should bring about gains in sentence construction as well as verb production.

Pre- and post-treatment assessments

Verb naming

EM's ability to access the 35 verbs was tested pre and post therapy in a picture naming task. In addition she was tested on 35 control verbs which were matched with the treated verbs for frequency and semantic "type".

Two stories were composed, one of which employed 14 of the treatment verbs and the other 14 of the control verbs. Both stories were approximately 150 words long. EM was told each story twice, first in its entirety and then in sections. After each section she was asked to try and retell what she had just heard. Then I asked EM questions aiming to elicit the target verb structures. These were designed to be minimally directive, e.g. "What did Bob decide to do?" (answer: drive home for Christmas) and "What happened in the station ticket hall?" (answer: a thief stole his wallet). EM's pre- and post-therapy attempts to retell the stories were recorded on video and "scored" for verb production and argument structure, as were her question responses.

A second procedure aimed to evaluate how effectively EM could communicate the stories to observers. Her recorded attempts were shown to four judges. Two (familiar) judges knew EM and were informed about aphasia. Two (naive) had not met EM and knew little about aphasia. The judges were asked to listen twice to EM's version of the story and then recall everything that they had understood. They were encouraged to attend to all features of her output, rather than just speech. Scoring evaluated the number of key propositions from the stories understood by the observers.

In addition to the story task a post-therapy "Cinderella story" sample was taken and analysed.

"Control" tasks

Two measures of spoken abstract word production were taken pre and post therapy. These evaluations were designed to investigate the extent of therapy changes. A number of positive outcomes were possible, for example:

1. Therapy might enable EM to access a set of trained verbs. This would manifest in enhanced naming of the treated verb pictures. The therapy hypothesis predicts an associated improvement in the structure of her picture descriptions when using the treated verbs.
2. Therapy might improve access to a corpus of verbs and make those verbs more available for spontaneous speech. In this case EM's story retelling should additionally improve, especially on the story which allows her to use the treated verbs. The therapy hypothesis states that both improved verb access and enhanced structure should be observed.
3. Therapy might bring about generalised benefits for verb access, in which case both the treated and the control verbs should improve in picture naming. The therapy hypothesis would also predict generalised gains in structure, e.g. across both stories and in the Cinderella task.

Evidence of improved verb access without structural consequences would challenge the therapy hypothesis and suggest that an additional factor is inhibiting output. Improvements on the "control" abstract word tasks would suggest that improvements are due to generalised therapy effects, or even spontaneous recovery.

THE FIRST THERAPY PROGRAMME

The selection of stimuli and rationale

The treated verbs were drawn from five "semantic types":

- non-action verbs that express sensory experiences, for example: "bore" and "pity" (five items)

- verbs expressing change of possession and communication, for example: "buy" and "learn" (these were grouped together since both express the transfer of an entity between and goal and source) (10 items=
- verbs expressing the movement of an entity to or from a location (locatives and verbs of removal), for example: "pack" and "peel" (10 items)
- verbs expressing changes of state, for example: "melt" and "cook" (five items)
- verbs expressing different manners of motion, for example: "spin" and "drive" (five items).

The different categories of verbs were used in order to equip EM with a group of predicates that could convey a range of events. It was presumed that EM would not be handicapped by their varying semantic and syntactic properties, since she displayed impressive verb knowledge during testing.

Investigations had revealed a number of residual skills which could be exploited in therapy. First, EM retained excellent semantic knowledge about verbs. I hypothesised that therapy might help her to recruit this knowledge for the purposes of phonological access. This view was supported by previous therapy studies which suggested that lexical retrieval can be promoted by semantic tasks, even when the subjects do not have a semantic impairment (Howard, Patterson, Franklin, Orchard-Lisle, & Morton 1985; Jones, 1989; Marshall, Pound, White-Thomson, & Pring, 1990). Second, EM's written verb production was comparatively preserved and she could read aloud virtually without error. It seemed therefore that the written modality offered her a potential route to phonology.

Throughout testing EM was very pessimistic about her performance and constantly surprised by success. This was partly due to her low mood, but also suggested that she was unaware of her retained skills. Consistent with this was the observation that she rarely attempted problem-solving strategies in response to her verb deficit, such as using writing. It seemed that therapy should aim to make EM's skills explicit to her and encourage her to use them when searching for phonology. Her sensitivity to failure indicated that treatment should employ tasks on which success was virtually guaranteed.

Semantic tasks

The first phase of therapy encouraged EM to explore the semantic properties of the 35 treatment verbs. This phase spanned 10 1-hour sessions, with intervening home work. The verbs were tackled in categories. Thus, each category of verbs was given two sessions.

Before introducing the tasks the general properties of the category were discussed. For example, with the locatives and verbs of removal I might say: "These verbs all talk about putting something into a new place, or taking it away. For example when you *pack* a bag you put your clothes into it. In other words the clothes end up in a new place. On the other hand when you *prune* roses you take away the dead bits of wood" (explanation accompanied by gesture).

EM was then asked to judge whether the remaining verbs expressed relocation or removal. She was also encouraged to think about what is relocated, or taken away, and whether the goal/source changes because of the action. Any intrinsic manner information was also considered, for example:

JM: when you *spray* a wall, what moves? The wall or the paint?
EM: the paint
JM: yes dumb question really and what changes?
EM: the wall
JM: yup. So that the paint moves onto the wall and the wall is changed. How come we say *spray*? What sort of painting is that?
EM: er (gestures the idea of dispersal) er … (writes aerosol)
JM: yes that's good. It sort of spreads out and it's often with an aerosol.

EM was not deterred by the apparently asinine nature of these exchanges—indeed she seemed to find this part of the therapy as interesting as the specific tasks.

In the first semantic task EM was given a picture of the target verb which she was asked to label from list of five written options. The options were: the target, two semantic distracters, one phonological/orthographic distracter, which wherever possible was also semantically related to the target, and a gross distracter. Thus, for "spray" the picture showed someone spraying a car and the options were: spray, polish (semantic), strip (semantic), spread (phonological/semantic), and post (gross). In order to make the semantic component of the task explicit, EM also had to explain why she eliminated the semantic distracters. She often needed cueing to accomplish this. For example, the therapist might encourage her to mime the different actions or ask her about different effects. Once the semantic judgements were complete EM was encouraged to read the target verb aloud, although she had often done this during the task. Feedback aimed to emphasise EM's skills, and suggest how she might use them when attempting verb access.

The second semantic task eliminated pictures. EM was presented with three written verbs from which she was asked to select the odd one out. In the first level of the task the judgement was based on manner information, for example:

spray   spatter   flow

In the second level, it was based on thematic information. Thus, in the following example "cover" is the odd one out since the theme is changed by an entity being moved towards it, rather than away from it:

strip   peel   cover

EM coped well with both levels. As in the first task she was asked to explain her judgements and read the target word aloud.

The third semantic task also eliminated pictures and involved more production. Here EM was given a written verb and encouraged to think of as many associated nouns as possible. Before attempting this she was invited to imagine an event which could be described by the given verb and then "look around in her head", to see which objects were involved. Once this was exhausted she was encouraged to think about a different event and repeat the process. This task exploited a behaviour which was already within EM's repertoire, namely the tendency to produce nouns when targeting verbs. It might, therefore, seem an odd therapeutic approach. However, it was hoped that the task would enable her to use her facility with nouns more productively when searching for verbs, first by connecting each target verb with a group of stimulus nouns, and second by encouraging her to link her noun production with the conscious imagining of an event.

All semantic tasks were introduced, in sequence, during a session and several different items were practised. EM was then asked either to complete, or repeat, the stimuli at home. Her efforts were discussed in the following session. EM made very few errors during this phase of the therapy, which was unsurprising given her good semantic skills. The tasks were not aiming to regenerate semantic knowledge. Rather they were encouraging EM to focus more on what she already knew about verbs and apply this knowledge to her word finding problem. EM's willingness to perform the tasks and her demeanour during therapy suggested that this rationale made intuitive sense to her.

Production tasks

The second phase of therapy involved verb generation. In the first task EM was given two written noun phrases and was asked to think of a verb that would connect them, for example:

complicated instructions for video recorders (confuse)	Jane
strippers (show)	their legs
graffiti artists (spray)	walls

Two levels of cue were supplied. In the first EM was encouraged to imagine an event involving the given nouns and then think about the properties and nature of the event, for example:

JM: Imagine me with the video instructions (EM mimes holding a book). Yes good. What am I doing (EM mimes reading then hurling the book on the floor—both laugh)? Yes

absolutely. So do I understand what I am reading?
EM: No (laughs)
JM: No not a hope. How do I look?
EM: Mimes sad/confused and writes "baffle".
JM: Yes that's excellent. Will that do for your word?
EM: (reading) instructions … baffle … Jane … yes.

If this form of cueing was unsuccessful EM was presented with five written options—which were the same as those used in the first semantic task—and asked to find the appropriate verb. The list was then removed and EM had to reproduce the target, either in writing or speech. In the second production task a situation was described to EM from which she had to generate a verb, for example:

"If you were a very keen gardener and your roses were full of greenfly what would you do?" (spray: note this was a non-organic form of therapy)

"A tourist is lost in London. He wants to find the Houses of Parliament. He notices a policeman. What might he do?" (ask)

The first level of cueing invited EM to gesture the action. If this was unsuccessful she was again shown the written options and asked to produce the correct target following a delay. It was anticipated that EM would depend on her writing in these production tasks. However, this was not the case. It seemed that EM was either unwilling or unable to exploit her writing, despite her apparent skills in this modality. Alternatively the semantic priming provided by the previous tasks may have eliminated the orthographic advantage. Indeed there was evidence that EM was applying the first stage of therapy to the production tasks. For example, when searching for a verb she occasionally "listed" associated nouns in order to cue herself or produced alternative verbs which were close to the one required. Some of these had been distracters in the previous tasks.

Ten "production" therapy sessions were offered. The first five focused on each category of verbs in turn. The second five targeted all the verbs at random. In addition EM was encouraged to repeat therapy tasks as home work. In all, the first therapy programme consisted of 20, 1-hour sessions spanning 14 weeks.

Results

Verb production – picture naming task

Table 11.3 shows pre- and post-therapy performance on the picture naming task. Overall, production of the treated verbs improved significantly following therapy (McNemar chi square = 9.09, $P < .01$). Although the untreated verbs showed some improvement this was not significant. The improvement in verb access was accompanied by an improvement in sentence production. Before therapy EM produced 14 correct sentences with the target verbs—despite the fact that this was a naming task. After therapy there were only seven responses in which she achieved the verb but not the sentence.

Story retelling task

Table 11.4 shows the breakdown of utterances in EM's pre- and post-therapy story telling attempts. There are five categories of utterance (Byng & Black, 1989):

1. Single phrases, e.g. "thirty pounds"
2. Verb alone, e.g. "stained"
3. Verb + arguments, e.g. "splash paint on the rug"
4. Arguments minus functions. These utterances combine two or more arguments

around a missing verb, e.g. "the paint on the carpet".
5. Conjoined phrases. Here at least one of the linked phrases is not an argument, e.g. "back in the garage".

EM's post-therapy stories showed a slight increase in utterances containing verb argument structure (from 18% to 34%) and a corresponding decline in single phrases. However, neither of these changes was significant. There was also no real increase in the number of utterances containing a verb, even with story 2, which enabled her to employ the familiar verbs. There were few utterances combining arguments without a verb both before and after therapy, which supported the view that structure was dependent on verb access.

Communicative effectiveness

The following evaluation aimed to determine whether her post-therapy stories were more communicatively effective. The video recordings of EM's pre- and post-therapy attempts to retell the stories were played, in sections, to familiar and naive observers. After each section the observers were asked to recount their understanding of the story so far and their production was recorded on audio tape. Each observer saw both stories, one pre therapy and the other post therapy (although they were unaware of this). Evaluation showed that observers' comprehension of the key propositions from the two stories was unchanged following therapy.

TABLE 11.3

Pre- and post-therapy verb production on the picture naming test

Assessment	Treated items		Control items	
	Pre	Post	Pre	Post
Non-action verbs	0/5	3/5	2/5	2/5
Change of possession/communication verbs	7/10	8/10	6/10	8/10
Locatives and verbs of removal	6/10	9/10	5/10	6/10
Change of state verbs	3/5	5/5	2/5	3/5
Motion verbs	3/5	5/5	2/5	3/5
Total	19/35	30/35	17/35	22/35

TABLE 11.4

Pre- and post-therapy analysis of the story retelling samples

| | Number of utterances | |
	Pre-therapy	Post-therapy
Story 1 (untreated verbs)		
Single phrases	9	9
Verb only	4	1
Verb + arguments	2	6
Arguments minus functions	–	1
Conjoined phrases	–	–
Total number of utterances	15	17
Story 2 (treated verbs)		
Single phrases	11	10
Verb only	3	3
Verb + arguments	4	7
Arguments minus functions	–	1
Conjoined phrases	1	–
Total number of utterances	19	21

TABLE 11.5

Responses to questions following the story retelling task

| | Story 1 (Untreated Verbs) | | Story 2 (Treated Verbs) | | Total | |
Assessment	Pre	Post	Pre	Post	Pre	Post
Verb production	6/14	8/14	5/14	11/14	11/28	19/28
Verb + argument structure	1/14	6/14	4/14	8/14	5/28	14/28

Response to questions

In addition to the retelling task EM was asked questions about each story, which were designed to elicit 14 propositions using either the treated or control verbs. Her responses were scored for verb production and for the number of utterances in which verbs were combined with argument structure. The results are shown in Table 11.5.

Over the two stories EM's responses showed significant gains in both verb production and predicate argument structure (verbs: McNemar chi square = 4.08, $P > .05$; verb + argument structure: McNemar chi square = 4.26, $P < .05$). There are no significant changes in her responses to the individual stories.

Cinderella task

EM was asked to retell the story of Cinderella. Her utterances were grouped into the five categories outlined earlier and are shown in Table 11.6.

Although EM's post-therapy output showed a slight increase in the number of utterances containing verb argument structure the change was not significant (4/46 vs. 8/32). There was also no overall gain in verb production. The number of isolated verbs declined after therapy. However, since the status of many of the pre-therapy "verbs" was ambiguous it is difficult to interpret this observation. These findings mirrored the results of the other story telling task. Verb production and structure remained unchanged. Even following

TABLE 11.6

Number of utterances in each category produced in the pre- and post-therapy fairy tale samples

	Number of utterances	
	Pre-therapy	Post-therapy
Single phrases	33	22
Verbs	8	2
Verbs + arguments	4	8
Arguments minus function	–	–
Conjoined single phrases	1	–
Total number of utterances	46	32

therapy EM's output consisted largely of single phrases.

"Control" tasks

EM's production of abstract words in response to definition and synonym cues was tested pre and post therapy. On both, performance was unchanged.

Summary and discussion

Therapy improved EM's ability to access the 35 treated verbs, at least in the picture naming task. This task also showed an improvement in sentence formulation, which was consistent with the therapy hypothesis. There was no generalisation to the untreated items.

Although EM had apparently gained access to a corpus of verbs she was unable to use those verbs in open narrative. On the story retelling task she displayed only minimal improvements, both in verb access and structure, even when the narrative was composed largely around the treated verbs. Furthermore her post-therapy stories were no more comprehensible to the four observers. The Cinderella task also showed only marginal gains. However, there was one further sign of progress. EM's responses to questions about the stories showed better structure and verb retrieval after therapy.

I noticed that EM's responses to the questions often did not employ the trained verbs, even when the questions were targeting those items (story 2). For example she produced "tail" for "follow",

"skidded" for "spun", "thieving" for "stole" and "paid for" for "buy". This suggested that the improved verb access might have generalised to verbs that were closely related to the treated items. Support for this view was offered by a synonym generation task. Here EM was shown an action picture and told the target verb. She was then asked to think of another word to describe this action or event. All the treated and control verbs were tested, using the same pictures as in the picture naming task. Two naive judges assessed whether EM's attempts were acceptable synonyms for the target. EM produced significantly more synonyms (or synonymous phrases) for the treated verbs than for the control verbs (treated 20/35, control 8/35, chi square = 7.2). Conclusions from this task are clearly tentative, since it was not conducted prior to therapy. However, it suggests that EM's facility with the treated verbs might have extended to their close semantic partners. This apparent gain might have been consequent on the semantic component of the therapy. Certainly many of the synonyms produced by EM had been used as distracters in the therapy tasks.

The most optimistic interpretation of these results therefore suggests that EM gained access to a corpus of verbs, and possibly their close semantic colleagues. However, her ability to use these verbs was strongly influenced by the nature of the task. She could retrieve them when describing pictures and when responding to questions, but not in open narrative.

Such effects of task are well known in aphasia (see Lesser, 1989 for review) and few clinicians will be surprised by these results. Yet they might be interpreted as a challenge to the original diagnosis. It had been hypothesised that EM had a "late" deficit in retrieving verbs' phonological representations. Her conceptual and semantic skills were deemed to be largely unimpaired. It is therefore difficult to see why the conceptual properties of the task so influenced success. When her thinking was directed, with picture or question, she was successful. When she was left to generate her own message structures, she was not.

It seemed that therapy should adopt different aims. Rather than familiarising groups of verbs, treatment should aim to adapt EM's message concepts and equip her with strategies for translating those concepts into verb structures.

THE SECOND THERAPY PROGRAMME

Rationale

EM's production was facilitated by picture and question cues. It was hypothesised that these were effective because they encouraged EM to focus on simple propositions which could be conveyed in single verb phrases. In spontaneous production EM often attempted more complex propositions, which demanded either embedded or conjoined structures. For example when describing baby sitting she produced: "take… the cuddle" (take the baby out of the cot and give him a cuddle). When she was prompted to break this up her output improved: "pick up the baby and cuddle". This suggested that therapy should promote the formation of simple, highly focused concepts at the message level, which would place minimal demands on her language system.

It was also observed that EM was very intolerant of failure. As previously mentioned her output was frequently aborted and contained numerous comments about her inadequacies. EM's poor phonological retrieval meant that episodes of delay and searching were inevitable. It seemed that therapy should aim to increase her tolerance to these episodes. Two strategies were applied. One was gesture. This strategy was suggested by EM herself. She already made some use of gesture—probably as a result of her previous therapy in the groups that encouraged non-verbal modalities. Furthermore, when she used gesture this tended to stimulate better verb production. The other strategy was the use of high frequency, non-specific verbs, which could be applied to a wide range of events and situations. A number of these verbs, such as "put" and "go" already featured in EM's output.

Thus, the second therapy programme had two aims. The first was to break down into component parts the types of ideas EM tried to convey, so that they were more "in tune" with her aphasic language

system. The second was to provide her with strategies to deal with phonological searching. Rather than equipping her with a body of verb vocabulary, I aimed to encourage the use of a few general verbs. The other strategy was the use of gesture, which would hopefully provide her with a means of holding on to a message concept during the inevitable processing delay. If successful, therapy should increase EM's production of verbs and verb structures in both constrained and spontaneous conditions.

Content

Therapy initially aimed to establish the general verbs. As in the first programme these were selected from a number of semantic categories. These were as follows:

- movement: go, come, leave
- change of possession: give, get
- removal and location: put, take, bring
- change of state: make, and change.

The verbs were introduced in their categories. EM was presented with the written infinitive form of each verb and asked to read it aloud and explain its meaning. A gesture was then generated for each verb. The applications of the verb were then discussed, and EM was asked to use the verb to describe recent life events. Cueing focused her on likely targets. For example, when working on the locative and removal verbs the therapist invited her to think about dressing (put the clothes on, take them off) and cooking (put the food in the oven, take it out). Additional tasks involved picture descriptions and completion exercises. For example, EM was presented with a number of written situations and asked to describe what she would do in each:

> "What would you do if someone gave you a Henry Moore statue?"

> "What would you do if you found a lost dog?"

Cueing encouraged her to focus absolutely consciously on the event; for example:

JM: Imagine yourself with the dog. There he is at your feet (points to the floor). You go and get some string and make a lead (gestures holding the lead). You set off…

EM: (copies the gesture and moves it away from body) "Take … yes take … take the dog to the house"

If this was unsuccessful EM was given the list of general verbs and asked to compose her answer around one. Interestingly EM's responses to the picture and completion tasks were not confined to the general verbs. For example, she suggested that she would "sell" the Henry Moore and when asked what she would do with a lost cat she offered: "shoot it". Further written completion tasks were provided for homework.

One dilemma in this phase of the therapy was whether to introduce the different tensed forms of the verbs. This was a particular issue given the irregularity of the targets. It was noted that EM usually produced infinitive forms, and conveyed time via supplementary phrases, for example: "last Saturday, go to Hounslow". As EM had a functional means of communicating time concepts and since she never produced regularisation like "goed" I decided not to introduce the additional complication of the tensed forms.

EM was not handicapped by the diverse argument structures of these general verbs. For example, she readily employed two argument or particle structures with "put". As before this confirmed her impressive knowledge about the properties of verbs. Ten 1-hour sessions were devoted to the general verbs.

The second phase of therapy aimed specifically to alter EM's conceptual preparations for language. The main task entailed recounting clips of commercial videos (*Roxanne* and *Ruthless People*). Prior to seeing the video clip EM was reminded of her general verbs. This involved giving her the written list and inviting her to generate a few sentences for each. Feedback emphasised the type of event described by the verb, for example:

"Yes you put your make up on. The make up starts in one place and ends up in another. So 'put' talks about moving objects from one place to another."

It was suggested that she might find these verbs useful in describing the video, although she was not restricted to them. The clips were selected so that at least some of the events could be conveyed using these verbs. EM was then shown the video clip. Before recounting the events a number of output strategies were introduced and discussed. These were condensed to three main tips:

- Think about one event at a time. Do not try to talk about the whole story at once.
- If you can't think of the verb don't give up. Mime it. Look at your mime and see if you can think of a word for that action.
- See if your general verbs help.

Most of the cueing during the task focused on the first two strategies. These seemed to provide EM with a means of tackling the task, for example:

EM: oh dear … no.

JM: OK. He's got to the door. Think about what he does next. Just the first thing. Try acting it out.

EM: (mimes putting something on the floor) put the bag in the ground … (mimes opening it) open the bag … (mimes reading in) pick up the credit card … oh no.

JM: (mimes inserting the card into the door)

EM: put the card in the … crack (both laugh).

Of course it is impossible to know exactly how gesture facilitated production here (if at all). It may have acted like a picture cue and focused EM on a specific, unitary proposition. Alternatively the gestures may have provided EM with a delay in which to accomplish phonological search and helped her to retain semantic level information during this delay. Feedback after EM's attempts recalled her successful production and emphasised the strategies that she had used. In addition, EM was videoed during the task and the tape was replayed to her. This enabled her to observe her use of gesture and see how it stimulated output.

The video task was made progressively more demanding by increasing the length of the clips. I also attempted to withdraw gradually the level of cueing and preparation provided. Instead EM was asked to recap the strategies independently before embarking on the task, e.g. "if you get stuck what strategies can you use?". Supplementary tasks were used to encourage the use of the output strategies in different contexts. In one, EM and I walked around the therapy area observing people in action. Periodically we would stop and focus on one person. EM was encouraged to copy or mime their actions and then describe them. In another, EM was required to apply the strategies to a description of events in her week. This phase of therapy occupied 10 90-minute sessions. In all the second therapy programme comprised 20 sessions.

Results

Verb production—picture naming tasks

The 70 verb pictures were readministered after the second therapy programme. With the previously treated verbs EM scored 28/35, which was still significantly better than her baseline score (19/35 vs. 28/35, McNemar chi square = 7.11, $P < .01$). On the untreated control verbs EM scored 24/35, which was not significantly different from baseline. This result suggested that the benefits of the first therapy programme had been maintained, with no generalised improvement in verb access.

This was evaluated further by readministering the Byng verb photographs, none of which had been specifically focused on in therapy. Prior to therapy EM had scored 25/42 with these pictures. After the

second programme her score rose to 37/42, which was a significant improvement (McNemar chi square = 10.08; $P < .01$).

The two picture tasks produced different results. The first showed maintenance of the training effect seen after the first therapy programme, with no gains in the untreated controls. The second suggested that verb access might have generally improved. This discrepancy may have been due to differences between the stimuli. The first set of pictures targeted items that were not easily substituted by EM's general verbs, whereas with eight of the Byng photos EM could and did make use of her non-specific verbs.

The story retelling task

EM was asked to retell the two "treatment" and "control" stories. Table 11.7 shows the number of utterances falling within five categories, with comparative pre-therapy and post first therapy data. As there were no significant differences between the two stories they were analysed together.

Comparing pre with post second therapy data shows a significant reduction in the proportion of single phrases (20/34 vs. 16/48, chi square = 4.25, $P < .05$) and a significant rise in the number of utterances with verb argument structure (6/34 vs. 23/48, chi square = 6.68, $P < .01$). Although there were more utterances containing a verb, this change was not significant.

Unlike the first therapy programme, the second programme produced significant changes in EM's narrative output, particularly in terms of verb argument structure. The achievement of structure seemed dependent on the verb, since

TABLE 11.7

Analysis of the pre-therapy, post first therapy and post second therapy story retelling samples

	Number of utterances		
	Pre-therapy	Post first therapy	Post second therapy
Single phrases	20	19	16
Verb only	7	4	3
Verb + arguments	6	13	23
Arguments minus functions	–	2	5
Conjoined single phrases	1	–	1
Total number of utterances	34	38	48

the number of utterances combining arguments without a verb (arguments minus functions) remained low. Overall, her verb production did not increase significantly, which apparently contradicts the therapy hypothesis. However, prior to therapy over half of EM's "verbs" were produced in isolation and were often ambiguous in status. It is therefore likely that the pre-therapy verb production was overestimated. In order to reduce the amount of testing the story questions were not readministered.

Communicative effectiveness
Video recordings of EM's pre- and post second therapy stories were played to familiar and naive observers (obviously these were not the same observers as used previously). After viewing the tape the observers were asked to recall everything that they had understood and their comprehension of the key propositions was scored. Table 11.8 presents their results.

Both pairs of observers comprehended significantly more propositions from EM's post second therapy output (Familiar: pre 12/35 vs. post 24/35, chi square = 6.92, $P < .01$; Naive: pre 10/35 vs. post 22/35, chi square = 6.96, $P < .01$). Also, considered individually, significantly more propositions were understood from each story following the second phase of therapy (Story 1 pre 12/34 vs. post 22/34, chi square = 4,76, $P < .05$; Story 2 pre 10/36 vs. post 24/36, chi square = 9.42, $P < .01$).

EM's stories after the second therapy programme were clearly more comprehensible to these observers than her pre-therapy versions. It is difficult to determine the source of this change. The observers may have benefited from the greater volume of her output (EM produced 157 words after the second therapy programme compared with 69 pre therapy). However EM's volume also increased after the first period of therapy (to 115 words). Yet then there was no improvement in the observers' understanding. Also the utterance analysis above showed that the increased word count occurred mainly because EM was producing more verb argument structures following the second therapy programme (the number of single phrases declined). This suggests that the quality, rather than volume of her output, may have been the crucial factor.

Cinderella task
In addition to the previously discussed story task, EM was asked to retell the story of Cinderella. Table 11.9 shows the number of utterances falling under five categories, with comparative pre-therapy and post first therapy data.

After the second therapy programme EM produced significantly more utterances with verb argument structure than at baseline (4/46 vs. 15/31, chi square = 13.62, $P < .001$). There was corresponding reduction in the proportion of single phrases (33/46 vs. 10/31, chi square = 10.14, $P < .01$). EM's production had also improved since the first therapy programme. A comparison of the results of the first and second therapy programmes shows a significant reduction in single phrases (22/32 vs. 10/31, chi square = 7.00, $P < .01$) and increase in the number of utterances containing a verb (10/32 vs. 19/31, chi square = 4.55, $P < .05$). The comparison of the number of structured utterances after the two therapy programmes fell short of significance.

"Control" tasks
The abstract word production tasks were re-administered after the second therapy programme and again showed no improvement.

TABLE 11.8

The number of propositions comprehended by observers from EM's pre- and post-therapy stories

	Story 1		Story 2	
	Pre	*Post second therapy*	*Pre*	*Post second therapy*
Familiar observers	6/17	12/17	6/18	12/18
Naive observers	6/17	10/17	4/18	12/18

TABLE 11.9

Number of utterances in each category produced in the pre-therapy, post first therapy and second therapy fairy tale samples

	Number of utterances		
	Pre-therapy	*Post first therapy*	*Post second therapy*
Single phrases	33	22	10
Verb only	8	2	4
Verb and arguments	4	8	15
Arguments minus functions	–	–	2
Conjoined single phrases	1	–	–
Total number of utterances	46	32	31

Summary and discussion

Evaluations of the second therapy programme showed promising gains in open narratives. The two story narratives revealed more structured utterances with an associated decline in the number of single phrases. These gains were also observed in the Cinderella task, together with a significant improvement in verb production. The linguistic changes in EM's speech seemed communicatively important. Familiar and naive observers found EM's post second therapy stories more comprehensible than her pre-therapy attempts.

Changes in verb naming were more difficult to evaluate. One picture naming task suggested that only the effects of the first therapy programme had been maintained, since the previously treated verbs were still significantly better named than at baseline, whereas the untreated items were unchanged. However, a second picture task indicated a general improvement in verb naming which was not confined to treated verbs, although here EM made use of the non-specific verbs focused on in the second programme of therapy.

The results of the second therapy programme were considerably more encouraging than those of the first. Then gains occurred only in constrained tasks, such as picture naming and question responses, with no carry over to more open conditions.

Why was the second programme more effective? It is possible that EM was simply benefiting from more therapy, rather than the different type of treatment. Here an examination of the trend in her improvements may be helpful. Fig.

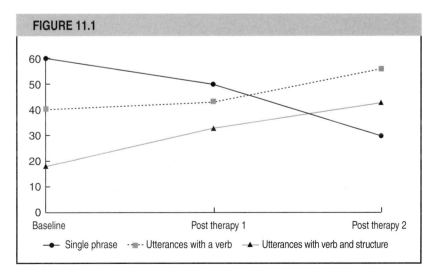

FIGURE 11.1

● Single phrase   ▪ Utterances with a verb   ▲ Utterances with verb and structure

Results of the story retelling task across the two therapy programmes.

11.1 displays the results of the story retelling task across the three evaluation periods. This figure reveals a remarkably steady increase in the two verb-related measures, together with a consistent decline in the production of single phrases. These results might support the view that the extent, rather than the nature of therapy may have been important. However, the Cinderella performance was different (Fig. 11.2). Here there was a significant "take off" in verb production between the two therapy periods, together with a significant decline in the number of single phrases. The trends on this task indicate that the second period of therapy particularly facilitated EM's output, presumably because of its specific content.

One aspect of the second therapy programme encouraged EM to exploit a small group of general verbs, such as "go", "come" and "put". It was hypothesised that these might be useful since they apply to a range of events and because EM was already showing some ability to access them. Yet there was little evidence that these verbs were responsible for the gains in EM's production. Although they were used quite heavily in one of the picture naming tasks, they appeared only seven times in all the post second therapy narratives. In retrospect this therapy hypothesis might be questioned. Verbs like "take" express a wide variety of meanings, which are determined largely through the structures employed with the verb, for example:

"take the pill"
"take the child to the dentist"
"take the knife from the child"
"take over"

These very diverse meanings and structures suggest that each sentence is employing a different (although homophonic) verb. In other words there may be several representations of "take" each with its own semantic and grammatical properties. This in turn suggests that therapy will have to train each version of these general verbs separately. Simply familiarising the phonological form of the verbs will be insufficient to ensure their use.

Another therapy component involved the use of gesture. This did not entail "teaching" gesture, since EM's previous group therapy had already established this medium. Instead, treatment encouraged her to use her gesture consciously as a verb cue. There was some evidence that this strategy was employed in the two post second therapy story tasks. Seventeen of EM's verbs and verb phrases were either preceded or accompanied by explicit gestures (65%), and on several occasions she repeated and refined a verb gesture until production was achieved.

It is difficult to determine the role played by gesture in EM's output. I speculated that gesture encouraged EM to create highly focused and imageable ideas, in preparation for language. In other words they acted like a picture cue. Yet why

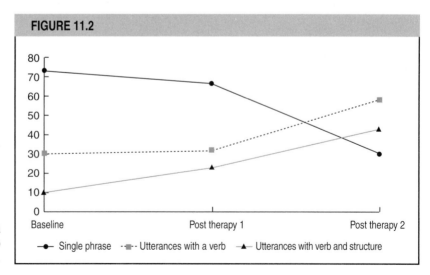

FIGURE 11.2

Results of the Cinderella task across the two therapy programmes.

Baseline   Post therapy 1   Post therapy 2

●— Single phrase   -■- Utterances with a verb   ▲— Utterances with verb and structure did this help her to accomplish phonological access? It may be that gesture enabled her to "hold onto" the semantic representation that she was attempting to convey. Without the gestural cue, this semantic information may "fade" before phonological retrieval can take place.

Alternatively, the benefits may have been "psychological", for example gesture may have relaxed EM and given her time in which to accomplish verb search. However, as indicated previously, gesture was not a new skill and EM's pre-therapy communication showed considerable use of this medium. It was only after the second therapy programme that she could "convert" her gestures into spoken output.

It seemed that providing EM with a strategy for assisting verb access, in this case gesture, constituted the most useful element of therapy. Familiarising groups of verbs improved her performance with pictures, but not her open narrative, even when the "trained" verbs had potentially widespread usage. However, this conclusion is necessarily guarded. The work on specific verb targets may have contributed to the development of a verb strategy and certainly many of the cues used during this therapy encouraged EM to focus on the event and use gesture.

Evaluations of both therapy programmes revealed a relationship between verb access and sentence structure. Tasks showing improved verb access also showed gains in structure and EM's attempts to combine arguments without the verb remained limited. Furthermore, improved structure was achieved without any specific work on either syntax or mapping. In both programmes the emphasis remained purely on verb access. These findings were consistent with the initial therapy hypothesis, which stated that EM's sentence output was hampered principally by her verb retrieval deficit. Once verb retrieval was facilitated output improved.

EMOTIONAL ASPECTS

Throughout this study EM's emotional state was fragile and she had episodes of quite severe depression. Six years prior to her stroke EM had lost her husband and mother in a car crash and it was clear that this bereavement was still a major factor in her mood. I felt that EM's emotional state interacted with her language presentation. Her spontaneous speech showed little evidence of her undoubted skills. For example, when blocked, she seemed unable to exploit her considerable ability with nouns, e.g. she did not fire helpful nouns at the listener in the hope that they would direct them to the missing information. She also made surprisingly little use of her writing. Finally, she rarely attempted to build sentence structures minus the verb, despite the fact that this type of output might have been anticipated by her deficit. Overall her main "strategy" during spontaneous speech was to abort and wait for assistance from her conversational partner.

Of course there may be numerous reasons for these signs. For example, it may be difficult to generate structure without the phonological form of the verb, and I have already considered the differences between spontaneous naming and naming to pictures. However, in addition, it seemed that EM's response to her deficit was quite passive. It appeared very difficult for her to experiment with adaptive strategies and maximise whatever skills were available to her. This, in turn, may have been due to her low emotional state.

In some ways EM's life style also displayed a degree of passivity and withdrawal. She had lost contact with many friends she had prior to becoming aphasic and she commented that she tended to remain silent, even with her family. Much of her time outside therapy was spent alone at home, usually watching television. She almost never used her speech with strangers. This led to quite a high degree of dependence on her daughter—who helped her with phone calls, complaints, and any negotiations involved in the running of her home. However, in contrast, EM had also undertaken some new activities since her stroke, such as pottery and keep-fit classes. EM suggested that she was able to take part in these because they imposed only minimal demands on her speech.

A sizeable component of EM's group therapy aimed to build her confidence and encouraged her to communicate in different settings. Group discussions identified situations which were felt to be problematic, such as using the telephone, asking for things in shops, and complaining. The group ranked these in order of difficulty. They were also invited to think about why each situation was problematic, e.g. because of the level of language required or the attitude of the people involved. These problem situations were tackled hierarchically, first through discussion and preparation, then through role play, and finally in assignments. Students accompanied the group members on the assignments in order to give them feedback about the strategies that they had used. This work also engendered some useful discussion about living with a disability. For example, one specific topic was whether having a Stroke Association card (which explains dysphasia) was helpful or stigmatising.

The profundity of EM's depression and the unresolved bereavement suggested that she needed specialised counselling. It was fortunate that, during this period, Action for Dysphasic Adults (ADA; a UK-wide voluntary sector organisation for people with aphasia) was running a counselling project for people with dysphasia. EM was initially resistant to being involved; however, after some discussion she agreed to be referred. Undoubtedly a factor which influenced her decision was the discovery that one of the workers was herself dysphasic. EM attended 14 sessions with the ADA project. She found the counselling enormously helpful, describing her feelings as "lighter" as a result. I also noted that she was now able to mention her husband without automatic tears. Following this experience, EM also decided to undertake further counselling from a different, external, source. Without a doubt, EM demonstrates the need for more counselling services for people with dysphasia.

FOOTNOTE

1   Throughout this study I based the analysis of spontaneous speech on narrative samples. This method was adopted since guidance is available about the elicitation and analysis of such samples, and because comparative data is available. In retrospect, I feel that

other samples, such as conversational speech, would have been far more appropriate, mainly because the narrative tasks is so difficult that it may not be sensitive to important functional changes in output. Furthermore, conversational speech is the type of output that most people with dysphasia would wish to improve.

REFERENCES

Byng. S. (1988). Sentence processing deficits: Theory and therapy. *Cognitive Neuropsychology*, 5, 629–676.

Byng. S., & Black. M. (1989) Some aspects of sentence production in aphasia. *Aphasiology*, 3(3), 241–263.

Caramazza. A., & Hillis. A. (1990). Where do semantic errors come from? *Cortex*, 26, 95–122.

Garrett, M. (1982). Production of speech: Observations from normal and pathological language use. In A.W. Ellis (Ed.), *Normality and pathology in cognitive functions*. London: Academic Press.

Howard, D., Patterson, K., Franklin, S., Orchard-Lisle, V., & Morton, J. (1985). The treatment of word retrieval deficits in aphasia: A comparison of two therapy methods. *Brain*, 108, 817–829.

Jones, E. (1989). A year in the life of E.V.J. and P.C. In E.V. Jones (Ed.), *Advances in aphasia therapy in the clinical setting. Proceedings of the Cambridge Symposium on Aphasia Therapy*. London: British Aphasiology Society.

Lesser, R. (1989) Some issues in the neuropsychological rehabilitation of anomia. In X. Seron, & R. Deloche (Eds.), *Cognitive approaches in neuropsychological rehabilitation*. Hillsdale NJ: Lawrence Erlbaum Associates Inc.

McCarthy, R., & Warrington, E. (1985). Category specificity in an agrammatic patient: the relative impairment of verb retrieval and comprehension. *Neuropsychologia*, 23, 709–727.

Marshall, J. (1995). The mapping hypothesis and aphasia therapy. *Aphasiology*, 9, 6, 517–539.

Marshall, J., Pound, C., White-Thomson, M., & Pring, T. (1990). The use of picture/word matching tasks to assist word retrieval in aphasic patients. *Aphasiology*, 4, 167–184.

Saffran, E., Berndt, R., & Schwartz, M. (1989). The quantitative analysis of agrammatic production: Procedure and data. *Brain and Language*, 37, 440–479.

Zingeser, L., & Berndt, R.S. (1990). Retrieval of nouns and verbs in aggramatism and anomia. *Brain and Language*, 39, 14–32.

12

Early stages in treating a person with non-fluent aphasia

Alison Greenwood

INTRODUCTION

IC was 71 years old when she experienced a left-sided CVA. She initially suffered mild weakness of the right arm and leg, but this resolved within 24 hours. She was not admitted to hospital, but was referred to a day hospital for assessment. Physiotherapy and occupational therapy were not required. IC's communication, however, remained severely limited.

Prior to her CVA, IC had been well, still working as a cook for a local nursing home. She had no relevant past medical history. She was a widow, living with her youngest unmarried son. She had three other married sons, living locally, and one married daughter who lived in America.

Presentation on initial referral to speech therapy (3 weeks post stroke)

IC was seen for initial assessment at the day hospital. She presented with good functional comprehension (as assessed on the Whurr Screening Test; Whurr, 1972), but severely limited expressive language: /tu tu/, /du du/, and an occasional single appropriate word. This had reportedly remained unchanged since the onset of her CVA.

It was arranged for her to attend the local aphasia clinic two days a week where she could receive individual therapy and participate in volunteer-run groups. IC began to attend the dysphasia clinic 6 weeks post lesion, where her case was taken on by a final-year student speech and language therapist.

She was assessed using the Boston Diagnostic Aphasia Examination (BDAE) (Goodglass & Kaplan, 1981). It was concluded that IC's major problem was one of oral execution of words; written output was considerably better then spoken output, comprehension was functionally good, but she showed some difficulties with complex ideational material and the longer, more complex commands.

Expressively, apart from /tu/ and /du/, IC had a small amount of automatic speech; she could sometimes supply a word within a sentence closure framework. Reading comprehension seemed better than auditory comprehension although there was some evidence of semantic errors in single word recognition.

As IC had appeared frustrated by her limited expressive ability, the initial aims of therapy were:

1. to develop a communication book and work on her use of gesture
2. to introduce a therapy programme for verbal dyspraxia
3. to use Melodic Intonation Therapy to improve spoken output (Sparks, Helm, & Albert, 1974)
4. to investigate further her reading skills.

IC was seen twice weekly over 3 weeks to work on the "dyspraxia" through use of imitation and articulograms. She was given sound production practice as homework and, in between individual sessions, she joined in "general" group work where she was encouraged to use a personal communication book and to gesture.

Initial contact with the current therapist 8 weeks post CVA

Prior to contact. It had been reported that IC was not getting on well with the sound production work; the previous session had been cut short as she had appeared "tired and frustrated", and her daughter-in-law had expressed concern that IC had been getting upset and depressed at home due to her inability to successfully produce the sounds given for home practice.

Observation of IC in a group. When I observed IC within a small group she seemed more relaxed, often using a combination of written words, gesture and her communication book to get her message across. As one of the more physically able of the group she had adopted quite a proactive role, organising the tea-making, the washing up, etc.

Conversation with IC. Understanding of spoken language was adequate in a conversational setting.

Spoken output was still limited to /du/ and /tu/ when volitional. A few nouns were uttered spontaneously but were usually triggered by a written word. IC showed a lot of frustration. Written output appeared to be a more effective means of getting a message across, but there seemed to be evidence of the following language difficulties:

1. some word retrieval problems, i.e. there were often long delays, sometimes with no results
2. semantic errors
3. spelling errors
4. IC appeared to use only single nouns (although these were usually adequate for the purposes of our conversation).

Written naming. IC's written naming of 20 object pictures (Winslow Press, 1982) produced quick and accurate responses which showed little evidence of any of the aforementioned errors. When asked to write down the *function* of these same object pictures, however, the following points were noted (see Table 12.1):

1. IC needed considerably longer to produce a response.
2. Verbs were omitted in 60% of the responses.
3. Function words were omitted, substituted, and mis-spelt.
4. Word order sometimes appeared bizarre, and the target phrase unclear.

TABLE 12.1

Writing the function of an object

Stimulus picture	Written response
Glass	milk
Scissors	scissor in cut hair
Book	read fur book
Matches	this matches but to cigerets
Chair	the chair to sit up
Pencil	the penicle write
Ball	the ball tennis
Radio	the records
Jug	the jug in the the milk
Mug	the mug or teas

Initial thoughts and hypotheses

My first and instinctive reaction to the observations in Table 12.1 and the previous reports was to take pressure off speech as much as possible, and concentrate on looking at her language through her written output and auditory and written input. It seemed, from the written output I had already observed, that IC's general output problems were not just "execution difficulties", i.e. there might be a more central language problem in need of further investigation.

IC appeared to have more difficulty accessing *verb semantics* and organising verb information into phrases/sentences. Could there also be a difficulty accessing the *phonology* of target words, accounting for her inferior spoken output?

Assessment

Picture word matching with semantic and visual distractors (PALPA; Kay, Lesser, & Coltheart, 1992). IC was shown a page containing five pictures to which she had to match a spoken or written word. The pictures represented either the target picture or pictures of objects either closely or distantly semantically related to the target, visually related or unrelated to the spoken or written word. IC had shown some semantic errors in her written output of single nouns, as well as in her recognition of single words (reported from the BDAE). Comprehension of both auditory and written single nouns in this test was, however, 100% correct.

Verb naming. Although I hypothesised that IC had more difficulty accessing verbs for output than nouns, I was not happy to conclude this from the results of my first contact, as the processing required to merely label the object as opposed to defining a function that was not itself pictured is obviously different. Maybe IC was helped to access the object labels by having the pictures to process "top down". I therefore wanted to replicate with action pictures (as much as possible) the task previously carried out with object pictures.

IC was therefore given 20 high frequency verb pictures (Table 12.2). She found this task difficult, taking more time than for the object pictures, and attempting only nine of them before indicating that

she had done enough! She did access verbs accurately in 55% of those attempted. Others she substituted with nouns, despite several attempts to access the verb. This did seem to indicate that verbs were more difficult for IC than nouns.

I wondered, however, whether IC would show similar word retrieval difficulties if given lower frequency nouns to name, so I followed this test with a task requiring naming of a greater range of objects.

Howard and Patterson's 100 picture naming test (unpublished). Howard and Patterson's 100 pictures were used to look at written naming of mixed frequency nouns. Generally IC's performance was good (85% correct), though there was some evidence of semantic (7%) and spelling (8%) errors, for example:

e.g. Hedge→Garden   Goal→Mouth

Stool→Stoop   Envelope→Enevople

At this stage there was beginning to be an increase in IC's spoken output. It seemed that, without any pressure to express herself verbally, and with the focus on written stimuli/responses, IC was producing more single words in speech. She was even starting to read aloud some of the words voluntarily.

This also allowed me more time to continue investigations into IC's language difficulties. Whereas it may have appeared inappropriate in

TABLE 12.2

Writing the verb names from pictures

Stimulus picture	Written response
Walking	WaLKing
Reading	Book MagRINE
Standing	attenion
Knitting	Knitting
Stroking cat	cat SToke
Drying hair	wasHing her HaiR
Winding watch	he windows his watch
Jumping	She Jumping
Drinking	Drink of milk

other circumstances to interrupt a therapy programme with extensive assessments, IC was pleased with her progress over the previous two sessions, and was therefore more than happy for the assessment to continue.

Picture description—"Cookie Theft" (BDAE). The Cookie Theft description (BDAE) is given in Table 12.3. I felt that I needed to look more closely at IC's connected writing. Again she took a long time to complete this task and needed two attempts within the session. The following observations seemed particularly relevant:

- Verbs took longer to retrieve than nouns.
- IC appeared to omit verbs or make verb substitutions.
- She omitted or substituted function words.
- She made spelling/"anagram"-type errors.

Spontaneous writing—making a cup of tea. The description of this is given in Table 12.4. The previously discussed difficulties were again observed with the addition of:

- substitution of verbs, e.g. "tough" for "put" and "that" for "add".
- perseveration difficulties.

Reversible sentence comprehension test. In this test (Byng & Black, 1999), IC was required to match a spoken NP (noun phrase) VP (verb phrase) NP (noun phrase) sentence to a picture from a choice of three (sometimes two). In each sentence the order of the two NPs is interchangeable, i.e. the sentence still makes sense regardless of which way

TABLE 12.3
Cookie theft picture—written description

First attempt	She
	There tools coppable
	he out cakes
	her water or sink of plain
Second attempt	he washing up the drain this owered
	he the to cake the the cole

TABLE 12.4
Making a cup of tea—written description

Boil the ketting
Tough the in the tea bag
Boil of the tea bag into the cup
That a milk and sugar

round the NPs are placed (e.g. "the swimmer splashes the nun", where the nun could also splash the swimmer). Different sentence types, and different verb and adjective types are included throughout the test. The three pictures comprise the target picture, a picture showing the reverse roles, and a lexical distractor where a different, unrelated verb is depicted. Based on the hypothesis that IC was having difficulty retrieving the semantics of the verb in order to successfully construct sentences, I needed to investigate further to see if there was a parallel problem in both written and spoken input, i.e. was it a *central* problem with verb semantics?

The results showed that this may indeed be the case. IC scored only 67% correct, with a significant percentage (24%) of her errors being reverse role errors compared with 9% distractor errors. This suggested that she had a problem determining who is doing what to whom when she cannot rely on pragmatic information but has to interpret the sentence fully.

Written sentence generation given verb infinitive. In order to further explore sentence construction, IC was asked to try to write a sentence given the verb. This would demonstrate whether there was any relationship between her difficulties with verb retrieval and sentence construction. In this task, IC showed evidence of verb nominalisation, difficulties with the ordering of arguments around the verb, and the omission/substitution of function words (Table 12.5). (In some cases, it was difficult to tell whether arguments were mixed up or whether it was a reflection of the function word difficulties.) IC appeared to cope better once she had produced one sentence giving her a syntactic framework/ model to work from. There was some evidence again of perseveration. The hypothesis relating to a

TABLE 12.5

Sentence generation with a verb provided

Given verb	Written response
To peel	I've a peel of oragenes
To post	I anywhere the post box
To light	I past light any it blackness
To persuade	I persuade to dog anythrine
To place	I place I lived up the noisely
To come	I come at party
To paint	I've a paint a to paint and window

difficulty with verb accessing and mapping information onto sentences seemed to be bearing out. It would have been interesting to see if she could have ordered a sentence when given all the phrases, e.g. two NPs and a verb, that is, when no independent generation of language was required, but I did not test this at the time.

Judgements of Phonology (PALPA). IC seemed also to have a problem with the phonology of words. I wanted to see if IC could access the *internal* phonology of the words she was not able to produce orally, i.e. could there be a problem at the level of the phonological output lexicon? I therefore asked her to carry out some tests of internal phonology, in which she was asked to judge whether two written words that were spelled differently sounded the same, e.g. pear and pair. IC scored barely above chance level with both irregularly spelled words and with non-word pairs, and she indicated that she was doing the task largely through guesswork.

Having watched IC perform some of the assessment, I was not totally convinced that she had fully understood the task involved. I therefore gave her a list of similar pairs of words *auditorily*. For real words this was not too difficult since the pairs of words of course sounded identical when they were the same; IC scored 95% correct. For non-words, however, she scored only slightly better than with the silent, written version. Does this show that IC needed to use semantics to mediate auditory input and thus make it recognisable as a group of sounds? Or was she unable to *hold* the sound combinations

in the phonological input lexicon without reinforcement from semantics?

Conclusions/hypotheses

1. IC had difficulty accessing the semantic system particularly for verbs. She was unable to access verb information for input and output, resulting in difficulty formulating sentence structure.
2. IC possibly had difficulty accessing the phonological form of the word, a problem which may then have been compounded by an articulatory timing deficit.
3. From observation I also tentatively questioned whether there was a problem accessing sentential stress/rhythm creating errors with unstressed components of the sentence, e.g. pronouns, prepositions, articles, auxiliaries, etc.

Further psychosocial factors taken into account when setting aims and planning therapy were:

- IC had not appeared to respond to a dyspraxia programme, and in fact, was becoming quite distressed by it. Spoken output had reportedly not improved since onset of her CVA and her determination to carry on sound production tasks that she was given for homework was resulting in increased failure and frustration.
- With the focus of investigation taken off spoken output and on to written language IC seemed more relaxed. Her spoken output was in fact increasing, and with it, her confidence.
- IC showed interest in, and a good tolerance for, the analytical type of investigative language tasks which had been carried out over the previous 2 weeks. Her lively sense of humour allowed a lighter side of the sometimes bizarre or repetitive nature of some of the tasks to be appreciated!
- IC's age and home environment meant that her communicative needs were predominantly related to her home and social life. Her interests were centred around her family and, to a lesser extent, around the local Women's Institute group. She did not express any desire to continue employment as a cook, indicating that

she had given quite enough years of service for little reward! However, she had in no way become passive; she was still an active and influential force in her family and in her home.

- IC, understandably, wanted to communicate through speech again. Given the improvement in her spoken output over the investigative sessions, she saw writing as a stepping stone to improved speech, and was therefore very keen to continue with writing tasks.
- IC had been attending the aphasia clinic two full days a week receiving an individual therapy session on each day and then participating in volunteer-run "stimulation" groups. In practice, many of the volunteers used structured exercises designed to give practice in various levels of word finding. Since IC relied on a limited source of volunteer transport, it was not possible to rearrange times or length of attendance at the clinic. Apart from the individual sessions with myself, therefore, IC needed a therapy programme that could be carried out in part by the volunteers who worked with her the rest of the time.

Overall aim of therapy

To improve written output and therefore, hopefully, spoken output, if the hypothesis about the nature of the underlying impairment was correct.

Overall strategy

To work on verb semantics at both single word and sentential levels in input and written output tasks.

THERAPY

Volunteer tasks

IC attended the aphasia clinic for two whole sessions per week, during which I would be seeing her for only part of the time. The rest of the time she was normally seen by volunteers either individually or in small groups for "general" language stimulation. My concern was three-fold:

1. I wanted to ensure that the *ad hoc* work done in these groups did not influence the

outcome of my therapy in an unspecified way.

2. Much of the group work carried out tended to focus on *spoken output,* and, although the volunteers had been encouraged to support IC in the use of her communication book and written output, this did not always happen; the "desired" mode was usually "peech", with writing accepted only if this could not be achieved. IC's sense of failure was therefore unwittingly being reinforced.

3. I felt that IC could benefit more from activities/tasks that took account of the results of all the previously discussed investigations and observations. A practical solution therefore seemed to be to draw up specific worksheets to be carried out with volunteers between therapy sessions which would complement and contribute to the work I was doing with IC.

I therefore devised a series of judgement and written output tasks that worked on verb processing and retrieval at a single word level.

Prior to the volunteer sessions, it was stressed that:

1. No attention was to be drawn to IC's spoken output. Judgement or written responses were all that was required from IC or any of the group members.

2. Work was concentrating on *single* word responses.

3. There was often no single correct response required. IC's judgement may well differ from that of other aphasic group members or the volunteer's judgement. This, in fact, could be encouraged.

4. Completed tasks, and any problems in carrying out the tasks, were to be taken for discussion in sessions with the therapist.

Written input/semantic judgement tasks

Categorisation of verbs, e.g. sorting verbs relating to eating, cooking, housework, etc. into their individual categories.

This was initially practised with pictures, though the nature and availability of such material obviously allowed only very highly imageable items to be used within a limited number of semantic fields. This task moved very quickly, therefore, on to categorising written words which could be more easily controlled for frequency and semantic relatedness.

Odd one out, e.g. deciding which of the following written verbs did not fit in the same category as the others:

whisking beating folding baking   kneading
running   standing walking skipping staggering

Again, as far as possible, high frequency items were chosen. Items within each judgement task were within the same superordinate category. Judgement therefore required IC to differentiate subordinate categories and items.

Sentence completion. Given a choice of semantically related responses, full processing of a given sentence was required in order to select an appropriate item. This test required access to the verb argument structure in order to determine which of the choice of verbs fitted the sentence most accurately. For example:

The telephone was ringing so he _____ it.
    replied
    rang
    answered

Pairing verbs given high frequency noun phrases. For example:

washing   a book
baking   a cup of coffee
reading   the cup final
watching   the sheets
drinking   a chocolate cake

IC found most of these worksheets relatively easy to complete. It proved somewhat difficult convincing the volunteers (and, therefore, IC) of the value of such input tasks, given the lack of traditional therapy task struggle. It did also meant that IC rarely needed to have the task or hierarchy of difficulty adjusted in order to achieve the desired

aim, i.e. conscious processing of the given verbs. Unfortunately, because these tasks were not implemented by the therapist, it was impossible to ensure that effective therapeutic modulation of the materials took place, such as capitalisation, expansion upon, or divergence from the processing during the task itself.

Written output

1. Given high frequency verbs, IC was to generate as many associated nouns as possible. For example:
    washing   drinking
    reading   knitting
    driving
2. Sentence completion without given alternatives. For example:
    His shirt was dirty so he _____ it.
3. Given high frequency nouns, IC was to supply as many associated verbs as possible. For example:
    cake
    jumper
    bus
    coffee
    plants
4. Given verbs, IC had to supply synonyms or antonyms. For example:
    sleep
    purchase
    run
    stop
    shout

Again, most of the items used or required as a response in the worksheets were high frequency for IC, and where possible relevant to her current situation and interests. A hierarchy of difficulty was again attempted, but since I was not always able to monitor her performance within these sessions, this was not always easy to achieve.

Therapist tasks

Whilst the volunteers worked on single word verb semantics, I concentrated on a hierarchy of tasks which aimed to develop IC's insight into the relationship between verb meaning and the sentence structure.

Recognition of the verb within the sentence. This task was undertaken in three stages. The first stage involved discussion of the terminology of the components of language in sentences, using simple SVO (subject-verb-object) sentences and their corresponding pictures. At this stage it was mutually decided that we would be identifying the "action word" (verb), "the person or thing which was doing the action" (agent), and "the rest of the sentence" (theme/goal) (e.g. Jones, 1986).

The second stage involved selection of the verb, agent and theme in simple *active* SVO type sentences controlled for semantic and pragmatic bias. For example:

The dog buried the bone (predictable, irreversible)

The cat chewed the newspaper (less predictable, irreversible)

The queen is splashing the nun (unpredictable, reversible)

Initially, pictures were used to help IC in her identification. When pictures were removed, IC was asked to visualise the action being carried out. Questions, for example, "Who is splashing the nun?", "Who gets wet?", etc. often helped to reinforce the concepts at each level of task.

Three groups of verbs were selected, using a hierarchy of difficulty suggested by IC's assessment performance, but involving, where possible, high frequency, high imageability and transitive verbs:

1. Agentive, non-directional verbs, for example:
   splash
   wash
   bake
   bury
2. Agentive, directional verbs, for example:
   push
   pull
   throw
   chase

2. Non-agentive verbs, for example:
   please
   worry
   frighten
   annoy

In the structured therapy tasks, more "complex" verbs, e.g. those taking more than one obligatory argument, phrasal verbs, etc. were avoided. However, such verbs were often discussed with IC when reviewing work done between these sessions.

The third stage involved selection of verb, agent and theme in *passive* sentences, using the same hierarchy of semantic and pragmatic bias, and using drawings where necessary to help IC's selection. For example:

The cake was burnt by the cook (predictable, irreversible)

The shirts were washed by her husband (less predictable, irreversible)

The daughter was buried by her father (unpredictable, reversible)

Selection of the correct sentence for a given picture. This was either active, for example:

The boy chases the girl

The girl chases the boy

or passive, for example:

The boy is chased by the girl

The girl is chased by the boy

Any difficulties in selection were overcome by guiding IC into systematically using the previously practised strategies, i.e. identifying verb, agent, theme, etc. to help her make a choice.

Ordering of written constituents for a given picture. This was either verb marked, e.g. Group 1 verb, predictable and irreversible, for example:

the girl

the apple   + picture

is eating

Or verb unmarked, e.g. Group 2 verb, reversible, for example

> the horse
> the cow   + picture
> is pushing

Again, where difficulties occurred, IC was guided through the basic strategies of identifying verb, agent, and theme, or the same task was used with a less "complex" verb, e.g. more predictable or irreversible.

Writing a sentence for a picture, given written nouns and verb infinitive. For example:

> girl, apple, to eat   + picture
> cowboy, indian, to hit   + picture
> horse, cow, to push   + picture

Only active sentences were required, with emphasis on correct ordering of constituents as in the previous task, rather than on correct use of function words, etc.

Writing sentence for a picture, given written verb infinitive only. For example:

> to eat   + picture
> to hit   + picture
> to throw   + picture

Again, only active sentences were required with emphasis on correct constituent ordering. Noun retrieval did not prove problematic.

Writing sentence for a picture, given nouns only. For example:

> girl, apple   + picture
> cowboy, Indian
> horse, cow

Although IC was now required to retrieve the verb, she was initially helped with pictures that depicted verbs used in previous tasks. Only when IC coped well at this level was she given pictures that required generation of new (although still high frequency) items.

Writing full sentence given picture only. Emphasis was still on retrieval and use of appropriate verbs and their arguments, not on use of function words.

Expansion of sentences to include two verbs, simple adjectival phrases, adverbial phrases, etc. (using all stages 1–7). This task was not attempted before the results of the therapy were evaluated.

EVALUATION OF THERAPY

IC was seen for nine sessions over 5 weeks with the therapist, working principally on the sentence construction tasks, and, where possible, the volunteers concentrated on single word verb semantics to support this. In practice the therapist was not able to monitor the volunteer sessions as closely as she would have liked due to caseload commitments. However, IC frequently brought along completed worksheets to the therapy sessions, and we were able to discuss and incorporate any difficulties into a sentential context.

Measuring effectiveness

IC's feedback. IC indicated that she enjoyed the therapy and was pleased with her progress; she felt more confident in and out of the home, she could now use the telephone (an important factor as her daughter lived in America), and she generally found that she could get her message across verbally most of the time. She still experienced periods of frustration, most of all with her youngest son who showed less understanding of her difficulties (and possibly therefore less tolerance) than the rest of her family. Although I had met other members of the family and discussed IC's difficulties and therapy, this son had so far eluded me, despite a visit to her home. IC's reluctance to involve her son suggested that, at this stage, it was inappropriate to pursue the matter. Perhaps the biggest indication of IC's improved self-esteem and confidence in her communication was a proposed trip to Florida to see her daughter and grandchildren.

Written output. IC's ability to describe the function of objects in pictures was reassessed at the end of the nine sessions (Table 12.6).

IC was asked to write a further description of the Cookie Theft picture (BDAE) (Table 12.7).

In both these cases IC showed improvement in the following:

- quicker and more successful retrieval of verbs
- clearer target sentences—improved word order
- greater awareness of continued areas of difficulty, e.g. function words which she had previously appeared to omit or substitute without any monitoring. She now indicated where she was unable to access, for example, a preposition, sometimes leaving a gap in the sentence in order to acknowledge its position
- a greater variety of sentence structures, showing an improved ability to generate new sentences.

TABLE 12.6

Writing the function of an object post-therapy

Stimulus picture	Written response
Glass	I shall drink glass of beer
Scissors	They cut this hair scissors
Book	I read my book
Matches	(not attempted)
Chair	My husband sat in this chair
Pencil	Teachers write with this pencil
Ball	They played at tennis
Radio	I liston to wireless to make liston Irish song
Jug	I got a jug full of milk
Mug	I shall drink a mug to coffee

TABLE 12.7

Written cookie theft picture description

The sink is overlowing
The women is washing up
The boy is looking for the cake this give that litte girl. The stool is falling on the floor.

Previously she had relied on a given example, or her first sentence, to provide a framework for the following sentences.

Spoken output. Although not directly worked on, it was hypothesised that IC's spoken output would benefit from the therapy programme described. IC was therefore asked to describe the Cookie Theft Picture (BDAE) and relate the story of Cinderella before and after therapy (Table 12.8).

Control tasks. IC was considered to be still within the period of spontaneous recovery. It was hypothesised that therapy would improve semantic access and not grapheme to phoneme conversion, therefore IC was asked to read aloud 10 non-words before and after therapy. On both occasions she scored 0 out of 10; on both occasions any attempts resulted in the production of phonologically similar real words.

Although this indicates the effectiveness of the semantic therapy, it is unclear whether such a function, little used in day-to-day activities, could be expected to spontaneously improve at the same rate as other language skills. For this reason I feel that IC's success could have been due to any one or a combination of the following factors:

1. positive effects of semantic therapy (single word verb semantics, sentence construction skills, or a combination of both)
2. reduced pressure on spoken output and therefore increasing receptiveness to therapy, and also allowing IC to focus on the processing of the language tasks rather than the struggle of output
3. spontaneous improvement.

Implications for continued intervention with IC

1. The positive gains so far suggested the programme should be continued into stage 8, with further attempts to control for spontaneous improvement.
2. Further investigation into IC's function word errors might determine whether these were part of a wider phonological problem with

TABLE 12.8

Spoken output

Spoken cookie theft

Before therapy:

/ni/... ooh ... one ... two ... oh ... two wer ... /kɜn/ ... er ... two two ... er ... /ɔdən/...takes two any ... thing ... um ... ooh ...

(AG: Try moving onto this, IC)

the /m.../ oh ... /i/ ... /sip/ ... the woman /di wənən/ washing up ... and the /wə/ /weits/ ... tə /tɛt/ um ... to know that ... he is o /ən/ over...

(AG: Right)

The cake ... what ... he /ɛ/ ... /tu/ anyth ... he ... um ... the what'sename ... with ...s... he ... /ku...ku/... k... the what'sname is ... going fall over.

(AG: Right ... the stool)

Um ... she is /---/ ... /---/ up /---/ /keɪts/ ... /bu/ here

After therapy:

Um ... um ... the sink is running over... she ... er ... wipe /mɔɪp/ the plates ... um... and the thing is just ... um ... pushing over, and she gets some cake for the girl.

Cinderella story

Before therapy:

Cinderella ... oH ... two ugly sisters ... they ... m ... more ... ooh ... gotten Buttons ... oh ... um ... [ti] ... um ... couldn't um ... um ... huh ... um ... /---/ ... um ...

After therapy:

/ə/ ... um ... old sisters and ... er ... she wouldn't let her /dəʊ/ go to dance. She got ... um ... some ... /tə/ ... fairy /frɛrɪ/ godmothers who ... um ... decked her all out ... and she went to the ball ... and she had ... um ... nice ... um ... um ... Prince Charming who ... um ... she didn't ... um ... um ... /----/ ... glass slipper ... ooh ... The glass sl... slipper ... /ə/ ... um ... she ... um ... fits the ... and they ... um ... happy ever after.

the unstressed elements of the sentence, or whether, given the improvement seen already, they constituted part of the semantic difficulties. A therapy programme might then be developed which would take into account the success of the previous programme in using the written modality.

3. Increased contact with IC's family, including her youngest son if appropriate, would continue to be important if they were to develop a better understanding of IC's difficulties.

4. Increased contact with the volunteers working with IC would be required, in order to better monitor their interaction with her, and to improve their understanding of the input and output tasks they were being asked to carry out with her.

REFERENCES

Byng, S., & Black, M. (1999). *The reversible Sentence comprehension test.* Buckingham: Winslow Press.

Goodglass, H., & Kaplan, E. (1981). *The assessment of aphasia and related disorders.* Philadelphia: Lea and Febiger.

Jones, E.V. (1986). Building the foundations for sentence production in a non-fluent aphasic. *British Journal of Disorders of Communication, 21, 1,* 63–82.

Kay, J., Lesser, R., & Coltheart, M. (1992). *PALPA: Psycholinguistic Assessments of Language Processing in Aphasia.* Hove: Lawrence Erlbaum Associates Ltd.

Howard, D., & Patterson, K. 100 Picture Naming Test. Unpublished.

Photographic Teaching Materials (1982). *Object Pictures.* Buckingham: Winslow Press.

Sparks, R., Helm, N., & Albert, M. (1974). Aphasia rehabilitation resulting from melodic intonation therapy. *Cortex, 10,* 303–316.

Whurr, R. (1974). *The Aphasia Screening Test.* London: Whurr Publishers.

13

"Who ends up with the fiver?"— a sentence production therapy

Jane Marshall

INTRODUCTION

MW was still in his 40s when he collapsed at work with a middle cerebral artery bleed. He had surgery to clip an aneurysm which left him with a severe dysphasia but no hemiplegia. He began therapy as an inpatient at Queen Mary's Hospital soon after his operation.

When MW was first referred he had a multiplicity of problems. He had no spoken output. He could write only a few useful written words such as family names. His comprehension began to fail at anything above a two-word stage. Most disabling were his problems of disorganisation and perseveration. He would get stuck on jargon words and phrases and get caught up in repetitive, meaningless gesture.

In the early stages we worked on improving attention and building up a useful vocabulary of Amer-Ind signs (Skelly, 1979). Slowly the perseveration and disorganisation resolved and with the manual output came some useful single word speech.

This chapter relates to the work undertaken when MW was about 6 months post onset. MW's communication at that time is typified in the following extract:

> "Weekend (points to self) ... airshow (writes ("airshow")) Maidstone (writes "Maidstone") ... (points upwards) ... aeroplane (makes a plane gesture) ... big (gestures "big") ... (writes "63 ft") ... Meths .. (gestures drinking and laughs) ... here seventy ... (writes "£80") ... (gestures using a hand held remote control while looking up at an imagined plane) ... Here"

MW's skill and resourcefulness as a communicator is excellently illustrated by this sample. He was very sensitive to the needs of his listener. Throughout the sample it can be seen that he supported and corrected his speech with gesture and writing thus cutting down the opportunities for misinterpretation. His output was colourful and lively, and he even had the range to incorporate a gestural joke. However, he seemed to have difficulty with sentence structure and possibly even with producing verbs.

In this sample the lack of sentence structure does not significantly hinder communication. MW got across all the key events of his weekend. However, in other aspects of his life the resulting communicative handicap was more evident. At this time MW was trying to sell his house. Once sold he planned to take over the mortgage of his parents-in-law's house. They in turn were seeking to emigrate and buy a bungalow in Australia. MW was not able to communicate this network of buying and selling. So much so that in desperation I was driven to phoning his wife to untangle our mutual confusion.

Certain events, such as buying and selling, can only be communicated with some degree of sentence structure. If MW was to become a functional communicator and be in control of his own affairs, we had to do something about his problem with sentences.

A review of sentence production, based on Garrett's model of sentence processing (Garrett, 1980), suggested a number of possible aspects of processing which could have acted as "sites" of breakdown. It was helpful to consider these options:

1. It was possible that MW had a specific verb deficit or a "verb anomia". In single word output it is often very difficult to know whether items are acting as nouns or verbs, therefore a speech sample alone may not tell us if a patient can access verbs. The following exchange illustrates this point:
    JM: "What did you do last night M?"
    MW: "Walk ... dog"

    Here the target could be "I took the dog for a walk'" in which case MW has accessed a noun, or "I walked the dog", which would make this an example of a verb construct. Certainly it is impossible to trace an unequivocal verb in MW's output at this time.

A verb deficit could take another form. It might be that MW was able to access verbs but was not able to retrieve the role information which is a prerequisite for sentence production. In normal processing it is argued that the first stage of lexical access retrieves not just the verb but also information about its required argument structures (Schwartz, 1987). So, for example the verb "eat" would specify an agent, and optionally a theme. In contrast "feed" would demand an agent, optionally a theme and a patient, or the person/animal being fed. Someone who is failing to retrieve role information would presumably view eat and feed as indistinguishable. MW may have been lacking this essential elaboration of verb meanings.

2. It was possible that MW's lexical access, including verbs, was intact but that he was unable to move on and create a predicate/argument structure. A deficit at this "stage" would mean that MW was not able to assign lexical constructs to the required verb roles. Given a picture of a man feeding hay to a horse he might appropriately access the semantics of "man", "horse", "feed", and "hay" but be unable to compose a structure that would make explicit the roles being performed by each character.

    Inability to decode the predicate/argument structure in comprehension would create difficulties with sentences in which the roles are not pragmatically obvious. In other words "the man feeds hay to the horse" would be understood, whereas "the man feeds soup to the woman" would cause problems.

3. MW's problem could have resulted from difficulties at Garrett's "positional level"— or the point at which the syntactic form is specified. A syntax deficit would have rendered MW incapable of composing an appropriate planning frame with which to express his predicate argument structure. A syntactic problem in comprehension would predict an inability to parse sentences.

4. MW's speech at this time not only displayed structural simplicity but also lacked morphology. There may have been an aspect of impoverishment in the creation of the planning frame. Alternatively, a phonological explanation might be sought. It is argued that the phonetic characteristics of minor items are processed immediately prior to articulation (Garrett, 1982). It may be that MW was unable to access or realise these subtle elements of sentence phonology. Were this true we might have expected an accompanying articulation problem. In fact MW's speech showed no evidence of dyspraxia or phonological groping. It seems more likely that the absence of inflections and articles, etc. was attributable to a structural poverty either at the level of the planning frame, or because of the lack of the higher predicate/argument structure.

I have tried to show how reviewing a psycholinguistic model of sentence production helped to generate a number of hypotheses about MW's problem. This in turn guided assessment selection and interpretation.

ASSESSMENT

I decided to look first into whether MW could produce verbs given the right circumstances. To do this I presented him with 10 action picture cards (Winslow Press, 1982) and encouraged him to give me one word to describe what was happening. The action picture cards have the virtue of extreme simplicity. Each contains just one person depicted performing a single action. The need to formulate decisions about the event is reduced to a minimum.

Under these conditions MW was entirely successful (10/10). It seems that he had some capacity to "name actions". However, as suggested earlier, it is difficult to judge verb competence from single word output. A word can only acquire the status of a verb by performing that role in a sentence. I therefore wanted to find out more about MW's verb knowledge. I attempted this through a sentence judgement task. In this task the assessor read aloud sentences; half the stimuli were correct, the other half contained violations (28 sentences in all). The task was to judge whether the sentences were right or wrong. The stimuli included a number of items containing anomalous verb argument structure, for example:

The vicar died the policeman.

The mother ate the rusk to the baby.

The girl fell the table.

MW identified all of these violations. When I asked him to point out the error in all cases he indicated the verb—in the first example he was even able to supply a correction. It seemed that he had some knowledge about the arguments required by verbs. For example, he knew that "die" was not a causative verb, and hence did not permit the inclusion of an agent. His performance with these stimuli suggested quite a sophisticated degree of verb knowledge. It seemed that MW did know about what roles are and are not permitted with individual verbs. So with the "died" stimulus MW seemed aware that only a theme is permitted; the presence of two noun phrases, one in the role of agent, alerted him to the violation.

The sentence judgement task illuminated other areas of linguistic competence. Despite the lack of morphology in his own speech MW was remarkably aware of any morphological errors in the stimuli, for example:

She wrote the letter didn't he.

They walks down the corridor.

It looked as if some morphological skills were intact. One might hypothesise that once able to generate sentence structure MW would begin to produce morphology.

MW also demonstrated surprising knowledge about the syntactic forms of sentences. He picked up violations in passive sentences:

The man was eaten by the dinner.

and in clefts:

It was the vicar that the sermon read.

MW revealed quite a subtle awareness about how the constituents are manipulated to generate these structures. Considerable skills at Garrett's positional level were suggested. MW's success with the sentence judgement task was surprising and difficult to explain. The task suggested that MW had intact skills in areas of verb role knowledge, morphology, and syntactic transformations. It was therefore surprising that his output was so structurally impoverished.

A task on which MW did show problems was in the comprehension of reversible sentences. On the Test for Reception of Grammar (Bishop, 1982), his failures were almost all on sentences where he had to decide who was doing what to whom, e.g. reversible passives, and reversible clause sentences. He also failed on reversible prepositions (in/on, above/below). On the Eirian Jones' test (Jones, 1984), using reversible action sentences, he made seven errors all of which were reversible.

MW was also asked to draw the sentence: "the dog is licking the boy". Here he simply drew a boy and a dog. When I pointed out the verb he incorporated it into the picture by drawing a bowl near the dog. It seemed that he was unable to represent the event described in the sentence or to interpret the predicate argument structure in a sentence. When this information was pragmatically obvious, he achieved some success, though even at this level he was vulnerable. Whenever the event was semantically reversible, he was likely to fail.

Why did MW fail on the comprehension of these comparatively simple sentences, while picking up violations on complex passives and clefts? I think one explanation rests with the nature of the event being described. The violation sentences deal with events that are non-reversible and have undisputed human agents. In contrast I asked MW to draw events in which either the human or the "lower status" animal might be acting as agent. His drawings showed a strong preference for placing the human in the agent role, suggesting that he may be using a pragmatic rather than linguistic system for assigning nouns to verb roles.

The assessment tasks illuminated surprising areas of competence. MW demonstrated skills in syntax, morphology, and verb knowledge. His main problem seemed to rest with reversible sentences in

which role assignment was either not clear or contrary to pragmatic expectations, (and one of MW's strongest expectations seemed to be that humans always play the role of agent in an event). If this analysis was right it suggested that MW needed help in clarifying "who is doing what to whom". Once helped to compose the functional level representation I speculated that he might be able to make use of his evident skills in other areas of syntactic processing. Good sentences should begin to emerge.

THERAPY

From my assessment I decided that I needed a therapy that would help MW to get inside the dynamics of an event and to see how that came to be expressed in a sentence. To do this I decided to exploit the "role reversal" family of verbs, e.g. give/take, send/receive, and buy/sell (I quickly dropped lend/borrow for socio-linguistic reasons) (Byng, 1988). These verbs are useful because they allow us to express the same event using different surface structures.

A core event such as the sale of a house might be represented as is seen in Fig. 13.1. Either the verb "buy" or "sell" can be used and in both instances the key actors occupy similar roles:

> source = Bob
> goal = Harry and Jean
> theme = the house.

However, the verb choice will influence how those roles are mapped onto the constituent structure of the sentence. In "Bob sells a house to Harry and Jean" the source occupies the subject noun phrase; whereas in "Harry and Jean buy a house from Bob" the subject is now the goal of the transaction. Using sentences of this kind I felt I might be able to help MW regain conscious access to the predicate argument structure of sentences.

Examples

"Give/got therapy"
Materials. I produced six people cards (Fig. 13.2). I also collected some magazine photographs of

FIGURE 13.1

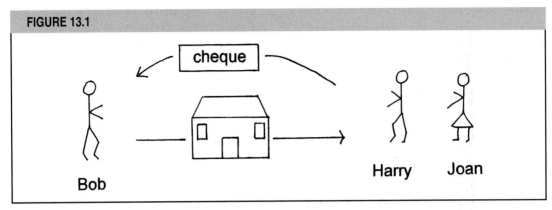

Drawing to represent the core event of "sale of a house".

FIGURE 13.2

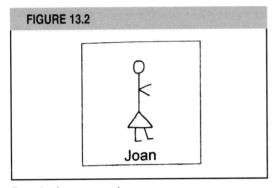

Example of a person card.

"presents", e.g. a tie, a bottle of whisky, a pen, a camera, a shirt, a bottle of scent, etc.

Hierarchy. For the first stage I presented MW with written sentences in which the goal was always represented in red:

Joan gave a tie to *Bob*
Bob gave a camera to *Jack*
Bob got a tie from Joan
Jack got a camera from Bob

MW was then required to select the appropriate people and present cards. He then had to compose the change of possession event by moving the present between the two people in the appropriate direction (Fig. 13.3). I also incorporated a checking procedure by asking questions about the event, e.g. "Who ended up with the tie?", "Who bought the tie?", "Who wrapped it?", etc.

Interestingly, at the beginning of this level of the therapy MW always set out his people cards in the same configuration as the written sentence. In other words he placed the Subject Noun Phrase person on the left and the person in the Prepositional Phrase on the right. As he

FIGURE 13.3

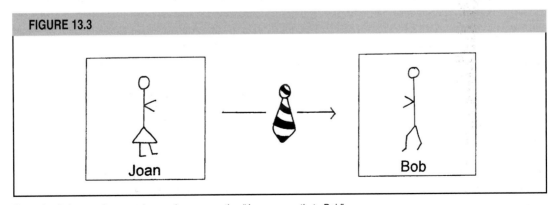

Example of change of possession cards, representing "Joan gave a tie to Bob".

became more adept he was able to be more flexible. His people cards now occupied either position and he was able to express the event by changing the direction of the movement of the present.

Once MW was consistent with the colour coding I moved on to the second stage in which it was eliminated. The task remained the same—MW still had to use the materials to represent the direction of the change of possession.

A third level involved the auditory input of sentences only.

The final stage was the production level. Here, I composed an event with the materials and MW was required to say what had happened.

At all levels the checking procedure was used.

Variations

"Buy/sell therapy"
Materials. The people cards remained the same. New item cards were drawn: a house, a car, and a record player. A card representing a cheque was also drawn.

Hierarchy. A very similar hierarchy was followed, which progressed from colour coded written sentences through to the auditory input alone and finally on to a production stage. However, now MW was asked to represent the double change of possession, with the goods moving in one direction and the cheque in the other.

Live therapy was a further variation. This became possible whenever a visitor or observer was present. Here the materials were three people and a £5 note. Again MW was given colour coded sentences, e.g. MW gives £5 to *Jane.* MW then had to act out the event. Checking went over the final ownership of the "fiver". The colour coding was then eliminated.

In the production phase I would enact an event with the third person, e.g. "Here you are Bob, I want you to have this" (handing over the £5). MW would then have to produce an appropriate sentence: "Jane gives £5 to Bob". Work on the reversal "take" was possible with me snatching the £5 back from Bob.

It was also possible to incorporate some work around MW's spontaneous output. At this time he was engaged in wranglings with the UK Government Department of Social Security (DSS) and was attempting to describe some of the correspondence that was taking place. This provided stimuli sentences such as: "The DSS sent a cheque to MW" for appropriate decoding.

Results

To discuss whether or not therapy had been useful I needed to review what kind of outcomes I was hoping for.

First, I was hoping to give MW improved access to the predicate argument structures of sentences. If successful he should have been less dependent on pragmatic assumptions to decode the direction of events. His comprehension of reversible sentences should have improved. From assessment I had speculated that MW's syntactic competence might be intact. In other words, were he able to compose a predicate argument structure he should then have been able to map this onto an appropriate syntactic form, without any further help at this level.

My therapy had targeted a very restricted range of drilled sentences. All input sentences were limited to the prepositional form. However, if MW's syntactic competence really was intact we would speculate that his output would generalise to both the drilled form and the undrilled double object dative. In other words we might have expected to hear sentences of the form: "Joan gave Bob a tie". One could go further to argue that improving awareness of predicate argument structures should generate a whole variety of syntactic structures in output.

Assessment had stimulated a second hunch that MW's morphology was intact. He was failing to produce much because without verb structures he had nothing to hang it on to. If therapy could remediate his structural difficulty auxiliaries, and inflections, etc. should have begun to emerge without additional training. In summary, if successful I was hoping that the therapy would produce gains in comprehension of reversible sentences and show improvements in structured and inflected output.

EVALUATION

Since I had not intended to write up this therapy for publication, I did not do an extensive amount of pre- and post-therapy evaluation, but rather carried out sufficient to indicate whether the gains that we could observe could be further demonstrated through formal evaluation.

Input

Test for Reception of Grammar: On retesting MW passed many of the sections he had previously failed, e.g. passives, comparatives, above/below. In a test of comprehension of reversible sentences (Jones, unpublished) MW now scored 100% correct. Thus, the predicted gains in comprehension seemed to have taken place.

Output

Although much of MW's speech remained "agrammatic" a far higher representation of structures began to emerge. Here are some examples of his output immediately post therapy:

> "When I've sold grandad's house money (gesture "sends") Australia."

> "Speaking to Ken C in the foyer."

> "I said to the girl ... stroke." (gestures to head)

> "Before I drove Emma to the doctor's ... now I can't drive."

> re DSS "Six month woman prosecute me."

> "Sent cheque to M."

> "Sent M cheque."

From this small amount of data, it would appear that the predictions about MW's output seem to have borne fruit. The suggestion that morphology would simply happen is certainly the case, most strikingly in the first sample with its sophisticated expression of tense. Similarly a generalisation of forms is seen. In the last two samples both the dative options are produced. MW is not confined to the forms that have been drilled in therapy.

An indisputable link between these gains and therapy cannot be proved. This is not a controlled study but rather a set of clinical observations and a cynic could argue that progress was simply an example of spontaneous recovery. A replication involving more in-depth investigation and evaluation with appropriate controls would be more convincing, but this study does suggest the potential utility of this type of therapy.

REFERENCES

Byng, S. (1988). Sentence processing deficits : Theory and therapy. *Cognitive Neuropsychology, 5(6),* 629–676.

Bishop, D. (1982). *Test for Reception of Grammar.* MRC, Oxford, & Thos. Leach, Oxford.

Garrett, M.F. (1980). Levels of processing in sentence production. In B. Butterworth (Ed.), *Language production.* Vol. 1. New York: Academic Press.

Garrett, M.G. (1982). Production of speech: Observations from normal and pathological language use. In A.W. Ellis (Ed.), *Normality and pathology in cognitive functions.* London: Academic Press.

Jones, E.V. (1984). Word order processing in aphasia: effect of verb semantics. In F. Clifford Rose (Ed.), *Advances in neurology: 42, Progress in aphasiology,* 159–181.

Schwartz M.F. (1987). Patterns of speech production deficit within and across aphasia syndromes: Applications of a psycholinguistic model. In M. Coltheart, G. Sartori, & R. Job (Eds.), *The cognitive neuropsychology of language.* Hove, UK: Lawrence Erlbaum Associates Ltd.

Skelly, M. (1979). *Amerind gestural code based on universal American Indian hand talk.* New York: Elsevier North-Holland.

14

An informal example of a successful therapy for a sentence processing deficit

Kate Swinburn

INTRODUCTION

Outlined here is a therapy method used with a 16-year-old boy with acquired aphasia and mild dyspraxia following a cerebral haemorrhage. Its purpose is to demonstrate, first, the effectiveness of this therapy programme based on a brief analysis of language and, second, that it can be valuable to write up therapy results regardless of whether one sets up a research design initially or not. I neither set up a research design nor kept a detailed record of untreated areas which could have been used for comparison to show specific treatment effects.

JH was 15 years old when he sustained a cerebral haemorrhage and underwent neurosurgery. The stroke resulted in him having a mild articulatory dyspraxia, a non-fluent expressive aphasia characterised by agrammatic speech

production and a mild to moderate receptive aphasia. There is no record of any work being done on sentence-level comprehension or production prior to that described here.

He received speech and language therapy for 18 months both in a hospital and in a rehabilitation unit. He was in mainstream education prior to his stroke but subsequently attended a school for children with physical impairments due to his hemiplegia. I began sentence processing therapy with JH 19 months post onset. He was well motivated and participated actively in therapy.

Functionally, JH communicated relatively well despite his impairments. When interpreting speech he relied heavily on non-verbal information and context. When expressing a message he utilised gesture, intonation, drawing, representative sounds (e.g. lateral clicks to represent a horse) and facial expression (see Appendix 1). JH's functional communication was clearly better than his verbal expression but it was obvious that he had some major difficulties in production of language.

SINGLE-WORD ASSESSMENT

Word recognition. Single word level abilities were tested using a variety of psycho-linguistic tests. On a lexical decision task assessing his word recognition abilties, JH scored 75/78 (95%) on the written presentation and 73/78 (93%) on spoken presentation. When tested on a same/different judgement he scored 20/20 (100%) when using function words, 30/30 (100%) when using one-syllable words, and 28/30 (93%) when using two-syllable words.

Semantics. Semantic knowledge was tested using a variety of tests. On Howard and Patterson's Pyramids and Palm Trees (1992) using the three-picture version to test comprehension of pictures, JH scored 49/52 (94%). Using the written word to picture matching version he scored 49/52 (94%) and with the spoken word to picture matching version, 51/52 (99%). On the picture to spoken word matching task in the PALPA (Kay, Lesser, & Coltheart, 1992), JH scored 31/35 (89%) (not all test items available). All errors made were close semantic errors. In a final test of semantic knowledge (Funnell, 1983), JH was presented with three spoken words, two of which were more closely related than the third. The test is in two parts; in the first part, the less related word of the three is unrelated to the related pair e.g. "mitten—plate — glove" (unrelated test). In the second part all three words are related but two are more closely related than the third e.g. "mitten—sock—glove" (related test). JH scored 16/16 (100%) on the unrelated test and 10/16 (63%) on the related test, indicating possibly some vulnerability of semantics when more specific knowledge was required or when no picture was available to support semantic access.

Phonology. Several tasks requiring knowledge of phonology were completed. Repetition of words and non-words was 100%. JH was asked to identify

rhyming pairs from a triad of pictures, e.g. "key—tea—shoe". He scored 13/16 (86%). He was asked to identify the number of syllables in a word from a picture of a common object. He scored 7/12 (59%). The target words ranged from one to four syllable words. In retrospect the value of this test is questioned as many people without language problems have difficulty making syllable judge-ments. JH was also asked to sort pictures into piles depending on their first sound. He scored 15/17 (89%). These tests demonstrate reasonably good phonological output ability.

Naming. When tested on confrontation naming there seemed to be a differential performance between nouns, verbs, and adjectives. Using a set of pictures of common objects and actions he named 15/23 objects, 4/16 verbs, and 9/16 adjectives.

Reading and writing. Reading and writing were not formally tested other than on lexical decision and the written version of Pyramids and Palm Trees Test. Informal observation of JH's reading showed that he had some whole word recognition skills, and that he combined this with use of a phonic system he had been taught previously by a speech and language therapist at the rehabilitation centre.

He was able to write words by using the meaning information to access the written words or by using letter to sound conversion (grapheme–phoneme conversion) which was laborious and often incorrect due to the prevalence of irregular words in the English vocabulary.

SENTENCE-LEVEL ASSESSMENT

JH seemed to have more difficulty with tasks at the sentence level. His output was agrammatic and non-fluent, lacking verbs, functors, and auxiliaries. JH often made word-order violations in spontaneous speech and verbal expression tasks (e.g. "apple … the boy … eating").

His performance on the Test for Reception of Grammar (TROG; Bishop, 1982) deteriorated beyond two item commands and he had difficulty comprehending reversible sentences. The Jones word order test (1984) was performed. This test is designed to examine the comprehension and expression of reversible sentences. The task is to identify, given a spoken or written sentence, a matching picture (e.g. "the nun pushes the vicar") from a choice of three pictures. The two other pictures represent a reverse role contrast (e.g. "the vicar pushes the nun") and a lexical contrast sentence (e.g. "the nun hits the vicar"). JH was generally unable to choose between the target and the reverse role contrast; the lexical contrast having posed no problem.

One explanation for his sentence comprehension problems could be a memory deficit. However, he had a digit span of four, suggesting some ability to hold on to and produce spoken items.

These observations suggested that JH had difficulty with the comprehension and expression of semantic relationships within sentences, e.g. who did what to whom. A number of factors suggested this. First, his questioning response when faced with reversible sentences (e.g. within Jones' Word Order Test). He would point to both the target picture, e.g. "the boy hits the girl", and the reversible contrast, e.g. "the girl hits the boy", and say "yes, but …" and gesture "which one?". Second, he often violated word order rules when talking spontaneously, e.g. "cutting … the woman … bread". Third, he had difficulty with understanding the reversible sections of the TROG and the Jones test. Fourth, he had difficulty accessing verbs in single word confrontation tasks and in spontaneous output. This was felt to be relevant to JH's sentence formulation difficulties, given data in the literature about the relationship between impairments in retrieving verbs and sentence formulation for other aphasic people with similar sentence comprehension and production problems (see Marshall, 1995).

JH appeared to share many of the characteristics shown by JG described by Byng (1988), by BB described by Jones (1986), and by AER described by Nickels, Byng, and Black (1991). They were all thought to have difficulty mapping semantic roles. As sentence processing therapy had proved successful with these people, I decided that this should be tried with JH.

THERAPY

Aims

The aim of therapy was to increase JH's awareness of the semantic roles within sentences and the relationship of these to word and component order. By doing this it was hypothesised that structuring of sentences within therapy tasks and spontaneous speech would improve, making it easier for JH to express himself more clearly. It was also hoped that lexical access for both nouns and verbs within sentences would increase as had been seen in the studies mentioned previously.

Method

Therapy took place over an 8 week period for 1 hour twice a week. Treatment was only curtailed because I moved to another post where I was unable to see JH.

Therapy was based on JH processing auditory input and using this to select written and picture material.

Sessions 1 and 2. The therapy performed in these two sessions was based on therapy used successfully by Jones with BB. The assessments had shown that JH had difficulty relating semantic relationships to word order. It was felt therefore that he needed a greater insight into what constituted a sentence and what aspects of a sentence were important to convey specific information. The concept of a sentence being made up of units (constituents) was introduced. Non-reversible, subject-verb-object (SVO) pictures and written sentences were included. SVO sentences were used initially as they were judged to be of more straightforward structure for interpretation and therefore useful to introduce the concept of the therapy. They also provided baseline measures for the rest of the therapy.

A system of colour coding was used whereby each phrase type was always the same colour regardless of the lexical item, e.g. verbs were always red. JH grasped the necessary concepts quickly and was soon successfully completing the following tasks:

1. selecting appropriate pictures from an array to correspond with the written and verbal input
2. dividing up sentences into their phrases when given the sentence verbally and written
3. selecting appropriate written constituents in response to question words "who" and "what" (colour-coded).

No verbal expression was allowed at this stage. J.H. had to point to a picture (1) or written constituent (2) or cut up a sentence into its constituents (3).

Session 3 and 4. Similar work was continued using non-reversible three-phrase written sentences with matching pictures but introducing the question word "where". This was done to broaden the sentence types JH had experience of and to consolidate the concepts of the therapy being used by him. JH had a tendency to attempt to express these sentences. This was discouraged as it was felt necessary for JH to concentrate on the meanings of the constituents and the interaction between them. It was thought that allowing expression would alter the focus of the task and reduce the concentration on sentence meaning. It was also noted that when he did produce any part of the sentence being worked on his errors generally involved omitting the verb and this led to confusion and frustration.

JH was very keen to work on production of sentences. To this end JH was given verb confrontation tasks to do at home. In the initial stages, he frequently retrieved the noun associated with the verb rather than the verb itself, e.g. "apple" for "eating" or "ball" for "throwing". JH was encouraged to gesture the action before attempting to retrieve the verb. It was hoped that by gesturing the verb this would focus JH on the action taking place and thereby facilitate the expression of the verb rather than the noun associated with the verb. This proved very successful and he was soon retrieving the spoken verb consistently (cf. Marshall, Chapter 13).

Sessions 5 and 6. It now seemed that JH had mastered the concept of the therapy and was understanding the relationships between constituents. Up until this point it was possible for JH

to use world knowledge to aid sentence comprehension and therefore aid his performance on the tasks in sessions 1 to 4. Reversible sentences were therefore introduced to increase the complexity of the task.

The task requirements were also changed at this point. Phrases were altered in various ways. They were either omitted (e.g. "the man is kicking …"), included with incorrect lexical items (e.g. "the boy is eating an apple" when the picture was of a girl eating an apple) or wrongly sequenced (e.g. "the apple is eating the man"). JH had to reorder the sentence to match them to SVO pictures, or indicate which phrases were missing or incorrect by pointing to the question words "who", "what", "where".

The aim was to focus JH increasingly on the meaning relationships within and between phrases. An attempt was made to mimic the errors of word selection or word order that JH had demonstrated in the past to emphasise the correct relationship. By this stage JH's verbal responses were more consistent and he was encouraged initially to say the verb alone and, if correct, then to attempt other parts of the sentence. JH had some difficulty with these tasks. Reordering incorrectly sequenced constituents was particularly difficult for him initially. However, this was soon overcome by discussion about the meaning relationships, reiteration of the colour codes, and description by the therapist of the focus of activity.

Sessions 7 and 8. I felt now that JH was mastering the concepts of the therapy well and was expressing whole sentences correctly within the confines of therapy tasks. It seemed however that to have any application to JH outside the therapy session work on more relevant lexical items should be included. To this end personal pronouns "I", "he", "she", and "they" were introduced in place of the noun phrases previously used. Family photos were also introduced so that real names could be used in place of the more formal noun phrases used to introduce and practise the therapy.

JH had some difficulty translating the techniques he had used when using less meaning-loaded noun phrases. Reiteration of the therapy aims and of the meaning relationships involved in word order and verb selection was needed, including reintroduction of the colour codes and pointing to the salient area of the picture. By the end of this stage JH was saying all these sentence structures correctly without prefacing them with the verb or needing the help described earlier.

Homework. Throughout therapy JH was given tasks to perform at home. From session 3 he had verb cards to take home. He was encouraged to gesture the action as mentioned under sessions 3 and 4.

Between sessions 5 and 6 he was given SVO pictures to say at home. He was told to say the verb first then try to produce the sentence. Between the final sessions 7 and 8 he was encouraged to go through magazines and family photos (depicting events that could be described using simple SVO structures) and produce the sentences aloud.

Results and discussion

There was a 9-week interval between pre- and post-therapy assessments. The assessments used included TROG and the Jones Word Order Test (1984) to assess changes in sentence comprehension, verb confrontation naming to assess lexical access and production, and a Cinderella story retell to test spontaneous output (Table 14.1).

Language samples obtained from his retelling of the Cinderella story show some of the changes in his spoken language abilities. The results were analysed using the method described by Byng and Black (1989) and the results are as illustrated in Table 14.2.

JH had taken 6.5 minutes to complete the pre-therapy language sample, compared with 12.45 minutes post therapy. Though this indicates important improvement in that he was giving more information, it was felt that to make analysis of pre- and post-therapy as comparable as possible, equivalent time spans should be analysed. Therefore, all of the pre-therapy language sample and 6.5 minutes of the post-therapy language sample was analysed. The results are shown in Table 14.2 and in Appendices 1 and 2.

Although the samples analysed are very small, some changes in ability to structure language are evident. After the therapy there is a shift away from relying on single phrases towards attempting to combine phrases into sentences. This is a pattern similar to that seen in Byng (1988). The proportion of verbs used has not changed but he can now attempt to combine verbs with other phrases to make simple sentences. However, he still relies heavily on the use of single phrases to convey information.

TABLE 14.1

Pre- and post-therapy assessments

Test	Pre-therapy	Post-therapy 1	Post-therapy 2
Verb confrontation naming			
Correct responses	4/16 (25%)	16/16 (100%)	
Test for reception of grammar (TROG)			
Number of blocks passed	6/20	8/20	
Number of correct responses	54/80 (67%)	61/80 (76%)	
*Jones Word Order Test**			
Correct responses (all errors were reverse role rather than lexical errors)	19/30 (63%)	12/12 (100%)	22/30 (73%)

*This test was administered three times, once before therapy and twice afterwards: once immediately after the therapy ended (post-therapy 1), and once (post-therapy 2) some 2 months after the end of sentence processing therapy.

TABLE 14.2

Analysis of the Cinderella story

	% of utterance type produced	
	Pre-therapy	Post-therapy
Single phrase*	75	51
Verb plus one argument*	19	20
Verb plus two arguments*	2	17
Two noun phrases without a verb*	4	11
Total number of utterances analysed*	48	35

*Significant at < .01 (Mann-Whitney U).

Through his increased awareness of semantic relationships, JH was now able to access more grammatically complex language within the constraints of a story retelling situation. He was moving away from a reliance on bare root nouns and verbs augmented with representational noises and actions. He was beginning to combine nouns and verbs, inflect verbs, add determiners and adjectives to nouns and thereby offer more information and context to the listener. The number of words he said nearly doubled and his speech rate increased—showing greater ease of lexical access as well as an increased semantic/grammatical control. He made no representative sounds post therapy as he now had access to the lexical forms previously unavailable to him (e.g. "riding", "twelve o'clock", and "here comes the bride", all previously signalled by representative noises).

I felt that therapy had focused on two things: first, increasing JH's awareness of semantic relationships signalled through grammatical construction, and second, increasing spoken access to verb labels through concentration on the main action and using an immediate mode of output, gesture, which was highly iconic and acting as both a "concrete peg" for the concept while somehow releasing the verbal label by focusing on a secondary mode of output. The combined effect increased comprehension of the relationships and enabled quicker more accurate access to a wider, richer vocabulary.

Other aspects of language production that have not been measured such as ability to produce function words, can, however, be observed not to have changed. Therapy did not focus on this aspect of production. Improvements in formal assessments were seen in the areas expected (reversible actives and passives). Positive changes specific to word order (not lexical choice) were seen in the Jones word order test (see Table 14.1).

From a purely subjective viewpoint the pre- and post-therapy language samples were rated on how well the story was conveyed regardless of grammatical correctness. Six raters (speech and language therapists and non-therapists), none of whom had been involved in JH's management, were asked to look at both samples without knowing which was produced pre and which post-therapy, and rate them on a scale between 1 and 5 (5 being the best and 1 being the worst). Individual ratings were then combined to give an overall pre- and post-therapy rating for how well the story was conveyed. The combined ratings were 10.5 (pre-therapy) as opposed to 21.5 (post therapy) showing a substantial change, when measured subjectively, in JH's ability to convey information.

In summary, it seems that the following changes have occurred in JH's language samples following therapy:

1. JH used more language and took longer to complete the language sample. There was an increase in the length and complexity of phrases used and a reduction in the single word phrases and non-linguistic items such as representative sounds.

2. It seems therefore that as JH's understanding of meaning relationships within a sentence improved, so the grammatical structure of the sentence improved. This improvement had a direct and positive effect on his ability to convey information verbally beyond the improvement in sentence structure.

3. It could be argued that the improvements seen in sentence comprehension and production were merely the result of spontaneous recovery. There are no control results to counter this argument. However, JH was 19 months post onset at the start of therapy and only completed an 8-week course of treatment. It therefore seems unlikely that this amount of improvement took place so rapidly and so late post onset.

I feel that these results demonstrate in a small way that work on the semantic relationships within sentences can improve both sentence comprehension and production, resulting in an increase in the linguistic complexity and the informativeness of language used. The therapy used was easy to perform and produced rapid rewards for both the client and the therapist.

REFERENCES

Bishop, D. (1982). *Test for reception of grammar.* (MRC, Oxford, & Thos. Leach, Oxford).

Byng, S. (1988). Sentence processing deficits: Theory and therapy, *Cognitive Neuropsychology, 5*(6), 629–676.

Byng, S., & Black, M. (1989). Some aspects of sentence production in aphasia, *Aphasiology, 3*(3), 241–263.

Funnell, E. (1983). Phonological processes in reading: new evidence from acquired dyslexia. *British Journal of Psychology, 74,* 159–180.

Howard, D., & Patterson, K.E. (1992). *Pyramids and palm trees.* Bury St Edmunds, UK. Thames Valley Test Company.

Jones, E.V. (1984). Word order processing in aphasia: Effects of verbal semantics. In F. Clifford Rose (Ed.), *Advances in neurology, 42, Progress in aphasiology,* 159–181.

Jones, E.V. (1986). Building the foundations for sentence production in a non-fluent aphasic. *British Journal of Disorders of Communication, 21,1,* 63–82.

Kay, J., Lesser, R., & Coltheart, M. (1992). PALPA: *Psycholinguistic assessment of language processing in Aphasia,* Hove, UK: Lawrence Erlbaum Associates.

Marshall, J. (1995). The mapping hypothesis and aphasia therapy. *Aphasiology, 9,* 517–539.

Nickels, L.,, Byng, S., & Black, M. (1990). Sentence processing therapy: A replication of therapy. *British Journal of Disorders of Communication, 26,* 175–199.

APPENDICES

APPENDIX 14.1

Telling the story of Cinderella pre-therapy

/ big um oh / /tæʊz/um queen um / baby but die / and weep weep um / um woman oh dear oh dear / but um oh..er oh man / woman meet um two er woman two woman / ugly really ugly / um right...dishes / um really cruel / um um oh dear oh dear um / crying crying crying um um / but.. magic woman um oh dear oh dear um / um why don't we um / oh why don't we /grɛs/ no dress / oh no man uh king um / um dishes um / magic oh um (draws a pumpkin) /pʌmplɪg/ (draws a wand and makes /ptʃu/ zap noise) / /bræ/ / no no /um goodie mouse (another zap noise) man man oh um / oh horses and oh dear dress/wɔtʃud/boring but (makes clip-clopping noise) / oh oh wonderful um um goodie goodie goodie / but um /.../lɛvən/ clock (makes sound of clock striking)/no um /dress gone gone gone bye bye / dance and dance and dance / wonderful man oh / but (whistles sound of clock striking) / oh quick um running um shoe slips / oh dear grass (sound of clock striking) / gone / man picks up ooo / I/ lev kɪgmʌm/ kingdom/ um whole world /.../ you know...kingdom / knocking knocking / you here um / shoes oh no / um try it no good / again again / oh given up / what is /draɪ/oh really awful / come here come /yes / this one...try...and fits / oh goodie goodie / I can / king queen (makes sound of peeling bells) happily end/

APPENDIX 14.2

Telling the story of Cinderella post-therapy

/ the man is dying / well oh dear oh dear oh dear / the man is // is dying and / oh dear oh dear / oh the lady is dead / but the man um / the lady meet / but this girl two girls is ratbag/ and um has horrible faces and um / but one girl nice and um / um clear up the mess and housework and / oh dear oh dear / one day the /plɪns/ the prince /...//pɛɪ/ play um party / and um two girls whoopee and um / dress and make-up and / girl one girl / oh potatoes now / oh dear oh dear boo-hoo boo-hoo / and / um and riding through the fields / boo-hoo boo-hoo knock knock knock who's there / Cinderella...oh / oh dear oh dear mess / wait oh um /.../ through no / magical um / whoopee um / magical er/dress um / whoopee um / oh dear / lovely dress style and / mouse mouse come here //mɪdɛɪ/ no / push no / magical men men / pumpkin oh dear /...// but whoopee / cars no / well um / horse and /græ/ no / horse and (writes letters C-H)/anyway um riding/ but...twelve o'clock midnight gone / um meet man and lady / um dance and dance whoopee whoppee / twelve o'clock oh dear running running / shoe oh dear * shoe /.../ running lady / um horror /no...no / ding ding ding / um dress ugly and / oh dear oh dear/ man / boo-hoo / tears / lovely girl / crying / I'm um send the whole world...house / door...ding ding / the shoe / oh knocking knocking / two girls ugly / let me try / let me try and / um / no way too long and / what about the girl...sweeping / oh no no / try..it fits / oh whoopee / kisses and kisses / and oh here comes the bride (sung) / boo-hoo tears and sad and oh // the end

* indicates end of language sample used for qualitative analysis.

Indexes

Author index

Albert, M., 132

Bailey, P., 76
Baxter, D.M., 80, 90
Berndt, R., 112, 113
Berndt, R.S., 107, 113
Best, W., 77
Bishop, D., 15, 146, 152
Bishop, D.V.M., 64
Black, M., 108, 112, 120, 134,
    153, 155
Byng, S., 6, 11, 77, 86, 108, 109,
    112, 113, 120, 134, 146, 153,
    155

Canter, G., 24
Caramazza, A., 91, 112
Certner Smith, M., 36
Coltheart, M., 15, 42, 80, 94, 133,
    152

Davis, G.A., 67
De Partz, M., 103
Dell, G.S., 43
Disimoni, F.G., 68
Duffy, J.R., 65
Duffy, R.J., 65

Edelman, G., 65
Ellis, A., 76
Enderby, P., 33

Fawcus, M., 68
Forer, S., 29, 39
Franklin, S., 76, 117
Funnell, E., 152

Garrett, M., 107, 114
Garrett, M.F., 144

Garrett, M.G., 145
Gilpin, S., 109
Goodglass, H., 101, 131

Helm, N., 132
Hillis, A., 112
Horton, S., 77
Howard, D., 15, 94, 117, 133, 152
Huber, W., 80
Huskins, S., 64

Ireland, C., 33
Ireland, C.M., 3

Jenkins, J.J., 5
Jiminez-Pabon, E., 5
Jones, E., 21, 95, 117
Jones, E.V., 109, 138, 146, 152,
    153, 155

Kaplan, E., 101, 131
Kay, J., 15, 42, 80, 94, 133, 152
Kraat, A.W., 68

Lesser, R., 15, 42, 80, 91, 94, 122,
    133, 152
Lyon, J.G., 51

Marshall, J., 11, 33, 107, 114,
    117, 153
McCarthy, R., 114
Miceli, G., 91
Morganstein, S., 36
Morris, J., 76
Morton, J., 117

Nickels, L., 77, 153

Orchard-Lisle, V., 117
O'Seaghdha, P.G., 43

Paradis, M., 32
Parr, S., 6, 109
Patterson, K., 15, 94, 117, 133
Patterson, K.E., 152
Poeck, K., 80
Pound, C., 6, 11, 91, 117
Pring, T., 117

Romani, C., 91

Sacchett, C., 11, 33
Saffran, E., 112, 113
Schuell, H., 80
Schuell, H.M., 5
Schwartz, M., 107, 112, 113
Schwartz, M.F., 144
Scott, C., 18
Skelly, M., 64, 143
Sparks, R., 132

Turner, J., 76

Villa, G., 91

Wallace, G., 24
Warrington, E., 114
Warrington, E.K., 80, 90
Wehigar, D., 80
Wepman, J.M., 5
White-Thomson, M., 117
Whurr, R., 131
Wilcox, J.M., 67
Willmes, K., 80
World Health Organisation, 3, 32,
    33

Zingeser, L., 113

Subject index

Abstract versus emotional stimuli, 24

Amer-Ind signals, 64

Apraxia, 43–44

Auditory perception impairment, 16, 24–25, 94, 95

Auditory perception tasks, 22–24

Bilingualism, 15, 32

Books, for communication, 27, 28, 52

Categorisation impairment, 45

Categorisation tasks, 18–19, 67
drawing, 45, 47–50
verbs, 136–137

Charting tasks, 19

Charts, 27, 28

Cognitive rigidity, 17–18, 25–26, 27

Communication books, 27, 28, 52

Communication charts, 27, 28

Communication method, patient's choice of, 68

Computer-based therapy
advantages of, 89–90
difficulties with, 83
keyboard familiarisation, 83
for spelling deficits, 81–82, 83–84, 85–86, 88–90

Computer software
"From Pictures to Words", 83, 84, 92
"Gapfiller", 84, 92
"Phraseflash", 85–86, 92
suppliers, 92

Computers
adapted word processors, 88

Conceptual judgements, 18–19

Conscious processing, 108

Constraint, 45, 47

Counselling, 130

Cueing
gestural, 119, 124, 128–129, 154
verb production, 115–116, 118, 119, 154

Cultural issues, 31–32

Definition selection task, 19

Diary keeping, 53

Dictionary use, 84–85

Drawing
categorisation tasks, 45, 47–50
for communication, 42, 44, 45–46, 51, 59, 65, 68
"free drawing", 52–56
as therapy, 10, 11, 46–59

Emotional expression, 59

Emotional state, 11, 30, 59, 71, 129–130

Emotional versus abstract stimuli, 24

Expletives, 61, 70

Facial expressions
charts of, 59
for communication, 69

FAM, 29

Family involvement in therapy, 14–15, 28, 31–32

Fatigue, 82, 85, 88

"From Pictures to Words", 83, 84, 92

Function of objects tasks, 132

Function word impairment, 101–104

Functional Assessment Measure, 29

"Functional" therapy, 33, 68

"Gapfiller", 84, 92

Gestures, *see also* Signing
for communication, 25, 44–45, 51–52, 64–65, 69
and constraint, 45
as cues, 119, 124, 128–129, 154
use during therapy, 64–65, 123, 124, 128–129, 154

Graphemic impairment, 80–81, 91

Graphic motor impairment, 80–81, 90, 91

Group therapy, 63, 64–68, 129–130, 136

Inconsistency of performance, 17–18, 21, 22

Insight, 20, 30–31

Interdisciplinary therapy, 27

Keyboard familiarisation, 83

Lifestyle, 129–130, 135–136

Melodic Intonation Therapy, 132

Mental health, 11, 30, 59, 71, 129–130

Mime, 65

Minimal pairs
word and picture, 21–22
written word, 22

Minimal sets
written word, 22

Mnemonic alphabet, 103

Naive observers of outcome, 109, 116, 120, 126, 156

Naming
oral, 94, 113–114
therapy, 95–98
written, 94, 114

Novel situations, communication in, 28

Odd one out tasks, 18, 137
Oral naming
    deficits, 94, 113–114
    therapy, 95–98
Oral spelling, 80–81, 82, 91
Outcome measures, 29–30
    Functional Assessment Measure,
        29
    naive observer use, 109, 116,
        120, 126, 156
    subject's feedback, 29, 139

Performance variability, 17–18, 21,
    22
Personally related stimuli, 24
Phonemic variation detection, 23
Phonological access assessment,
    43–44, 152
Phonological processing therapy,
    20–25
Phonological simularity tasks, 23
"Phraseflash", 85–86, 92
Pointing, 25, 26
Proxy therapists, 77, 136
Psychosocial adjustment, 30–33,
    59

Reading aloud, 95, 96, 102
Reading therapy, 102–104
Relations, involvement in therapy,
    14–15, 28, 31–32
Reversible sentences, 134, 146,
    152–153, 154

Self-monitoring, 30, 95, 97
Semantic processing assessment,
    15–16, 44, 94, 152
Semantic representation
    preservation, 10
Semantic therapy, 18–20, 65, 67
    for verb impairment, 118–119
Sentence-category task, 19
Sentence completion, 103, 137
Sentence comprehension, 134,
    145–146, 152–153
Sentence production, 134–135,
    143–145, 152, 153–157
Sentence therapies, 19, 103, 108,
    137, 138–139, 146–149,
    153–157
Sentences, reversible, 134, 146,
    152–153, 154
Signing, 64–65, 67, 69, *see also*
    Gestures
Skywriting, 69
Social factors, 31, 129, 135–136,
    see also Psychosocial
    adjustment
Software, *see* Computer software
Spelling deficits, 80–81, 102
    computer-based therapy, 81–82,
        83–84, 85–86, 88–90
    dictionary use, 84–85
    oral spelling, 80–81, 82, 91
    therapy, 81–91
Story retelling, 116, 120, 122,
    125–126

Swearing, 61, 70

Tape recordings, 97
Task effect, 122
Therapy
    length of, 77
    timing, 11
    by unqualified volunteers, 77,
        136
Total communication approach,
    61–71

Variability of performance, 17–18,
    21, 22
Verb categorisation, 136–137
Verb impairment, 112–116, 133,
    144, 145
    therapy, 116–129, 136–137, 138
Verb production
    cueing, 115–116, 118, 119, 154
    tasks, 119–120
Verbs, role reversal, 146–148
Volunteer therapists, 77, 136

Word books, 27, 28, 52
Word charts, 27, 28
Word length tasks, 23
Word/picture minimal pairs, 21–22
Word processors, adapted, 88
Writing to dictation, 82
Written naming, 94, 114
Written word minimal pairs, 22
Written word minimal sets, 22